KOREAN IMMIGRANTS IN CANADA

Perspectives on Migration, Integration, and the Family

Edited by Samuel Noh, Ann H. Kim, and M~~~

Korean Canadians are one of the fastest-growing visible minority populations in Canada today. However, very few studies of their experiences in Canada or their paths of integration are available. To fill this gap, *Korean Immigrants in Canada* provides the first collection of scholarly essays on Korean immigrants and their offspring.

The contributors explore the historical, psychological, social, and economic dimensions of Korean migration, settlement, and integration across Canada. A wide variety of topics are covered: included are demographic profiles and in-depth examinations of entrepreneurship, mental health and stress, elder care, language maintenance, and the experiences of students and second-generation Korean Canadians. Providing a wealth of quantitative and qualitative research from an interdisciplinary perspective, this collection serves as a springboard for future study on the Korean diaspora in Canada.

(Asian Canadian Studies)

SAMUEL NOH is the David Crombie Professor of Cultural Pluralism and Health in the Department of Psychiatry at the University of Toronto.

ANN H. KIM is an associate professor in the Department of Sociology at York University.

MARIANNE S. NOH is a postdoctoral scholar in the Arthur Labatt Family School of Nursing at the University of Western Ontario.

Korean Immigrants in Canada

Perspectives on Migration, Integration, and the Family

EDITED BY SAMUEL NOH, ANN H. KIM, AND MARIANNE S. NOH

UNIVERSITY OF TORONTO PRESS
Toronto Buffalo London

© University of Toronto Press 2012
Toronto Buffalo London
www.utppublishing.com
Printed in Canada

ISBN 978-1-4426-4218-8 (cloth)
ISBN 978-1-4426-1115-3 (paper)

Printed on acid-free, 100% post-consumer recycled paper with
vegetable-based inks.

Asian Canadian Studies Series

Library and Archives Canada Cataloguing in Publication

Korean immigrants in Canada : perspectives on migration, integration, and
the family / edited by Samuel Noh, Ann H. Kim, and Marianne S. Noh.

(Asian Canadian studies)
Includes bibliographical references and index.
ISBN 978-1-4426-4218-8 (bound). ISBN 978-1-4426-1115-3 (pbk.)

1. Koreans – Canada – History. 2. Canada – Emigration and immigration –
History. 3. Korean Canadians – Ethnic identity. 4. Korean Canadians –
Cultural assimilation. 5. Korean Canadians – Psychology. 6. Korean
Canadians – Social conditions. 7. Korean Canadians – Economic conditions.
8. Immigrant families – Canada – Case studies. 9. Immigrants – Family
relationships – Canada – Case studies. I. Noh, Samuel, 1946– II. Kim, Ann
H., 1972– III. Noh, Marianne S., 1977– IV. Series: Asian Canadian studies

FC106.K6K67 2012 971'.004957 C2012-903469-X

 Canada Council   Conseil des Arts   ONTARIO ARTS COUNCIL
for the Arts   du Canada   CONSEIL DES ARTS DE L'ONTARIO

University of Toronto Press acknowledges the financial assistance to its
publishing program of the Canada Council for the Arts and the Ontario
Arts Council.

University of Toronto Press acknowledges the financial support of the
Government of Canada through the Canada Book Fund for its publishing
activities.

Contents

Tables

Figures

Foreword

PYONG GAP MIN

Research on Korean immigrants in the United States started in the early 1970s, leading to the publication of several books and many journal articles. A comprehensive annotated bibliography prepared by this author in 2010 shows that more than 110 books, 30 of them edited volumes, and nearly five hundred journal articles and book chapters focusing on Korean-American experiences have been published. By contrast, owing to a shorter immigration history, a much smaller population size, and a lack of scholars dedicated to the subject, research on Koreans in Canada started much later, in the early 1990s. There is no social science book focusing on Korean Canadians, and only five or six dozen journal articles have been published up to now.

Despite presence of a small number of Korean scholars studying their own population and a thin social science literature on Koreans in Canada, there is one positive aspect of Korean-Canadian research. It is a collective effort by a small number of Korean scholars in Canada to organize workshops and conferences on research issues, and collaborate on research during recent years. The collaboration of the co-editors of this current volume is one good example of the collegial spirit of this small group of scholars.

This anthology has twelve substantive chapters covering different aspects of Korean-Canadian experiences. Chapter 2 provides a comprehensive demographic profile of Koreans in Canada. The following four chapters in Part I cover the immigration, socio-economic characteristics, and settlement of the Korean diaspora internationally and in Canada. Three chapters in Part II examine the adaptation of Korean immigrants. The additional two chapters cover ethnic identity and psychological well-being among Korean-Canadian young people. Three chapters in Part III respectively cover Korean elderly people, fathers, and transnational *kirogi* families.

The fourteen chapters of the book as a whole provide a great deal of general information about Korean-Canadian experiences. Considering that neither a single social science monograph nor an edited book focusing on Korean Canadians has been previously published, this anthology is significant. It is likely to be of great use to Korean community leaders, Canadian and Korean governmental policymakers, and researchers who are interested in the Korean-Canadian population.

Among others, two interesting features of the community that emerge in this volume for me include the extent of self-employment and the large presence of international students and their family members. In fact, Korean foreign students make up the largest international student group in Canada (18 per cent of all international students in Canada in 2006, as shown in chapter 6). International students also compose a greater proportion of Korean residents in Canada than they do in the United States.

Another significant feature of the Korean community, and one that I raise as an important topic for future consideration, is the Korean Protestant church and other religious institutions. In the United States, Korean churches serve multiple sociocultural and economic functions in the community. These include fellowship, retention of Korean cultural traditions, social services for church members, and the provision of social positions for many Korean immigrants who have experienced downward mobility in their social status. Thus, without understanding Korean immigrant churches, including second-generation Korean churches, fully comprehending Korean immigrants' adaptation in Canada is difficult. Although this subject has not been addressed in this book, it is one needing future research. It would be a welcome contribution in a future anthology on Korean Canadians.

Finally, a comparison between Korean-American and Korean-Canadian experiences with regard to several areas would produce meaningful findings. Such a comparison would be ideal, for example, on the topic of entrepreneurship. Korean-owned businesses in the United States are heavily dependent on Latino employees. Is similar reliance on a particular group of workers true for Korean-owned businesses in Canada? Korean immigrants running stores in racially black neighbourhoods in the United States experienced a great deal of conflict with black customers in the 1980s and early '90s. Did Korean business owners in Canada serve many minority customers in the 1990s and have conflicts with them? I hope to learn the answers to these and other questions in future work.

KOREAN IMMIGRANTS IN CANADA

Perspectives on Migration, Integration, and the Family

1 Introduction: Historical Context and Contemporary Research

ANN H. KIM, MARIANNE S. NOH, AND SAMUEL NOH

Judging by our conversations with people from all walks of life across the country, from Moncton to Victoria, the Korean population seems to be a bit of a mystery. Korean communities have been generating greater interest among scholars, policymakers, and local residents, likely because of their increased presence and visibility in Canadian cities. The 2006 census and immigration statistics showed a rapidly growing community, particularly in selected metropolitan areas including Toronto and Vancouver (J. Park, chapter 2, this volume) and increasingly in smaller cities and towns. Statistics Canada also projects Koreans to be one of the fastest growing visible minority groups to 2031 (Statistics Canada, 2010).

The chapters of this volume were collected to showcase a body of systematic social-science research that offers insight into the growth and development of the Korean population and some of the challenges facing Korean immigrants. Ours is an inclusive approach, as we consider immigrants to be those who have arrived in Canada for the purposes of education (for themselves or their children), employment, and/or settlement. As a whole, this collection of papers examines contemporary issues in Korean immigration and proposes some directions to advance research and scholarship in the areas of migration, integration, and the family. Much of the large body of research on immigration more generally fits into these areas, and we add to this body of knowledge the Canadian case of Korean migration and settlement for comparative purposes. Moreover, these are the areas that offer a solid foundation for understanding additional migration-related issues for Korean and other immigrants in Canada as well as for Korean diasporic populations and future generations. Readers will notice that the common thread among all the papers is the approach to bring to light the shared experiences, perceptions, attitudes, and behaviours of Korean immigrants. At the same time, there is recognition of the diverse ways in which their place in Canadian society is negotiated and manifested. To set the context for the chapters in this volume, we start with a historical overview.

A Historical Overview

Immigration is a complex process that is determined by the social, economic, and political forces of both receiving and sending nations, as well as by personal motivations and opportunities. The history of Korean emigration, including immigration to Canada, shows a dynamic shift in the nature and volume of migration over time (I.-J. Yoon, chapter 3, this volume). Korean migration to Canada may be best illustrated by outlining four time periods that can be characterized according to the social-class origins of immigrants and to contemporary immigration policies of the two countries, South Korea and Canada. To be sure, flows from one phase to the next cannot be demarcated precisely, nor is it possible to pinpoint the exact timing of shifts due to regional variations in flow patterns across Canada. Thus, arguably, there are multiple ways of defining the history of Korean immigration (see Kwak, 2004, and I.-J. Yoon, chapter 3, this volume). Yet, in our view, the following four periods represent the changing patterns of Korean immigration to Canada more generally: the period prior to 1963; 1963 to 1985; 1986 to 2003; and 2004 to the present. Although we show that these periods reveal substantial changes in immigration patterns, we do not use this breakdown as rigid and definitive. Rather, it serves the heuristic purpose of organizing the data on the history of Korean immigration and enhancing our understanding of Korean communities.

The Pre-Migration Period (Prior to 1963)

It has generally been acknowledged that the genesis of Korean immigration to Canada lies with the initiation of diplomatic relations between the two governments in 1963 (Yoo, 2002). However, contact between the people of Canada and Korea began much earlier, at the end of the nineteenth century and the early twentieth century – close to the end of the Chosôn (or Yi Dynasty) period, when missionary workers from Canada entered the Korean peninsula (Yoo, 2002). It was around this time that Korea began to allow American and Canadian missionaries into the country. It was also the context within which the first known

Figure 1.1. Yearly Total Immigrants, Korean Immigrants, and Korean Student Flows (in Thousands)

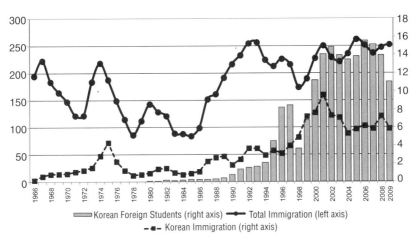

Source: Immigration Statistics Reports yearly 1966 through 1996, Facts and Figures 2005, 2008, and customs tabulations. The Korean migrants include both North and South Koreans by last place of residence.

Koreans came to Canada. Since it was too costly to continue to send Canadian missionaries back and forth from Canada to Korea, Canadian missionaries decided that they would educate and train Korean missionary helpers by sending them to study abroad in Canada. Thus, Korean migration to Canada was, in fact, initiated by education migrants who visited Canada on a temporary basis.

During this pre-migration period, contact between Korea and Canada was not limited to the religious sphere but was also characterized by political involvement. Specifically, the Canadian military participated in the Korean War, and prior to that it assisted the United Nations in supervising free elections at the end of Japanese colonial rule in 1947 (Price, 2004; Yoo, 2002). While Canada had a presence in Korea over this period, Korea's presence in Canada was mostly limited to missionary students who were generally not permitted to stay on a permanent basis. Many of them moved back to Korea or on to the United States.

It is interesting that those Korean migrants who first entered Canada were on temporary visa permits, particularly since migration for educational purposes has also been a strong motivation for contemporary Korean emigration. Figure 1.1 illustrates that the yearly flow of foreign students from South Korea, from 1996 onward, was, for the most part,

Table 1.1. A Brief Chronology of Selected Events in Canada's Immigration History

1962	Canada abolishes national origin as a criterion for immigration.
1963	Diplomatic relations between the Republic of Korea (South Korea) and Canada begin.
1967	Canada introduces a points system for admitting immigrants.
1973	Canada opens its first embassy in South Korea.
1976	Immigration Act of 1976 permits federal-provincial agreements with respect to immigration policy.
1978	Business Class immigration is introduced and expanded throughout the 1980s.
1994	Canada grants a visa exemption to visitors from South Korea staying less than six months.
2009	By August 2009, nine provinces and two territories have Provincial Nominee Programs in place (Quebec has had its own agreement with the federal government since 1975).

Note: For further description and analysis of Canada's immigration policy, see Kelley & Trebilcock (2010) and Simmons (2010).

nearly double that of the permanent migration flow. Also, as described by M.J. Kwak (chapter 6, this volume) and by J. Jeong and D. Bélanger (chapter 14, this volume), it is clear that education has re-emerged as the predominant motivation behind Korea-to-Canada migration. With the exception of the 1998 to 1999 period, the annual number of student entries has exceeded the total number of immigrants from South Korea since 1995.

Permanent Pioneers (1963 to 1985)

The initiation of diplomatic relations between Canada and South Korea in 1963 provided Koreans with the opportunity to consider Canada as a destination for permanent settlement. Canada abolished national origin as a criterion for immigration and as a basis for family sponsorship in 1962 and 1967, respectively (see table 1.1 for a chronology of selected events in Canada's immigration history). At the same time, the movement of labour was facilitated by the policies of the South Korean government. By then, the traditional and autocratic government of South Korea had planted the seeds of emigration among its residents via an emigration policy that encouraged people to disperse (Choi, 2003; Yoo, 2002). South Korea, at the time, was facing increasing population pressures caused by a decreasing mortality rate, the post-war baby boom, and an influx of North Koreans (Yoon, 1997). In addition, the South Korean government also wanted to secure foreign exchange that was crucial to their goals for economic development, and they saw the spreading of Koreans overseas as a way of facilitating this process.

Yet, despite contact between the two countries dating back more than a half-century and the number of significant changes in the migration policies of both countries, very few immigrants came from South Korea in the 1960s. Koreans who did arrive in the early part of this second period primarily came to study or came after having worked temporarily as miners or nurses in the *Gastarbeiter* ("guest worker") program in Germany (Yoo, 2002). It was only after 1973 that Canada received larger flows of Korean permanent migrants (see figure 1.1), as it was in 1973 that the Canadian embassy opened its doors in South Korea. After this point, the first relatively large wave of immigrants arrived, and they formed the basis of the Korean community today. It should also be pointed out that their unique form of economic integration, i.e., self-employment (E. Chan & E. Fong, chapter 7, this volume), has shaped the livelihoods of subsequent waves.

These new migration policies of South Korea and Canada, coupled with poorer economic conditions, political instability, and military dictatorship in South Korea, may explain why permanent migration from South Korea shot upward in the early 1970s, peaking in 1975 with 4,331 migrants (figure 1.1). After this peak, however, levels dropped just as dramatically and stayed low to the end of the period, which follows the total migration pattern. This rapid decline may be explained by subsequent changes in the emigration policy of the South Korean government, which likely resulted from the realization that the floodgates had opened. By 1975, the South Korean government revised their emigration policy to restrict the movement of wealthy Koreans, that is, persons owning properties worth more than US$100,000, military officers, retired generals, and high-ranking government officials. Furthermore, they restricted how much money each person could take with him or her (Kim, 1987 in Yoon, 1997, 82). More important, the mirrored decline in flows from South Korea to total migration flows to Canada suggests that the decline had more to do with the recession in Canada and consequent restrictions in immigration targets (Kelley & Trebilcock, 2010). During this part of the period, overall immigration to Canada stayed low until the mid-1980s.

This first wave of more than 26,000 Korean immigrants came through two primary avenues: as sponsored family members; and via the independent class with their educational and occupational qualifications. Based on available micro-data from the Permanent Resident Data Sys-

Figure 1.2. Korean Immigrants Landing in Canada by Immigrant Class

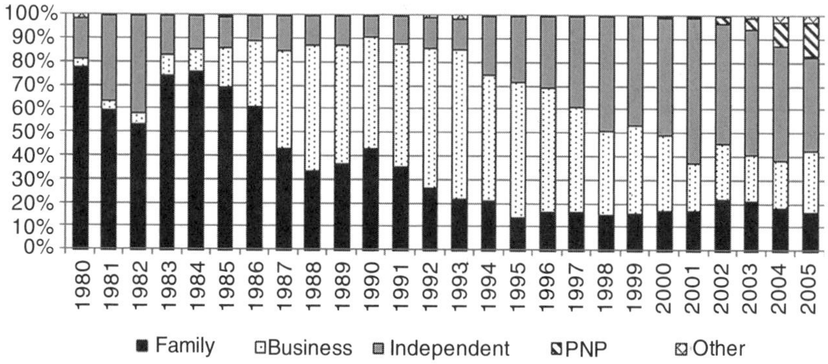

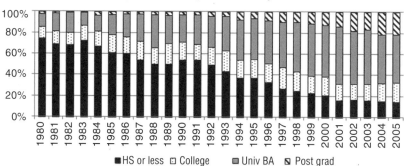

■ Family   ▫Business   ▨ Independent   ▨PNP   ▨ Other

Source: Permanent Resident Data System (PRDS) 1980–2005. Includes both North and South Koreans by Korean native language and last place of residence or country of birth (N=97,479).

Figure 1.3. Korean Immigrants Landing in Canada by Education

■HS or less   ▫ College   ▨ Univ BA   ▨ Post grad

Source: Permanent Resident Data System (PRDS) 1980–2005. Includes both North and South Koreans by Korean native language and last place of residence or country of birth, 25 years and older (N=56,225).

tem (PRDS), which contains information from landing files, more than half of the immigrants arriving between 1980 and 1985 were family-class migrants, with the independent class the second-largest category of entrants (figure 1.2). Over the same limited period and with year-to-year fluctuations, approximately 13 to 22 per cent had at least a university degree (figure 1.3) and 20 to 50 per cent listed a technical, skilled, or paraprofessional occupation (figure 1.4). Also in this second period,

Figure 1.4. Korean Immigrants Landing in Canada by Occupation

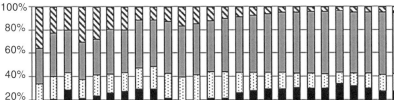

Source: PRDS 1980–2005. Includes both North and South Koreans by Korean native language and last place of residence or country of birth, for those who identified an occupation (N=17,503).

Figure 1.5. Korean Immigrants Landing in Canada by Age Group

Source: PRDS 1980–2005. Includes both North and South Koreans by Korean native language and last place of residence or country of birth (N=97,479).

about half of adult immigrants were over the age of fifty (figure 1.5). This second wave, which consisted of primarily permanent migrants, settled in Ontario and in the western provinces, namely British Columbia and Alberta (figure 1.6).

The Period of Business-Class Dominance (1986 to 2003)

In the third period, the permanent migration flow from Korea generally moved in an upward direction from an annual inflow of about

Figure 1.6. Korean Immigrants Landing in Canada by Intended Destination

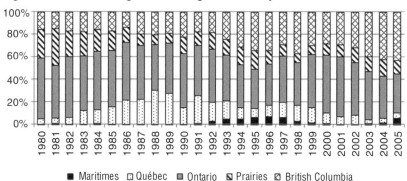

■ Maritimes ▫ Québec ▦ Ontario ◩ Prairies ▨ British Columbia

Source: PRDS 1980–2005. Includes both North and South Koreans by Korean native language and last place of residence or country of birth and excludes the territories (N=97,450).

1,100 in 1986, peaking to more than 9,600 in 2001 and then down to 7,000 in 2003 (figure 1.1), reaching an eight-year total of over 78,000 persons. However, this is an underestimation, since tourists and visiting students without permanent-resident visas are omitted from the calculation. If we include the foreign-student flow, the yearly volume of Korean migration numbered approximately 20,000 in the early 2000s. The small surge in the earlier part of this period can be attributed to the expansion of the business-class immigration program in Canada and the government's efforts to boost the numbers in this class. As we can observe in figure 1.2, the majority of Korean immigrants arrived under the business-class program during the first half of the period until the mid-1990s, and this increase was associated with a relative decline in family migration.

During this time, trade between Canada and South Korea was also on the increase (Han, 2002). Trade relations between South Korea and Canada grew well into the 1990s with the creation of the *Canada–South Korea "Special Partnership"* in 1993 (Bohatyretz, 2004; Yoo, 2002). While the previous migration period was marked by political linkages between South Korea and Canada, this period was marked by the establishment of economic linkages.

The dominance of business-class immigration was also a product of structural changes in South Korea as much as it was due to Canadian immigration policy. Conditions in South Korea had altered dramatically: there was strong economic growth during the late 1980s; democratic presidential elections took place in 1987 following two decades of military control; and the 1988 Seoul Olympic Games put South Korea on the world stage (Kong, 2000; Lee, 1996). Not surprisingly, these broader changes led to shifts in the migration flow as well as in the socio-economic characteristics of Korean immigrants. Generally, migration flows to Canada from South Korea rose only incrementally while total immigration more than doubled in the same period (figure 1.1). These diverging trends suggest that many Koreans might not have felt the need to leave, as there were sufficient economic opportunities at home. For those who did leave, expanding economic opportunities in South Korea meant they had greater resources than their predecessors and were able to meet the financial obligations under the business-class stream.

Later in the period, the impact of the 1997 Asian financial crisis (International Monetary Fund or IMF crisis) on flows is clear (figure 1.1). This crisis saw a severe devaluation of the South Korean won, which hit the country after many years of rapid economic growth and subsequent to its being labelled an "Asian Tiger" owing to its aggressive economic policies. The crisis shook South Korea's national confidence, and the resulting emotional shock and sense of economic instability led to increased numbers of migrants going abroad, with the majority of those arriving in Canada coming from the professional class (see figure 1.4). This rush, however, was short-lived, and by the end of the period the flows had decreased.

Within this context, it is not surprising that one distinction between this group of immigrants and the previous is their access to capital. The latter group was more likely to have the financial means to migrate and invest in Canada after benefiting from advances in South Korea's economy. This result is obvious since immigration under the business-class stream meant applicants had to demonstrate their financial viability as entrepreneurs, investors, or in self-employment, which may also explain why they might have been more sensitive to currency exchange rates as tested by J.D. Han and P. Ibbott (chapter 4, this volume). At the same time that educational levels of permanent migrants were rising (figure 1.3), there was a shift in the occupations of immigrants from predominantly managers prior to 1994 to a majority of professionals (figure 1.4). In this period, we also see the shift in the age of adult immigrants such that those over fifty became the smallest group of

Figure 1.7. Korean Immigrants Landing in Canada by Intended Metropolitan Area

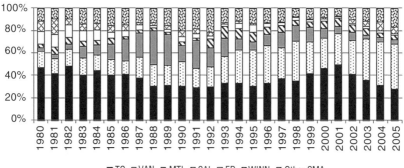

■TO □VAN ▣MTL ◨CAL □ED ▨WINN ▨ Other CMA

Source: PRDS 1980–2005. Includes both North and South Koreans by Korean native language and last place of residence or country of birth and excludes non-metropolitan areas (N=95,366).

Korean immigrants (figure 1.5). Furthermore, in addition to these shifts in composition is the large number of educational migrants on short-term stays; they are not visible in the official counts owing to the visa exemption granted since 1994 for visits of under six months' duration. Thus, compared with those arriving in the previous period, this third group of migrants was relatively young, wealthy, highly educated, and professional.

As shown in figures 1.6 and 1.7, like earlier immigrants, most of those arriving during this period indicated their place of settlement as Ontario, namely Toronto. Although Montreal, Quebec, appeared to be growing as a potential second destination early in the period, it was consistently replaced by the western provinces by 1992, particularly British Columbia and, more specifically, Vancouver.

Regionalization and Transnational Migrants (2004 to the Present)

The beginning of this period is identified by what appears to be another rise in migration flows from Korea (see figure 1.1), as well as shifts in the patterns and composition of flows in light of recent changes in Canada's immigration policies. These changes, primarily in regard to the regionalization of immigrants through the Provincial Nominee Programs (PNP), are described by A.H. Kim and C. Belkhodja (chapter

5, this volume) and can also be detected in the growing rates of PNP migrants in figure 1.2. In effect, such efforts to disperse immigrants across Canada have led to a slow decline in the significance of Toronto as the key destination for those coming from South Korea. We can observe the growing importance of Vancouver throughout the 1990s (see figure 1.7), and beginning in 2003, Korean immigrants intending to go to Vancouver outnumbered those indicating Toronto as a place of destination. As of 2004, Winnipeg became the third most popular intended destination for Koreans landing in Canada. Once again, the Maritimes appeared on the "map" of immigrants (see figure 1.6).

In this period, Korean migrants appear less likely to migrate under the business-class stream, according to federal immigration statistics (figure 1.2). However, this classification scheme belies the extent to which Koreans are continuing to come to Canada with financial capital. For example, many apply as business-class migrants under the various PNPs. Korea also continues to be one of the top two or three source countries for business-class immigrants. And like their more recent predecessors, post-2003 arrivals are highly educated and relatively young, and there has been a shift back to those with management experience versus professional work experience (figures 1.3, 1.4, and 1.5).

While future Korean immigrants' educational and occupational qualifications are likely to remain high, whether this trend of regional dispersion will continue to be a distinguishing feature of this period remains to be seen. One additional feature of Korean immigration makes this period distinctive from the past: the modern transnational family and the migration of younger foreign students. This shift in family migration is hidden in the data shown here but can be seen in chapter 14 of this volume, by J. Jeong and D. Bélanger.

For Koreans, the transnational family generally takes one of two forms. One is the "parachute" child or children who migrate alone without their parents and are placed with legal guardians. A second form is the *kirogi gajok*, or "wild goose family": one parent remains and works in Korea, typically the father, while the mother accompanies the children, who acquire student visas. For Koreans, the term is heavily imbued with cultural connotations, as wild geese symbolize family loyalty and marital harmony. Wild geese engage in seasonal migration, they make long trips to bring food back for their young, and they are monogamous and remain loyal even after the death of a mate. This term has been used in the news media, in Koreans' references to themselves, and in the scholarly literature.

The growth in transnationalism stems from the high value placed on education in Korea. More important, like the leaders in the late nineteenth century who first opened Korea's borders to Christian missionaries as a way to facilitate social and economic goals, the South Korean government enacted a globalization (*segyewha*) policy in 1994. Along with economic liberalization, the policy entailed the opening-up of social, cultural, diplomatic, and security sectors (Cho, 2005; Kim, 2000; Lee & Koo, 2006). Since then, the perception that the English language is essential for employment and economic advancement, also known as "English language mania" (Park & Abelmann, 2004), has become widespread. Foreign credentials are a mark of prestige and status, and access to professional occupations and upward mobility appears to be challenging without English-language fluency and its associated cultural capital. The issues of transnational families have become paramount for understanding the contemporary Korean diaspora (I-J. Yoon, chapter 3, this volume).

In summary, this historical outline of Korean immigration to Canada illustrates the importance of education for historical and contemporary flows. It demonstrates that permanent migration to Canada from South Korea did not occur, for the most part, in large sweeping waves. Rather, Korean migration has generally occurred in small peaks and valleys. There have also been gradual shifts in the composition of migrant flows depending on social, economic, and political conditions in South Korea and Canada, and on the political, social, and economic relations between the two countries and in the world economy. In this overview, we have provided some background and context for understanding the situation of Korean immigrants across Canada and touched on some of the issues to be explored in greater depth in subsequent chapters.

Research Themes and Organization of the Book

This book has three major research themes: migration, social-psychological adjustment, and the family. Although distinct, the contributions overlap and intersect in their focus on experiences, perspectives, and issues for various segments of the Korean population. In its richness, the collection illustrates the commonality yet diversity of Korean immigrants' experiences, attitudes, and behaviours, which should spark comparisons with other immigrant experiences in Canada and with Korean diasporic experiences around the world. The research studies reported here incorporate Korean immigrant experiences across the wide span of this country at a national level but also at finer geographic levels, including large urban centres and smaller mid-size cities, with the most common research location being Toronto, where most Korean immigrants have settled.

To complement the historical context offered above, this collection begins with J. Park's chapter 2, which provides a socio-demographic profile of the community. Using the 2006 census data, Park gives us a comprehensive illustration of Koreans' social and economic character-istics. Through his analysis, we discover that there is a degree of Korean disadvantage in the Canadian context that deserves attention.

In "Part I: Understanding Korean Migration," the four chapters focus on various push-and-pull factors of emigration from Korea. The section opens with I.-J. Yoon's chapter 3, which encourages all of us to think in comparative terms and offers a global context within which to situ-ate Korean migration to Canada. As others in this volume show, there is value in juxtaposing Korean migration experiences in Canada not only in relation to other immigrants on Canada but also cross-nation-ally. Yoon traces both the historical and geographic evolution of Korean emigration. He describes four major periods of the Korean diaspora, beginning in the 1800s, and details the flows of Korean migrants in the Commonwealth of Independent States (CIS), People's Republic of China, Japan, and North America. It is distinct from the other chap-ters in this collection as it provides a broad and sweeping overview of Korean migration history, yet we find it to be as important as the more specialized chapters, for it allows us to see how migration to Canada forms a small but growing part of the bigger picture.

Individually, each of the other chapters in this section provides a detailed analysis of the various migration experiences of Koreans in Canada. J. Han and P. Ibbott's chapter 4 frames Korean migration in eco-nomic terms, testing human-capital theory. A. Kim and C. Belkhodja's chapter 5 examines Atlantic Koreans' migration decisions within the policy context of the Provincial Nominee Program. Finally, M. Kwak's chapter 6 highlights Korean international students' migration experi-ences in Vancouver. Each paper provides unique perspectives and findings. Together, however, they point to the cultural non-price value of the Canadian educational system for the children and young adults of Korean immigrant families.

In "Part II: Immigrant Socio-economic and Social-Psychological Integration," we have a collection of papers that requires us to ques-tion further whether immigrant integration into Canadian society is, for one, predominantly occurring, and two, socially and psychologically advantageous. From a socio-economic perspective (E. Chan and E. Fong's and S. Noh and M. Moon's chapters 7 and 8, respectively), Koreans are not fully integrating into the Canadian system, owing to their lower levels of participation in the labour market. However, from a cultural perspective (M. Jeon's chapter 9), Korean-language maintenance is decreasing across generations in the Greater Toronto Area, which indicates some degree of acculturation. In addition, similar to findings of other studies on recent immigrants, racialized experiences in Canada have been found to impede the integration process, even for second-generation Korean Canadians who are fully proficient in the English language and are attaining high levels of Canadian education (M.S. Noh's chapter 11). Alongside these various patterns of integration, we must question to what degree the patterns benefit or hinder Koreans, and in what ways. The findings in E. Chan and E. Fong's chapter 7, in S. Noh and M. Moon's chapter 8, and in S. Noh, A. Kimura-Ida, R.F. Falk, N.B. Miller, and M. Moon's chapter 10, imply that integration in Canada – that is, greater participation in the primary labour market through employment, and not self-employment, as well as advanced education in Canada and attachment to Canada are beneficial for the settlement experiences of Korean immigrants. However, the chapters in this section also describe the difficulty in achieving full integration for Korean immigrants, and they provide some insight into the newcomers' behaviour and the decisions they make.

In "Part III: Social Roles and Relationships in Korean Families," the processes of adaptation and innovation are documented in various aspects of Korean family life. G. Kwak and D. Lai's chapter 12 sheds light on the importance of family relations, particularly parent-child relationships, for enhancing a healthy outlook held by the Korean elderly residing in Calgary. Y. Kwon and S. Chuang's chapter 13 examines meanings of fatherhood and the ideal father among Korean men in Toronto. They find that Western or Canadian values of fatherhood are adapted as a part of their constructed identities. Finally, J. Jeong and D. Bélanger's chapter 14 provides an empirical description of *kirogi* families in a mid-size city and identifies adjustments made by Korean immigrants in their family roles and their gender definitions to innovatively reclaim the legitimacy of their family form. While each paper highlights different aspects of family function, each study presents results of resilience and resourcefulness among Korean-Canadian families. Similar to the chapters in part I of this book, part II shows just how Korean families place values around education at the centre of their migration decisions.

As a whole, this collection gives readers a set of multidisciplinary investigations into the lives of Korean immigrants. The methodological approaches that have been applied are varied and include both qualitative and quantitative methods and reports of descriptive data as well as sophisticated analytical models. And while there are different subjects, results, and interpretations, there are also common underlying themes, and one such theme is culture. We did not seek a paper devoted to this topic, as culture, in all its complexity and fluidity, is a pervasive theme and permeates all the contributions.

In this collection we have just scratched the surface of the Korean diaspora in Canada. At the same time, the papers provide much-needed knowledge and enrich the literature on immigration and ethnic studies. Our volume is intended to be accessible to academic, student, research, policy, and community circles alike. Finally, the successful completion of the book would not have been possible without the research participants from the Korean community who shared their circumstances, personal experiences, observations, and feelings. The book is a collective endeavour to present the findings and conclusions back to them.

REFERENCES

Bohatyretz, S. (2004). Tiger by the tail? Canada's trade with South Korea. Analytical Paper. Ottawa: Statistics Canada International Trade Division.

Chan, E., and Fong, E. (2012). Social, economic, and demographic characteristics of Korean self-employment in Canada, chapter 7, this volume.

Cho, U. (2005). The encroachment of globalization into intimate life: The flexible Korean family in "economic crisis." *Korea Journal* 45(3):8–35.

Choi, I. (2003). Korean diaspora in the making: Its current status and impact on the Korean economy. In C.F. Bergsten and I. Choi (Eds.), *The Korean diaspora in the world economy, Special report 15*. Washington, DC: Institute for International Economics.

Han, J.D. (2002). Korean-Canadian trade: Before and after the Asian financial crisis. In R.W.L. Guisso and Y.-s. Yoo (Eds.), *Canada and Korea: Perspectives 2000*. Toronto: Centre for Korean Studies, University of Toronto.

Kelley, N., and Trebilcock, M. (2010). *The making of the mosaic: A history of Canadian immigration policy*, 2nd ed. Toronto: University of Toronto Press.

Kim, A., and Belkhodja, C. (2012). Emerging gateways in the Atlantic: The institutional and family context of Korean migration to New Brunswick, chapter 5, this volume.

Kim, S.S. (2000). Korea and globalization (*segyehwa*): A framework for analysis. In S.S. Kim (Ed.), *Korea's globalization*. Cambridge: Cambridge University Press.

Kong, T.Y. (2000). *The politics of economic reform in South Korea: A fragile miracle*. London: Routledge.

Kwak, M.-J. (2004). An exploration of the Korean-Canadian community in Vancouver. Working paper series 04–14. Vancouver: Research on Immigration and Integration in the Metropolis (RIIM).

———. (2012). International student experiences of migration and consuming Canadian education, chapter 6, this volume.

Lee, H.-K. (1996). *The Korean economy: Perspectives for the twenty-first century*. Albany: State University of New York Press.

Lee, Y.-J., and Koo, H. (2006). Wild geese fathers and a globalised family strategy for education in Korea. *International Development Planning Review* 28(4):533–53.

Park, J. (2012). A demographic profile of Koreans in Canada, chapter 2, this volume.

Park, S.J., and Abelmann, N. (2004). Class and cosmopolitan striving: Mothers' management of English education in South Korea. *Anthropological Quarterly* 77(4):645–72.

Price, J. (2004). The "Cat's Paw": Canada and the United Nations Temporary Commission on Korea. *The Canadian Historical Review 85*(2): 297–324.

Simmons, A. (2010). *Immigration and Canada: Global and transnational perspectives*. Toronto: Canadian Scholars' Press, Inc.

Statistics Canada. (2010). *Projections of the diversity of the Canadian population: 2006–2031*. Ottawa: Statistics Canada Demography Division.

Yoo, Y.-s. (2002). Canada and Korea: A Shared History. In R.W.L. Guisso and Y.-s. Yoo, eds., *Canada and Korea: Perspectives 2000*. Toronto: Centre for Korean Studies, University of Toronto.

Yoon, I.-J. (1997). *On my own: Korean businesses and race relations in America*. Chicago: The University of Chicago Press.

———. (2012). The Korean diaspora from global perspectives, chapter 3, this volume.

2 A Demographic Profile of Koreans in Canada

JUNGWEE PARK

Introduction

This chapter provides a demographic profile of individuals of Korean origin living in Canada.[1] It describes the basic social and economic characteristics of members of the Korean community. Characteristics discussed in the chapter include population growth, immigration status, geographic distribution, age distribution, language proficiency, family status, religion, educational attainment, employment, occupation, and income of Canadians of Korean origin. Most information presented in this chapter is derived from the 2006 Census of Canada. Statistics Canada conducts the census every five years. Information on ethnic or cultural origin was obtained from a long questionnaire of the census that at the time one in five Canadian households answered.

For the purpose of this chapter, the term *Canadians* refers to all persons with a usual place of residence in Canada, regardless of their citizenship.

Population Growth

The Korean community in Canada has been growing fast. There were

1 The author would like to thank Siméon Akinseloyin, Ibukun A. Sorinmade, and Michelle Carman for their assistance in the preliminary data analysis for this chapter.
    All statistical information in this chapter referring to Koreans, the Korean community, Canadians of Korean origin, people of Korean origin, or Korean Canadians denotes those who reported Korean origins, either alone or in combination with other origins, in response to the question on ethnic origin in the 2006 census.

Figure 2.1. Population of People of Korean Origin in Canada, 1981–2006

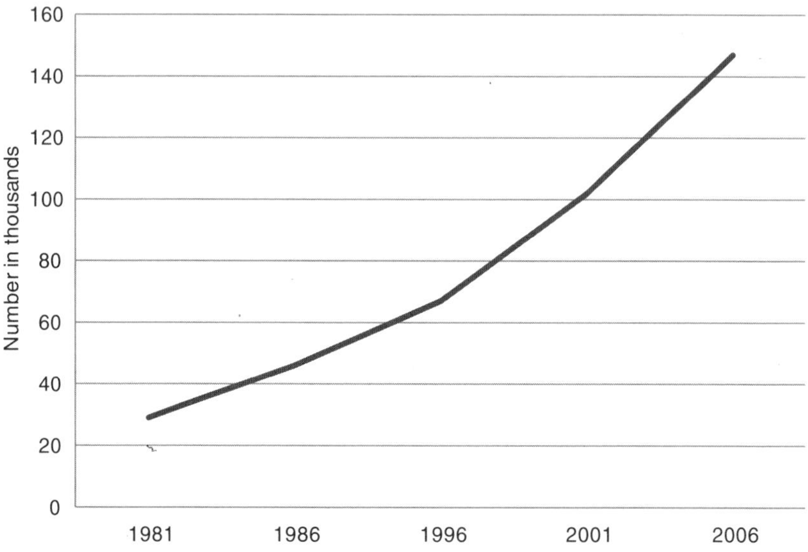

Source: 1981, 1986, 1991, 1996, 2001, 2006 Census – 20% sample data.

146,550 people of Korean origin in 2006.[2] The number increased by 44 per cent from 2001 and more than doubled from 1996; and for the past quarter-century, the number of Canadians of Korean origin more than quintupled (figure 2.1). This is a remarkable increase, given that the population growth of the total Canadians between the censuses of 1996 and 2001 was only 5.4 per cent. In 2006, the Korean community was the seventh largest among non-European ethnic groups.[3] Unlike other ethnic population groups, almost all people of Korean origin (94 per cent) indicated that they had only Korean origin.[4] According to single ethnic origin responses, the Korean population in Canada was the fourth

---

2 However, Korean community sources in Canada claim that the census may have undercounted the number of temporary visitors, especially students for English training (Yoon, 2006); moreover, according to the number of overseas Koreans published by the Korean government, there were 223,322 Korean descents in Canada (Ministry of Foreign Affairs and Trades, Seoul, 2009).

3 In 2001, as well, the Korean community was the seventh-largest non-European ethnic group in the country (Lindsay, 2001).

4 Almost 40 per cent of the overall Canadian population has multiple ethnic origins.

Figure 2.2. Period of Immigration: People of Korean Origin in Canada, 2006

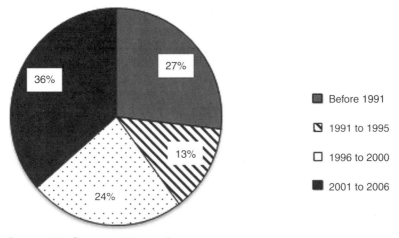

Source: 2006 Census – 20% sample.

largest among non-European groups after Chinese, East Indian, and Filipino.

Immigration Status

Of 146,550 people of Korean origin in Canada, 70 per cent were immigrants and 16 per cent were Canadian-born. Non-permanent residents accounted for 15 per cent. Non-permanent residents include those who hold a student authorization, an employment authorization, or a Minister's permit and family members living with them.

Among Koreans fifteen years and over, 91 per cent were first-generation Korean Canadian while 8 per cent were second generation. Only 1 per cent of them were third generation. Thus, the majority of the Korean population in Canada was born outside the country. Among the total of immigrants of Korean origin, about 97 per cent emigrated directly from Korea.

The large share of Koreans in Canada comprises recent immigrants. More than a third arrived in the past five years, and about 60 per cent landed in Canada between 1996 and 2006 (figure 2.2). And as shown in figure 2.3, most Koreans immigrated to Canada while at their core economic age (twenty-five to forty-four). This circumstance may be a result

Figure 2.3. Age of Immigration: People of Korean Origin in Canada, 2006

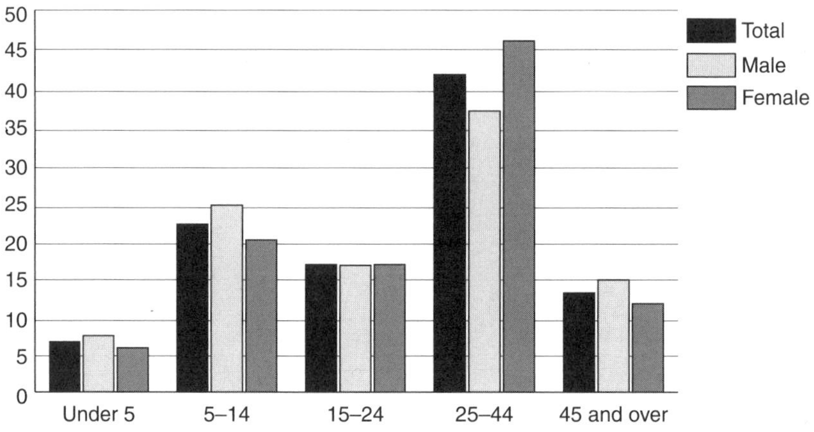

Source: 2006 Census – 20% sample.

of Canada's immigration points system assigning the highest score to applicants aged between twenty-one and forty-nine years.

Fifty-seven per cent of all people of Korean origin were Canadian citizens: 16 per cent of them were citizens by birth, while 41 per cent became Canadian citizens by naturalization (table 2.1). Older members of the Korean community (aged forty-five and up) were more likely than younger members to be citizens, which may result from the longer period of immigration of older Koreans. Compared with the total Canadian population, a much greater proportion of the Korean community population were non-citizens – 6 per cent versus 43 per cent. A great number of Koreans residing in Canada prefer to keep permanent-resident status instead of obtaining Canadian citizenship, probably because of South Korean government rules: under current law, South Korea does not allow adults and foreigners living in the country to hold multiple citizenship; and Koreans who obtain foreign citizenship at birth in other countries, or after emigration, must choose a single nationality by the age of twenty-two.

Geographic Distribution

Like many other immigrant groups, Canadians of Korean descent tend to be geographically concentrated. In 2006, out of the 146,550 Canadian

Table 2.1. Citizenship Status of People of Korean Origin and the Total Canadian Population

	Korean origin (%)					Total Canadian (%)
	Under 25	25–44	45–64	65 or older	Total	
Citizen by birth	30.5	10.7	1.2	3.6	16.1	79.4
Citizen by naturalization	22.4	41.6	62.3	79.1	40.8	15.0
Non-citizen	47.1	47.7	36.5	17.4	43.1	5.6

Source: 2006 Census – 20% sample data.

Table 2.2. Provincial Distribution of People of Korean Origin and the Total Canadian Population

Province	People of Korean origin (%)	Total Canadian population (%)
Ontario	49.2	38.5
British Columbia	35.4	13.0
Alberta	8.4	10.4
Quebec	3.8	23.8
Manitoba	1.6	3.6
Nova Scotia	0.6	2.9
Saskatchewan	0.5	3.1
New Brunswick	0.4	2.3
Prince Edward Island	0.1	0.4
Newfoundland and Labrador	0.1	1.6
Northwest Territories	0.0	0.1

Source: 2006 Census – 20% sample data.

residents of Korean origin, about half lived in Ontario, 35 per cent in British Columbia, and about 8 per cent lived in Alberta (table 2.2). The population growth for the previous five years occurred especially in British Columbia and Alberta. Despite a slight decrease in proportion since 2001, about half of the Korean population still lived in Ontario (54 per cent in 2001) in 2006. British Columbia was home to 35 per cent of people of Korean origin (32 per cent in 2001). British Columbia may be attractive to Korean immigrants since the province has warmer winters and is close to the Asia-Pacific Rim. For the years from 2001 to 2006, Koreans in Alberta increased from about 8,000 to 12,000.

This trend of concentration in the two provinces (Ontario and BC) among people of Korean origin seems remarkable compared with the distribution of the total Canadian population. A much smaller proportion of Koreans lived in the other provinces. For example, only 4 per

Table 2.3. People of Korean Origin in Major Cities

City	Number	% of total Koreans
Toronto	57,235	39.1
Vancouver	46,035	31.4
Calgary	7,005	4.8
Montreal	4,850	3.3
Edmonton	3,865	2.6
Ottawa	2,440	1.7
Hamilton	2,285	1.6
Winnipeg	2,205	1.5
London	2,190	1.5
Kitchener	1,725	1.2
Abbotsford	1,665	1.1
Victoria	1,270	0.9

Source: 2006 Census – 20% sample data.

cent of Korean Canadians lived in Quebec, while about a quarter of the total Canadian population resided in the province. Only a few members of the Korean community lived in the Atlantic Provinces and in the North.

As shown in table 2.3, many persons of Korean origin resided in two cities, Toronto (39 per cent) and Vancouver (31 per cent). This high concentration of Koreans in Toronto and Vancouver is related to the sociocultural environment of the two metropolitan cities. In the two cities, they tend to find a well-established network of people of Korean heritage. In addition, Vancouver is favoured because of its easy access to a natural environment, a fair climate, and geographical proximity to their country of origin (Kwak, 2004).

Age Distribution

In 2006, there were slightly more women than men in the Korean community (52 per cent versus 48 per cent). The Korean population in Canada is relatively younger than the total population. Of all Korean Canadians, 41 per cent were under the age of twenty-five, while 31 per cent of Canadians were under twenty-five (table 2.4). Only 13 per cent of people of Korean origin were aged fifty-five and over, whereas a quarter of the total Canadian population belonged to that age group. Likewise, the elderly population aged sixty-five and over was only 6 per cent of all Korean Canadians, compared with 14 per cent of the total Canadian population.

Table 2.4. Age Distribution of Population of Korean Origin and the Total Canadian Population

| | Korean origin | | | Total Canadian | | |
	Total	Male	Female	Total	Male	Female
Under 15	21.1	23.7	18.6	17.6	18.5	16.9
15 to 24	19.6	21.0	18.3	13.4	13.9	12.9
25 to 34	14.4	13.5	15.2	12.7	12.7	12.7
35 to 44	16.3	13.4	19.0	15.2	15.3	15.2
45 to 54	15.5	14.9	16.0	15.8	15.8	15.7
55 to 64	7.3	7.4	7.2	11.6	11.7	11.6
65 to 74	4.0	4.5	3.5	7.2	7.0	7.4
75 and over	1.9	1.5	2.2	6.4	5.2	7.7

Source: 2006 Census – 20% sample data.

Table 2.5. Official Language Proficiency among People of Korean Origin and the Total Canadian Population

| | Korean origin (%) | | | | | Total Canadian |
	Under 25	25–44	45–64	65 or older	Total	(%)
English only	85.8	87.3	83.3	62.1	84.3	67.6
French only	1.2	0.3	0.3	0.4	0.6	13.3
English and French	8.3	5.9	1.7	1.7	5.7	17.4
Neither	4.7	6.6	14.7	35.9	9.4	1.7

Source: 2006 Census – 20% sample data.

Language Proficiency

An overwhelming majority of people of Korean origin in Canada speak English. As well, 91 per cent of Korean Canadians can speak at least one official language (table 2.5). Nine per cent of members of the Korean community in Canada were not able to conduct a conversation in either of the official languages. Not surprisingly, more individuals with language barriers were found among seniors. More than a third of seniors aged sixty-five or older in the Korean community reported that they spoke neither official language; they are the ones who immigrated either very recently or late in life. In the Chinese community, 14 per cent indicated the inability to speak an official language. Compared with the Canadian total, far fewer Koreans speak French (31 per cent versus 6 per cent). This difference may be related to the relatively small size of the Korean population in the province of Quebec.

Many of the people of Korean origin (86 per cent) reported that their

Table 2.6. Language Most Often Used by People of Korean Origin

	At home	At work
English	26.4	82.8
French	0.9	1.5
Non-official (Korean)	69.4	14.9
Others	3.3	0.8

Source: 2006 Census – 20% sample data.

mother tongue is neither English nor French. As a result, their language-use patterns are different at home and work (table 2.6). In 2006, about 70 per cent of all ethnic Koreans in Canada most often spoke Korean at home; but at work, 84 per cent of Korean workers aged fifteen or older used one of the official languages. Fifteen per cent of Korean Canadians who indicated their use of a non-official language at work may be employed at ethnic businesses serving mostly Korean compatriots.

Family Status

More than 40 per cent of people of Korean origin in Canada are married, and another 40 per cent are children living with their families; almost 90 per cent of Canadians of Korean descent belonged to a census family (table 2.7). For male Korean Canadians, the biggest category of family status is children living with families (45 per cent). This percentage seems quite high compared with 34 per cent of total Canadian men. The proportion of lone-parent families increased from 2001 to 2006. Single mothers accounted for 7 per cent of the total female population in the Korean community in 2006, whereas the rate in the 2001 census was 4 per cent.

Overall, people of Korean descent in Canada are less likely than the total population to live alone. Only 5 per cent of Koreans reported that they live alone, compared with 11 per cent of the national average, which may be related in part to differences in marital status of the two population groups. More than half of Korean Canadians aged fifteen and over were legally married, and about 6 per cent were separated, divorced, or widowed. On the other hand, of all Canadians, 48 per cent were married, and 17 per cent were separated, divorced, or widowed. As well, the percentage of elderly Koreans living alone was only half of their Canadian counterpart (14 per cent versus 28 per cent), which may reflect the cultural emphasis on family shared by Koreans.

Table 2.7. Family Status of People of Korean Origin and the Total Canadian Population by Sex

	Korean origin			Total Canadian		
	Total	Male	Female	Total	Male	Female
Married	42.2	41.7	42.6	39.3	40.1	38.6
Living common-law	1.8	1.4	2.1	8.9	9.1	8.7
Lone parent	4.2	1.0	7.3	4.6	1.9	7.2
Child living at home	39.8	44.7	35.3	31.3	33.9	28.8
Living with relatives	3.2	2.5	3.9	2.1	1.7	2.4
Living with non-relatives	4.1	4.3	3.8	3.2	3.7	2.7
Living alone	4.7	4.4	5.0	10.7	9.7	11.7

Source: 2006 Census – 20% sample data.

Table 2.8. Religious Affiliations of People of Korean Origin in Canada, 1981, 1991, 2001

	1981	1991	2001
Catholic	21.2	24.4	24.5
Protestant or non-Catholic Christian	58.5	57.5	50.7
Buddhists	2.2	2.2	3.9
Other religions	0.6	0.3	0.6
No affiliation	17.6	15.7	20.3

Source: 1981, 1991, 2001 Census – 20% sample data. No question regarding religion was included in the 2006 census.

Religion

The question on religion is not asked in the quinquennial censuses, thus the most recent census data on religion are provided in the 2001 census. These data show that 51 per cent of Canadians of Korean descent reported that they belonged to a Protestant or non-Catholic Christian denominations, and 25 per cent indicated that they were Catholic. Four per cent were Buddhists; and about 20 per cent had no stated religion. High percentages of Christian membership among Koreans in Canada were more marked in the previous two censuses that collected information on religion (table 2.8). This profile of religious affiliation among Korean Canadians contrasts with Koreans in South Korea, where 23 per cent of the population in 2005 reported that they were Buddhists, 47 per cent said they had no religious affiliation, and only 29 per cent were members of Christian denominations – 18 per cent Protestants and 11 per cent Catholics (Ministry of Culture, Sports and Tourism, 2009). Korean ethnic churches in Canada may play a significant role in making Christianity the dominant faith among Korean Canadians. Many Koreans join their ethnic churches to seek practical social supports for immigrant life as well as for religious accommodation.

Education

Canadians of Korean origin are more likely to have a higher academic education than the average Canadian. In 2006, only 5 per cent of Canadians of Korean origin aged twenty-five or older did not have an academic certificate, diploma, or degree, whereas 21 per cent of total Canadians fell under the same category (table 2.9). Also of interest is the fact that people of Korean origin were twice as likely as other Canadians to have a university degree. For instance, among the Korean population, 52 per cent had a bachelor's degree or higher, whereas only 20 per cent of the total Canadian population had the same level of education. Almost one in seven Korean Canadians had a professional degree (in areas such as medicine, dentistry, veterinary medicine, or optometry), a master's degree, or an earned doctorate. The educational attainment of Korean Canadians was much higher than most other ethnic groups.[5] For example, 36 per cent of Japanese Canadians and 37 per cent of Chinese Canadians had a bachelor's degree or higher.

Korean Canadians' educational attainment is especially high among its first- and second-generation members. Rates of university graduation or higher for first- and second-generation Koreans aged twenty-five or older was 52 per cent and 60 percent, respectively. As high as 20 per cent of second-generation Korean Canadians held a professional degree. The third generation of Korean Canadians showed much lower educational attainment than their first- and second-generation counterparts. Only 16 per cent of third-generation Koreans was composed of university graduates. This rate is even slightly lower than the Canadian average.

Interestingly, members of the Korean community are much less likely than the total Canadian population to engage in practical education such as apprenticeship. Eleven per cent of total Canadians have an apprenticeship or trade certificate, compared with only 3 per cent among Canadians of Korean origin.

---

5 Given that many Korean Canadians are recent immigrants, it is not surprising that the majority (67 per cent) of post-secondary graduates obtained their degrees outside Canada. Other ethnic groups from East Asia showed a much lower rate of foreign degrees (47 per cent for Chinese Canadians and 37 per cent for Japanese Canadians) as they are more established groups with longer immigration histories in Canada.

Table 2.9. Educational Attainment of People of Korean Origin and the Total Canadian
Population Aged 25 and Over

	Korean origin (%)			Total Canadian (%)		
Education level	Total	Male	Female	Total	Male	Female
No certificate, diploma, or degree	4.8	3.5	5.8	20.6	20.3	20.9
High school certificate	18.8	15.8	21.4	23.4	21.8	24.9
Apprenticeship or trade certificate	3.1	3.1	3.1	12.2	16.1	8.4
College, CEGEP, or non-university diploma	10.3	9.7	10.8	18.5	16.5	20.4
University certificate or diploma below bachelor's	11.2	11.5	11.1	4.9	4.3	5.5
University degree at bachelor's	34.8	34.5	35.0	12.8	12.5	13.1
University certificate or diploma above bachelor's	4.4	4.6	4.3	2.2	2.1	2.3
Degree in medicine, dentistry, veterinary medicine, or optometry	1.2	1.7	0.8	0.6	0.8	0.5
Master's degree	9.6	12.8	7.0	4.0	4.5	3.6
Earned Doctorate	1.8	2.8	0.9	0.8	1.2	0.5

Source: 2006 Census – 20% sample data.

Employment and Occupations

Despite their high levels of educational attainment, Canadians of
Korean descent are less likely than the general population to find jobs
in the Canadian labour market commensurate with their education and
training (Yoon, 2006). Compared with the total Canadian population,
members of the Korean community in Canada showed a lower labour
participation rate and a higher unemployment rate in 2006 (table 2.10).
In particular, the unemployment among women was 8 per cent, and the
jobless rate among youth (aged fifteen to twenty-four) of Korean origin
was at a staggering 16 per cent.

About 57 per cent of Korean adults aged twenty-five and over were
employed in 2005. Among those employed, full-year and full-time
workers[6] were only 50 per cent. By contrast, 63 per cent of the total
Canadian adult population had a job, and 58 per cent of them were
full-time workers all year-round. Compared with about 49 per cent full-

---

6 Those who work forty-nine to fifty-two weeks mainly full-time – thirty hours or
   more a week.

Table 2.10. Employment Characteristics of Workers Aged 25 and Older, People of Korean Origin, and the Total Canadian Population

	Korean origin			Total Canadian		
	Total	Male	Female	Total	Male	Female
Labour participation rate	61.5	71.4	53.4	67.1	73.7	60.9
Unemployment rate	7.0	6.2	7.9	5.4	5.3	5.5
Wage earners	66.2	63.5	69.1	86.2	83.1	89.5
Self-employed	32.3	35.5	28.8	13.5	16.8	9.9
Unpaid family workers	1.6	1.0	2.1	0.3	0.1	0.5

Source: 2006 Census – 20% sample data.

time employment among first- and third-generation Korean Canadians, second-generation members showed a much higher rate of 72 per cent.

While the vast majority of Canadian workers were wage earners (83 per cent for men, 90 per cent for women), a considerable number of people of Korean origin (32 per cent) were self-employed.[7] Many of them work for small businesses in retail, restaurants, and hotels. Apparently, most of the self-employed Koreans were members of the first generation. Less than 10 per cent of the second- and third-generation Korean workers were self-employed.

Compared with other visible minority groups, a much higher rate of self-employment was found among members of the Korean community. For instance, more than one-third of the first-generation Korean workers were self-employed, compared with no more than 20 per cent of any other visible minority groups. A distant second were West Asian groups, with 18 per cent of the population in self-employment.

The percentage of unpaid family workers was high among Korean Canadians compared with the Canadian average – 2 per cent versus 0.5 per cent. Such unpaid individuals may work for their family-owned small businesses.

High rates of self-employment are evident among workers of Korean origin. And as shown in table 2.11, the biggest occupation category for Korean Canadians was management for men (30 per cent), and sales and service for women (31 per cent) in 2006. In these occupational groups, many Koreans were engaged in self-employment and in small businesses. It is expected that many held managerial positions in their unincorporated self-employment, such as family-owned small busi-

---

7 The total rate includes self-employed unincorporated and incorporated. About two-thirds of those self-employed were in unincorporated businesses.

Table 2.11. Occupations Held by Workers Aged 25 and Older, People of Korean Origin, and the Total Canadian Population, 2006

Occupation	Korean origin			Total Canadian		
	Total	Male	Female	Total	Male	Female
Management	25.9	30.4	21.2	10.8	13.1	8.3
Business, finance, and administration	12.5	8.0	17.4	19.0	9.9	28.9
Natural and applied sciences	8.0	12.3	3.4	7.0	10.4	3.2
Health	5.6	4.5	6.8	6.1	2.3	10.3
Social science, education, government services, religion	10.1	9.0	11.2	9.3	5.8	13.2
Art, culture, recreation, and sport	3.7	2.7	4.8	2.9	2.5	3.3
Sales and service	25.9	20.8	31.4	19.9	15.9	24.3
Trades, transport, and equipment operation	5.1	8.6	1.3	15.4	27.3	2.3
Primary industry	0.7	0.9	0.5	3.6	5.4	1.8
Processing, manufacturing, and utilities	2.5	2.9	2.0	6.1	7.5	4.5

Source: 2006 Census – 20% sample data.

nesses. Also, a high percentage of sales and service work may be a result of job changes necessarily made by Korean immigrants whose education and skills were not recognized in the Canadian labour market. This occupational pattern reflects the patterns exhibited by first-generation Korean Canadians. For second-generation members of the Korean community, the biggest occupational category was business, finance, and administration.

Compared with the national average, a much smaller proportion of Korean-Canadian workers were in occupations related to trades, primary industry, and manufacturing.

Income

As table 2.12 indicates, in 2005, the total average income for Korean Canadians aged twenty-five or older was $23,741 (median income, $14,081), about $14,000 less than or about 60 per cent of the national average of $37,937 (median, $28,543). Among full-time workers[8] aged twenty-five or older in 2005, Korean-Canadian men and women ($39,534 for men, $30,546 for women) earned much less than the Canadian aver-

---

8 Those who worked mainly full-time weeks in 2005.

age ($57,916 for men, $40,878 for women). A similar income differential is observed among part-time workers.[9] On average, Korean-Canadian part-time workers earned $16,985, which was considerably less than the national average, $25,059.

Moreover, average total incomes of most other visible-minority groups were significantly higher than that of Korean Canadians. For example, total incomes of Chinese Canadians ($31,095), African Canadians ($30,197), and Filipino Canadians ($30,485) were over $30,000. The total income of Japanese Canadians (average $41,823; median $29,211) was almost twice that earned by members of Korean community.

Given the higher educational attainment, the overall lower income level of Korean Canadians seems quite ironic. Income differentials still existed among those with a bachelor's degree or higher. The average income of individual Korean Canadians in 2005 was $27,391, while the Canadian average was $60,873, so the Korean-Canadian income was about $33,500 less than or about 45 per cent of the national average. The income gap was even greater among university graduates.

It is reported that Canadian employers tend to require immigrants to have job experience and schooling in the host country, more even than employers in the United States (Yoon, 2006); thus, the lower income level of Korean Canadians may be related to the fact that many of their higher degrees were earned outside Canada.

However, the relatively lower income of Korean Canadians is not entirely explained by recent immigration and the attainment of post-secondary education outside Canada. Even when the generation factor was controlled for, the income differential still remained. Let us take an example of second-generation Korean workers aged twenty-five or older with university education (bachelor's degree or higher). Most have received a Canadian education. However, their average income was significantly lower than that of other Canadians with the same education levels ($45,864 versus $67,936).

Many Korean families and individuals fell below Low-Income Cut-offs (LICOs).[10] In 2005, Korean-Canadian families were about four times more likely than other Canadian families to live in low-income families; 41 per cent of members of the Korean community were below the offi-

---

9 Those who worked mainly part-time weeks in 2005.
10 LICOs represent an income threshold at which families, or persons not in economic families, likely spend 20 per cent more of income on food, shelter, and clothing than the average family, leaving less income available for other expenses such as health, education, transportation, and recreation. LICOs are calculated for families and communities of different sizes (Statistics Canada, 2007).

Table 2.12. Income Statistics for People of Korean Origin and the Total Canadian
Population Aged 25 and Over, 2005

	Korean origin			Total Canadian		
	Total	Male	Female	Total	Male	Female
Average total income	$23,741	$29,754	$18,764	$37,937	$47,790	$28,854
Median total income	$14,081	$17,597	$12,035	$28,543	$36,214	$20,460
Low-income – family (%)	40.6	39.7	41.3	9.6	8.5	10.6
Low-income – unattached individual (%)	59.5	57.8	61.0	33.3	30.2	36.0

Source: 2006 Census – 20% sample data.

cial LICOs, compared with 10 per cent of the total Canadian population. Similarly, Korean-Canadian unattached adults were twice as likely to have low incomes as other Canadian unattached individuals (60 per cent versus 33 per cent). Particularly high rates of low income were found among elderly members (aged sixty-five and over) of the Korean community who lived alone. Four out of five Korean unattached seniors lived under the LICOs. Even after taxes, more than 70 per cent of them had low incomes, whereas only 17 per cent of the total Canadian unattached seniors had low incomes.

The lower income level of Korean Canadians in spite of their higher educational attainments is so puzzling that, some argue, it may be related to the under-reporting of income. This argument might be supported by Korean-Canadian workers' high percentage of self-employment. Some studies indicated that the self-employed are often able to conceal income and increase expenses to reduce their taxes because of the absence of a third party reporting income (Schuetze, 2002). However, this argument has been largely refuted by new findings revealing the pervasiveness of under-reporting of income, regardless the type of employment (Dunbar & Fu, 2008). There is no reason to speculate that a systemic misrepresentation of income information exists in the national census by certain population groups.

Conclusions

The Korean community in Canada has been rapidly growing. Their population has more than doubled since 1996 owing to the arrival of new emigrants from Korea. In 2006, its number was close to 150,000. Most Koreans landed in Canada while they were in the core working age group. Compared with the total Canadian population, the Korean-

Canadian population structure is much younger; its proportion of people under twenty-five was more than 40 per cent. Ninety-four per cent were able to speak English or French. Korean-Canadian adults were more likely than others to be married, and Koreans in all age groups were much less likely than other Canadians to live alone. More than 40 per cent of Canadians of Korean descent earned a university degree or higher. In short, compared with the overall Canadian population, the Korean-Canadian population is a relatively young, strongly family-based, and highly educated group.

Despite their advanced level of educational attainment, people of Korean descent in Canada do not seem to gain fair returns from their human capital. Their performance in the labour market has not been so successful: the average income of Korean-Canadian adults in 2005 was $23,741, which is about $14,000 less per capita than the average Canadian, only half of the adult population worked full-time, and more than 40 per cent of Korean families fell under the low-income cut-off. The maximization of potential and opportunities for members of the Korean community is yet to come in Canadian society.

REFERENCES

Dunbar, G.R., and Fu, C. (2008). Income illusion: Tax evasion in Canada. Working Paper. Department of Economics, Simon Fraser University.
Kwak, M.J. (2004). An exploration of the Korean-Canadian community in Vancouver. Vancouver Centre of Excellence. Research on Immigration and Integration in the Metropolis. Working Paper Series 04–14.
Lindsay, C. (2001). The Korean community in Canada. Statistics Canada. 1996, 2001, 2006. Census data. Ottawa: Statistics Canada.
Ministry of Culture, Sports, and Tourism. (2009). Republic of Korea, religions, the present conditions. Seoul: Ministry of Culture, Sports, and Tourism.
Ministry of Foreign Affairs and Trades. (2009). Current status of overseas Koreans. Seoul: Ministry of Foreign Affairs and Trades.
Schuetze, H.J. (2002). Profiles of tax noncompliance among the self-employed in Canada: 1969 to 1992. *Canadian Public Policy, 28*(2), 219–37.
Statistics Canada. (2007). *2006 Census Dictionary.* Statistics Canada Catalogue no. 92-566-XWE. Ottawa, Ontario. February 14. http://www12.statcan.ca/english/census06/reference/dictionary/index.cfm (accessed June 3, 2008).
Yoon, I.-J. (2006). Understanding the Korean diaspora from comparative perspectives. Paper presented at the Asia Culture Forum, Gwangju, South Korea.

PART I

Understanding Korean Migration

3 The Korean Diaspora from Global Perspectives

IN-JIN YOON

Introduction

According to the 2009 statistics of the Ministry of Foreign Affairs and Trade of South Korea, approximately 6.8 million Koreans are said to be residing abroad. This population of overseas Korean residents is equal to roughly 10 per cent of the total combined populations of South and North Korea. Overseas Koreans are regionally concentrated in four superpowers: China (2.3 million), the United States (2.1 million), Japan (912,655), and the Commonwealth of Independent States or CIS (created at the breakup of the Soviet Union in 1991) (537,889). The international migration and settlement of Koreans was an unintended consequence of unfortunate events in modern Korean history. However, because of the global community of overseas Koreans, Korea now has an invaluable pool of worldwide human capital and a competitive edge over other countries with respect to globalization.

Overseas Korean immigrants have dealt with issues such as immigration, discrimination, adaptation, cultural assimilation, acculturation, communities, ethnic cultures, and ethnic identities. Each of these topics deserves an independent study of its own. In fact, studies have been in progress, and in disciplinary areas other than history, anthropology, folklore studies, sociology, political science, economics, and linguistics. A synthetic approach from a holistic point of view is needed, as the multiple disciplines are closely associated. To connect them, *diaspora* is the concept employed here to embrace both the diverse overseas experiences of Korean immigrants and their inter-relations.

The colloquial notion of diaspora originated with Jewish experiences as a dispersed people who maintained their common ethnic and religious identity and sought return to their ancestral homeland. As diaspora studies became active in the 1990s, the term itself became a comprehensive concept comprising international migrations, expatriation, refugees, migrant labourers, ethnic communities, cultural diversity, and identities of other ethnic groups beyond the Jews (Safran, 1991; Tölölian, 1991). In recent studies, immigrant groups that either have given up on repatriation to their homeland, or have not considered such a possibility from the beginning, are also considered as diasporas (Clifford, 1994). As an analytic concept, *diaspora* is used here to refer not only to the ways in which members of the same ethnic group disperse in different parts of the world but also to the migrants themselves, as well as the locations and communities within which they live.

The history of the Korean diaspora goes back to the mid-nineteenth century. The Korean diaspora, however, has been shorter than those of other ethnic diaspora groups such as the Jews, Chinese, Greeks, and Italians. Koreans, however, present an unusual historical case, because unlike other ethnic groups they have sought to adapt to a range of dissimilar political and economic systems of nations including, but not limited to, the United States, Canada, Japan, China, and the CIS.

Recent studies on the topic of overseas Koreans have been in progress in various research areas including anthropology, sociology, history, political science, and linguistics. The existing research on overseas Koreans, however, has focused largely on regional case studies (e.g., Korean Japanese, Korean Americans, Korean Russians), without much emphasis on comparative analysis to theorize about the diverse experiences of the Korean diaspora in different parts of the world. The Korean diaspora needs to be evaluated from a global perspective based on well-reasoned theories in order to move beyond localized and descriptive knowledge. Furthermore, the Korean diaspora – which is not merely a Korean experience in that it has also affected the places to which the migrants have relocated – presents a great opportunity to facilitate understanding of diasporas of other ethnic groups in general.

This study, therefore, aims at presenting from comparative perspectives the history and characteristics of international migration and settlement of overseas Koreans in China, the CIS, the United States, Japan, and Canada, which have longer histories of Korean immigration and larger numbers of Koreans than elsewhere. After reviewing similarities and differences among the five groups of overseas Koreans, this chapter attempts to generalize overall patterns of adaptation that Koreans have shown in their host societies.

The History and Characteristics of the Korean Diaspora

The history of the Korean ethnic dispersion is largely divided into four periods. The first begins in the 1860s and ends in 1910 (the year of annexation of the Korean peninsula by the Japanese), when the late Chosôn farmers and labourers began emigrating to China, Russia, and Hawaii in order to escape famine, poverty, and oppression by the ruling class. Koreans who crossed the borders to Manchuria and the Russian Far East, however, were economically displaced illegal migrants who earned a precarious living by cultivating land in restricted areas (Lee, 1994). Between 1902 and 1903, Koreans began moving to Hawaiian sugar plantations, only to be prohibited three years later, in 1905, when the Japanese government banned Korean emigration to protect the interests of Japanese labourers in Hawaii. Those who arrived in Hawaii between 1903 and 1905 numbered 7,226 and were by and large single males in their twenties. In turn, almost a thousand Korean women went as "picture brides" to marry these men and have families in Hawaii (Patterson, 1988). This pattern continued until 1924.

The second period is that of the Japanese colonial era, from 1910 to 1945, when farmers and labourers deprived of land and other means of production migrated to Manchuria and Japan. Also, political refugees and activists moved to China, Russia, and the United States to lead the independence movement against the colonial rule. Japan, on the other hand, forced the migration of Koreans en masse to assist in the development of Manchuria, since the Manchurian Incident in 1931 and the establishment of Manchukuo in 1932. The Korean population in the region, as a result, increased rapidly to approximately 500,000 in the late 1930s. Of that total, 250,000 were forced migrants (Kwon, 1996). Koreans also moved to Japan as labourers, since the Japanese economy boomed during the First World War, and with the onset of the Sino-Japanese War in 1937 and the Pacific War of 1941, the Japanese government conscripted Korean males to work in coal mines and fight on the battlefronts (Han, 2002, p. 107). The Korean population in Japan increased in an unprecedented manner and reached about 2.3 million in August 1945 before this number plummeted sharply to 598,507 by 1947, when many of them had repatriated after Japan's defeat in the war (Lee, 1997, pp. 66–70).

The third period is from 1945 to 1962, the year when the South Korean government established its first immigration policy that enabled students to study abroad, war orphans to be adopted, and interracial children and wives of the military officers to be united with their families in the United States or Canada (Yuh, 2002). There were about 6,000 Korean women who immigrated to the United States as spouses of American military officers between 1950 and 1964, as well as about 5,000 children, including war orphans, interracial children, and those adopted by American families. These two groups of immigrants account for two-thirds of Koreans admitted to the United States during this period. From 1945 to 1965, about 6,000 Korean students also stepped on American soil to receive higher education in colleges and universities in the hope of gaining social power and success when they returned to Korea after finishing their education in America. A considerable number of them, however, ended up settling in the United States after receiving their degrees, some even without completing their studies. These persons, along with the women who married the American military officers, paved the way for subsequent generations of immigrants: later in 1965 American immigration policy permitted the sponsorship of family members (Yu, 1983, pp. 23–4).

The fourth period continues from 1962 to the present, as Koreans left their country to seek permanent residency abroad. In 1962, the South Korean government initiated group and contract emigrations to Latin America, Western Europe, the Middle East, and North America. The two main purposes of the 1962 emigration policy were first to relieve the population pressure by sending surplus population abroad, and second to secure foreign currencies sent home by those working or living abroad. Under the sponsorship of the South Korean government, Koreans began to immigrate to Brazil, Argentina, and Paraguay beginning in 1963 as agricultural immigrants who were contracted to cultivate farmlands in interior regions. Many of them did not have experience in farming and headed to metropolitan areas to find jobs as soon as they arrived (Hong, 1992, p. 31). Also, starting in 1963, Koreans began to arrive in West Germany as coal miners and nurses to fill shortages in the local labour market, which experienced rapid growth after the Second World War (Lee, 2008). Many of the Korean contract workers in West Germany headed to Australia, the United States, and Canada after their contracts expired instead of returning to their homeland (Kim, 1981). When in 1965 the Americans changed the policy that discriminated against immigrants from countries other than those in Northern and Western Europe, more Koreans in search of upward social mobility moved to North America. The most active group of immigrants to the United States and Canada subsequently came from the educated middle class who held white-collar occupations in Korea (Yoon, 1997). Immigration to the United States, however, began to decline after the 1988 Seoul Olympic Games, as an increasing number of Koreans moved back to South Korea, and many others reconsidered their plans to emigrate. It was only following the 1997 Asian financial crisis that the number of immigrants began to increase again. However, there was a change in the immigrants' choice of host countries; more Koreans today prefer Canada, Australia, and New Zealand to the United States. Many now choose to go abroad to seek employment and business opportunities rather than to re-unite with family members abroad.

Thus, Korean dispersion can be seen as an ongoing process that will continue to transform in response to political, economic, and social changes within South Korea and in the international community. The introverted nature attributed to Korea as "the Land of Morning Calm" or "the Hermit Kingdom" is indeed a myth of the past, since the country today is as globalized as many others. Although the Korean diaspora is distinguished by its own particularities, it also offers an excellent case for studying the ways in which three elements – immigrants themselves, home and host countries, and time of immigration – interact to transform the lives of the first and subsequent generations of any immigrant group.

As seen above, each period of the Korean diaspora differs significantly depending on the conditions of the home and host countries, and each period is as diverse as the motivations of each immigrant. Koreans abroad have adapted to host countries in different ways and have faced a range of disparate social problems. In the case of Korean Chinese, unresolved problems include unemployment and poverty brought about by being excluded from the economic revolution, as well as population decline caused by the declining birthrate and population movements out of Yanbian Korean Autonomous Region in the three northeastern provinces in China (Han & Kwon, 1993). Koreans in Central Asia and the CIS have faced a serious economic crisis after the dissolution of the Soviet Union in 1989, and experienced racial discrimination after the independence of countries in Central Asia in 1991, and the loss and disappearance of the Korean language and culture. Koreans in the Maritime Province of Siberia and Russian Volgograd also share difficulties in obtaining employment, housing, income, and education (Yoon et al., 2001).

Koreans in Japan, on the other hand, are not declining in number but experience discrimination in employment, public service, and participation in politics. A rising number of the second and third generation have become naturalized through marriage and have assimilated rapidly to Japanese society and culture due to the decline in ethnic education (Han, 2002). Korean Americans, in contrast to Koreans in other places, enjoy an affluent lifestyle and a liberal environment. Making a living no longer presents serious challenges, and racial discrimination is proscribed and discouraged at least on legal and institutional fronts. On the other hand, psycho-social problems such as ethnic identity, interracial marriage, generational conflicts, and political participation remain (Hurh, 1998). Rising racial tension with Hispanics presents another ongoing challenge and increases the risk of conflicts breaking out for Korean Americans whose relationship with African Americans has been improving since the Los Angeles Riots of 1992.

Korean Canadians, on the other hand, are still working in the initial stage of settlement since their immigration history is considerably shorter than that of Koreans in the United States. Economic problems, therefore, remain the crux of the matter in areas including unemployment and discrimination in the labour market. Many of the recent immigrants, in particular, consist of educated white-collar workers in their thirties and forties who must turn to alternative ways of livelihood such as self-employment and manual labour since Canadian employers require Canadian work experience. A great number of elementary and secondary students also stay in Canada as temporary residents with the purpose of early study abroad, but some experience difficulties in adapting to the new society because of difficulties in school, anxiety caused by separation from parents, and lack of parental supervision (Yoon, 2001).

At the risk of oversimplification, table 3.1 compares categories including motivation for immigration, class background, minority policies of host countries, and levels of cultural assimilation by each period of immigration and host country.

If we compare the categories by periods, the most visible difference lies between the earlier immigrants who migrated to Russia, China, America, and Japan from the mid-nineteenth to the early-twentieth centuries, and the new immigrants who migrated to the United States and Canada after the 1960s. The earlier immigrants were farmers from the lower classes whose residency in the host countries had been temporary rather than permanent. The new immigrants, on the other hand, are mostly educated middle-class urbanites who at the outset have sought permanent residency in host countries that offer higher living

Table 3.1. The Korean Diaspora by Destination

	Commonwealth of Independent States	People's Republic of China	Japan	United States	Canada
First Period	1863–1904	1863–1910	Prior to 1910	1903–1905	Prior to 1967
Second	1905–1937	1910–1930	1910–1937	1906–1945	After 1967
Third	1937–1945	1930–1945	1937–1945	1945–1964	
Fourth	1945–1991	1945–1992	1945–1989	After 1965	
Fifth	After 1991	After 1992	After 1989		First
Mainstream Generation(s)	Third and fourth	Second and third	Second and third	First	
Area(s) of Origin	Present North Korea (Hamgyŏng and P'yŏng'an Provinces)	Prior to 1930: present North Korea (Hamgyŏng and P'yŏng'an Provinces) After 1930: entire Korean peninsula	Present South Korea (Kyŏngsang, Chŏlla, Cheju Provinces)	Present South Korea at large with exceptions of a few whose hometown is in North Korea (the displaced)	Present South Korea
Reasons for Immigration	Mostly economic / partly political (independence movement)	Mostly economic / partly political (independence movement)	Mostly economic / conscription during 1937–1945	Mostly economic / partly sociocultural (education)	Mostly economic / partly sociocultural (education and social welfare)
Class Backgrounds	Mostly economically displaced farmers suffering famine and oppression	Mostly economically displaced farmers suffering famine and oppression	Mostly farmers, laborers, and sojourners forced to move	Early stage: farmers and laborers seeking temporary stay Mid stage: international marriage, war orphans, and students Later stage: educated middle class seeking permanent residency	Educated middle-class professionals seeking permanent residency

Table 3.1. The Korean Diaspora by Destination (*concluded*)

	Commonwealth of Independent States	People's Republic of China	Japan	United States	Canada
Minority Policy of the Host Country	Assimilation	Pluralism (autonomous rule by the ethnic minority)	Assimilation	Assimilation	Pluralism (cultural diversity)
Level of Cultural Assimilation	Assimilation to Russian culture	Preservation of Korean culture	Assimilation to Japanese culture	Assimilation to American culture and preservation of Korean culture	Assimilation to Canadian culture and preservation of Korean culture
Appellation	*Koryŏ saram*	*Chosŏnjok*	*Zainichi* Korean	Korean American	Korean Canadian

standards and educational opportunities for their children. While the reasons to expatriate might vary, these new middle- class immigrants have experienced rapid upward social mobility in the host country even within the first generation.

Another significant distinction between the earlier and later immigrants is shown through the changes in location. The earlier generation of immigrants, in most cases, opted to migrate to countries in the vicinity of the Korean peninsula; in contrast, the more recent generation of immigrants chose alternatively geographically distant locations such as North and South America, Europe, and Australia. It is, however, not as simple as it seems for the new immigrants because they may have experienced a greater degree of culture shock and faced more challenge in adapting to white-dominant culture than non-white minorities.

Immigration and ethnic policies of host countries have affected the mode of assimilation of Koreans. The countries that have developed pluralistic policies to acknowledge and protect ethnic cultures and minority identities include China, the United States, and Canada: after the 1920s for China, and after the mid-1960s for the United States and Canada. Koreans in these countries have achieved high social and economic status as minorities since they have had considerably open access to the opportunity structures of mainstream society. They have also preserved, to some extent, Korean culture and identity. In China, an ethnic minority policy allows high degrees of autonomy and affirmative action for major ethnic groups. In recognition of their contribution in establishing the People's Republic of China, Koreans were able to create Yanbian University as the first minority university in 1949 and established Yanbian Korean Autonomous Prefecture on September 3, 1952 (Zheng, 2000). Inside the Autonomous Prefecture, Koreans created what Breton (1964) called a "community of institutional completeness" (p. 194). They were allowed to appoint Koreans as governors, judges, mayors, or superintendents, as well as use Korean as the primary language and maintain Korean culture.

Koreans in the CIS, in contrast, have been discriminated against as citizens of the enemy state during the former Soviet Union period. Stalin, who feared that Koreans would work as Japanese spies, forced the migration of 171,781 Koreans from the Maritime Province to Central Asia in 1937. He also wanted to utilize Koreans to improve the underdeveloped regions of Central Asia with their labour (Kim, 2001; Yoon, 2000). Despite their treatment, hundreds of young Korean men voluntarily enlisted when the Second World War began, and some were selected and dispatched to the front line. The majority of Koreans, who could not participate, volunteered for the industrial battlefront called the "Work Army." Through such attempts of loyalty in the battlefield and on industrial sites, many Koreans tried to shed discrimination and the oppression of being labelled as citizens of the enemy.

Koreans in Japan have been discriminated against as people of the colonized state and forced to assimilate into mainstream society and culture. One example of the degree of oppression they faced is during the Great Kanto earthquake in 1923 when it was alleged that Koreans poisoned the wells, and 6,000 Koreans were massacred by the Japanese militia corps who believed the Koreans to be malicious (Lee, 1994). Discrimination against Koreans continued after the Japan's defeat in the Second World War. In 1947, the Japanese government deprived Koreans of Japanese citizenship, began to treat them as foreigners, and excluded them from social benefits (Han, 2002).

Koreans without Japanese citizenship have long been denied employment in both the public sector and large private companies. A prime example of their attempt to gain rights for the Korean Japanese was the Hitachi incident of Jong-Seok Park in 1970. Although Park, a second- generation Korean Japanese, was accepted as a new employee at Hitachi and received a letter of acceptance, his acceptance was cancelled when it was later revealed that he did not have Japanese citizenship. Korean and Japanese citizens and Christian organizations inside and outside Japan actively carried out a protest and boycott of Hitachi products. In May 1974, Hitachi surrendered to the worldwide pressure (M. Lee, 1997). As anti-discrimination opinion gained ground, the problems that Koreans faced became arguments for the universal values of human rights, and movements protecting the human rights of Koreans spread. Movements demanding the employment of Koreans at public universities, correct pronunciation of Korean names in broadcasting, the right to vote, opposition to fingerprinting, and so on spread and were to some extent successful (Han, 2002, p. 132). Although prejudice and discrimination against Koreans in these states have diminished, there is still work to be done in order for minority cultures and identities to be accepted.

Modes of Incorporation of Overseas Koreans

Despite such regional and temporal differences in the Korean diaspora, the above-mentioned five groups of overseas Koreans seem to similarly exhibit the following patterns of adaptation.

First, overseas Koreans experience disadvantages and discrimination at an early stage of adaptation, but they overcome such obstacles with their strong work ethic and aspiration for upward mobility. Many believe that discrimination against racial minorities is inevitable and members of racial minorities need to have competitive skills and knowledge to achieve independence. Yet, in spite of their drive, Koreans seldom enter the upper classes of the host country. Their socio-economic position is generally middle class. The high levels of educational attainment, as well as the intermediate occupational and income statuses of Koreans in the five countries examined, support this argument.

Second, faced with disadvantages and discrimination in the labour market, overseas Koreans seek occupations that are relatively sheltered from systemic discrimination and governmental authority. They avoid politics, the military, and government and prefer independent work such as private farming, academia, or self-employed businesses. The high rates of self-employment among Koreans in the above five countries point to the fact that Koreans secure an economic foothold first in areas where they can rely on themselves. Even in self-employed businesses, they are concentrated in areas that members of the dominant group are reluctant to engage in because of low profit margins and low social prestige. Dry cleaning, fruit and vegetable stores, liquor stores, grocery stores, beauty supply stores, and so on are typical enterprises among Koreans in the United States and Canada, and Korean barbecue restaurants and Korean-owned slot-machine businesses in Japan are good examples.

Third, after members of the first generation accumulate capital either through small business or wage employment, Koreans tend to invest in their children's education. And to provide better educational opportunities for their children, they show a strong propensity to live in large cities and particularly middle-class suburbs known for having good schools. In other words, independent work, investment in children's education, and urbanization seem to be common survival strategies of overseas Koreans in unfriendly environments. For their efforts, children of Korean immigrants have demonstrated high rates of employment in professional occupations.

Fourth, Koreans maintain a strong ethnic identity while accommodating to the host society's culture and opportunity structures. Ethnicity is not merely a cultural and symbolic expression, but it can also affect lifestyles and the life chances of individuals in such areas as occupation, marriage, friendship, and church affiliation. For Koreans, their ethnicity is a dual identity that emphasizes ethnic origin and culture as well as collective experience in a host society. As a result, second and subsequent generations of Koreans maintain strong levels of ethnic identity and attachment even after they have been culturally and structurally assimilated. Their ethnic identity is a reactive and emergent response to an externally imposed distinction and societal discrimination rather than a primordial, cultural, or symbolic expression. These findings illustrate that minority status constitutes an important component of Korean ethnic identity.

Paradigm Shift from Diaspora to Transnationalism

Looking at the experiences of overseas Koreans through a diasporic lens provides a consistent analytic framework to compare and examine their diverse experiences. A diasporic lens is not limited to immigration, but incorporates community, culture, and identity. I would like, therefore, to define the Korean diaspora as the "dispersion of ethnic Koreans in which the consanguineous people of the Korean peninsula leave their homeland to immigrate and live in various parts of the world," and to encourage the study of its varied phenomena such as adaptation, assimilation, identity, and community.

However, when we examine a contemporary Korean diaspora like the one in the United States and Canada, there are new dimensions that make it difficult to explain by applying the concept of diaspora. For example, classifying the Korean diaspora by time of immigration raises striking differences between earlier immigrants who migrated to Russia, China, America, and Japan during the late-nineteenth and early-twentieth centuries, and newer immigrants who moved to the United States and Canada after the 1960s (Yoon, 2004). Earlier immigrants moved owing to "push" factors in Korea such as famine, government oppression, and colonial rule. They were also likely to come from a class of farmers and from the lower classes, and the orientation in the country of settlement was such that the predominant character was of a "temporary sojourn" rather than "permanent settlement."

On the other hand, newer immigrants are strongly drawn by "pull" factors in the country of settlement (higher standards of living and educational opportunities) as much as by the push factors in Korea. They are typically the highly educated middle class from cities, and their decision for migration from the start is based on the goal of permanent settlement. Newer immigrants acquire middle class status in their host country within the first generation. In this way, there are at least two experiential variants in the Korean diaspora. Earlier immigrants can be seen to be what Cohen (1997) calls a "victim diaspora." In contrast, new immigrants fall into other categories of diaspora that Cohen terms "trade," "labour," "imperial," and "cultural." To describe newer immigrants (including Koreans, Chinese, Indians, and Mexicans) who spontaneously move to find opportunities for a rise in status in countries such as the United States and Canada after the 1960s, we will have to think of "immigration diaspora" as a new form of diaspora.

Lastly, the main factor in defining an ethnic minority group as a diaspora is ethnic/national identity, but in the case where a group resides in the host country for a long period of time and proceeds to assimilate to a great degree, we have to consider the dual identity. In the case of first-generation immigrants, they maintain a national identity that strongly leans toward the home country regardless of the length of residence in the country of settlement, but the second or third generation expresses a dual identity that combines the cultural heritage of their ancestral country with the ethnic and national identity of the host country. For example, the following are dual identities: Korean Chinese are *Chosônjok*, Central Asian Koreans are *Goryeo saram*, overseas Koreans in the United States or Canada are Korean Americans or Korean Canadians, and Koreans in Japan are *Zainichi* Koreans.

Here, dual identity can lead to a marginalized status where a person does not belong to society. Alternatively, it can act as a bridge and facilitate creative leadership that crosses both identities. In times when discrimination was severe against minorities and earlier immigrants, dual identity was a product of social discrimination and prejudice, but in today's circumstances, with state and national borders weakened through globalization, bilingualism and the ability to function in more than one culture have become internationally competitive advantages. In a worldwide global system where cosmopolitanism prevails, members of a diaspora easily traverse diverse cultural systems, and are able to stimulate new ideas and forms of expression. In this way, the current situation of overseas Koreans reveals that although there are aspects that are sufficiently explained by the existing concept of a diaspora, there are new dimensions that are not. Even though the gap between the concept and the phenomena can be addressed by expanding the original concept, there is concern that the analytic value of the original concept will then be diminished. For this reason, rather than proceeding too far in expanding the original concept of diaspora, I think it is more appropriate to introduce new concepts that are able to properly explain new dimensions such as transnationalism.

The focus of sociological research on human migration that uses a "transnational" model is mostly on the network of relationships that are formed in across borders and on the life strategies of the immigrant groups (i.e., their livelihoods). Transnational phenomena appear prominently in many economic, social, and cultural domains of overseas Koreans today. Human interchanges and the movement of capital between South Korea and the country of residence are increasing daily. For example, Los Angeles' Koreatown has grown into a central area of economic exchange between South Korea and the United States, and is now more than just an ethnic community of Korean Americans. Culturally, overseas Koreans have combined cultures from the homeland with those in the country of residence to make new cultural styles, forms, and spaces. Finally, overseas Koreans have come to have a transnationalized social identity: as second- and third-generation overseas Koreans create new forms of culture, social identities may not align with discrete national identities. Thus, new forms of transnational identities can be expected to increase, and to further explore them we need explanations that not only use the concept of diaspora but also the concept of transnationalism.

For the time being, the situation of overseas Koreans is expected to contain both diasporic and transnational elements, and the relationships between the two may become complicated and occasionally conflicting. One example is the relationship between the "old-timer" and the "newcomer" Koreans in Japan. The old-timers, especially those affiliated with the pro–North Korea organization called the General Association of Korean Residents in Japan, are likely to hold their diasporic orientation, while the newcomers who entered Japan toward the end of the 1980s try to strengthen transnational networks with their homeland for greater economic opportunities and for social support. Similar cases can be found in many Korean communities across the United States and Canada, where earlier cohorts who arrived in the 1960s and '70s maintain old and pessimistic memories and images of Korea, and live relatively isolated lives in their host societies. By contrast, more recent cohorts who arrived after the 1990s left South Korea as a G20 country, and sustain multi-stranded social relationships and multi-layered networks that link their societies of origin and destination, transcending localities and national boundaries. The long-term trend would be a movement toward greater integration between the homeland and the host society as a result of globalization, and thus transnationalism can be expected to become the dominant mode of incorporation of overseas Koreans.

REFERENCES

Association of the Koreans of Kazakstan. (1997). *The Koreans of Kazakstan: An illustrated history.* Seoul: STC.

Breton, R. (1964). Institutional completeness of ethnic communities and personal relations of immigrants. *American Sociological Review, 70,* 193–205.

Clifford, J. (1994). Diasporas. *Cultural Anthropology, 9*(3), 302–38.

Cohen, R. (1997). *Global diasporas: An introduction.* Seattle: University of Washington Press.

Han, K.K. (2002). The history and current situation of the Korean diaspora and migration: Japan (in Korean). In I.Y. Yim (Ed.), *New concepts and approaches to national integration (Part II): National integration in the period of globalization and information* (pp. 91–149). Chunchon, South Korea: Hallym University Research Institute of National Integration.

Han, S.B., and Kwon, T.H. (1993). *Chosonjok in Yanbian of China: Social structure and change* (in Korean). Seoul: Seoul National University Press.

Hong, S.H. (1992). Life and ethnic consciousness of Korean-Brazilians (in Korean). *Koreans Abroad, 51,* 30–4.

Hurh, W.M. (1998). *The Korean Americans.* Westport, CT: Greenwood Press.

Kim, G.N. (2001). The deportation of 1937 as a logical continuation of Tsarist and Soviet nationality policy in the Russian Far East." *Korean and Korean American Studies Bulletin, 12*(2/3), 19–44.

Kim, I. (1981). *New urban immigrants: The Korean community in New York.* Princeton: Princeton University Press.

Kwon, T.H. (1996). *The Koreans in the world: China* (in Korean). Seoul: Ministry of Reunification.

Lee, K.K. (1994). *Koreans in Japan: An anthropological approach* (in Korean). Seoul: Ilchokak Publishing.

Lee, M. (1997). *The Koreans in the world: Japan* (in Korean). Seoul: Ministry of Reunification.

Lee, S. (2008). Theoretical research on the otherness of female migrants and interaction of tolerance: With the case study of Korean female migrants in Germany (in Korean). *Society and Theory, 12,* 73–107.

Ministry of Foreign Affairs and Trade. (2009). *The Present State of Affairs of Overseas Koreans* (in Korean). Seoul: Ministry of Foreign Affairs and Trade.

Patterson, W. (1988). *The Korean frontier in America: Immigration to Hawaii, 1896–1910.* Honolulu: University of Hawaii Press.

Safran, W. (1991). "Diasporas in Modern Societies: Myths of Homeland and Return." *Diasporas, 1*(1), 83–99.

Tölölian, K. (1991). The nation state and its others: In lieu of a preface. *Diasporas, 1*(1), 3–7.

Yoon, I.-J. (1997). *On my own: Korean businesses and race relations in America.* Chicago: University of Chicago Press.

———. (2000). Forced relocation, language use, and ethnic identity of Koreans in central Asia. *Asian and Pacific Migration Journal, 9*(1), 35–64.

———. (2001). Conditions and perceptions of immigrant life of Koreans in Toronto (in Korean). *Studies of Koreans Abroad, 11,* 5–56.

———. (2004). *Korean diaspora: Migration, adaptation, and identity of overseas Koreans* (in Korean). Seoul: Korea University Press.

Yoon, I.-J., Jang, W.C., Lee, K.K., Rhee, J.H., and Sim, H.Y. (2001). Political and economic situations of the Commonwealth of Independent States and confronting tasks for Koreans (in Korean). *Journal of Asiatic Studies, 44*(2), 145–73.

Yu, E.Y. (1983). Korean communities in America: Past, present, and future. *Amerasia Journal, 10,* 23–51.

Yuh, J.Y. (2002). *Beyond the shadow of Camptown: Korean military brides in America.* New York: New York University Press.

Zheng, X. (2000). *Ethnic Koreans in China: Their future* (in Korean). Seoul: Siningansa.

4 Is There Evidence of Price Substitution in Migration? The Case of Korean Immigration to North America in the 1990s[1]

J.D. HAN AND PETER IBBOTT

Introduction

THE NEW COLOSSUS

Not like the brazen giant of Greek fame,
With conquering limbs astride from land to land;
Here at our sea-washed, sunset gates shall stand
A mighty woman with a torch, whose flame
Is the imprisoned lightning, and her name
Mother of Exiles. From her beacon-hand
Glows world-wide welcome; her mild eyes command
The air-bridged harbor that twin cities frame.
"Keep, ancient lands, your storied pomp!" cries she
With silent lips. "Give me your tired, your poor,
Your huddled masses yearning to breathe free,
The wretched refuse of your teeming shore.
Send these, the homeless, tempest-tost to me,
I lift my lamp beside the golden door!"

—Emma Lazarus, 1883

These are the famous words inscribed on the Statue of Liberty. While this New York City beacon still shines, it no longer welcomes the "wretched refuse" or "homeless" to North America. Instead, the millions who continue to come are often the "best and brightest," and they scarcely ever

1 Parts of the empirical results reported in this chapter may also be found in Han, J. D., & Ibbott, P. (2005b). Korean immigration to North America: Some prices that matter. *Canadian Studies in Population, 32*(2), 155–76.

arrive empty-handed. And yet, this image of the poor migrant wage labourer seeking to pass through "the golden door" of the high-wage factories of the New World continues to colour thinking about international migration. If "differences in net economic advantages, chiefly differences in wages, are the main causes of migration" (Hicks, 1932, p. 76), then migration patterns can be understood by examining the factors influencing the present value of a family's human capital at home and abroad. If the present value of a family's human capital abroad exceeds its worth at home by more than the full moving costs, then migration becomes economically attractive.

This human-capital framework presents straightforward and testable implications for the pattern of migration flows. The most obvious are these: migrants tend to be young; migrants move from areas where the return to human capital is low to areas where the return to human capital is high; reductions in the costs associated with migration will increase migration flows; greater physical and cultural distances increase the costs and, hence, reduce the rate of migration. Further implications, brought forth by Todaro (1969) and Harris and Todaro (1970), pointed to reduced migration flows. High unemployment in the migrant's destination reduces the expected net present value of the migration investment and, hence, likely reduces migration flows. Not surprisingly, the evidence from a large body of empirical literature strongly supports these standard predictions of the Human-Capital Model (Ghatak et al., 1996).

While the flow of migrants from Canada to South Korea does seem to be consistent with many of the predictions of the Human-Capital Model, in this paper we provide evidence that the recent increase in migration to Canada cannot be explained by this model. We propose an extension of the Human-Capital Model of migration to explain the rapid rise of Korean immigration to Canada in the 1990s and examine these recent migration patterns to test the validity of the model.

Recent Korean Immigration to Canada

During the 1990s, Korean immigration to Canada rose dramatically.[2]

---

2 The large Korean-American community recently celebrated a century of Korean immigration to the United States. The earliest migrants went to Hawaii in the early part of the twentieth century. Today, the Korean-Canadian community is more than 10 per cent of the size of the Korean-American community. The 2006 Canadian Census indicates that there are 146,545 persons of Korean descent, while the 2000 U.S.

Figure 4.1. Korean Arrivals in Canada

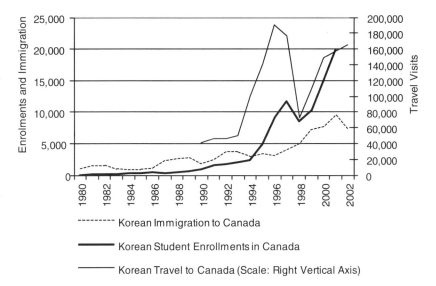

-------- Korean Immigration to Canada

▬▬▬ Korean Student Enrollments in Canada

▬▬▬ Korean Travel to Canada (Scale: Right Vertical Axis)

Source: Citizenship and Immigration Canada.

This rise coincided with a large and sudden increase in Korean visitors and students to Canada (figure 4.1). Remarkably, this rise in Korean migration to Canada occurred while Korean migration to the United States was in decline (figure 4.2).

The difficulty this presents to the Human-Capital Model is that during the 1990s Canadian earnings fell and unemployment rose relative to those of the United States. The Human-Capital Model predicts that Canada should have seen Korean immigration fall over the period and fall more quickly than the United States. With immigration to Canada quadrupling over the decade, the evidence challenges the legitimacy of the simple Human-Capital Model.

Other economic models of migration offer no easy solution to this puzzle. A more sophisticated model of heterogeneous labour that self-selects was introduced by Sjaastad (1962), and developed by Borjas (1987, 1989, 1994) and Chiswick (2000). The usual predictions of the human-capital story carry through, along with some unexpected pre-

---

Census reports 1,076,872. Additional demographic details on the Korean-Canadian community can be found in chapter 2 of this volume.

Figure 4.2. Korean Immigrants to Canada and the United States

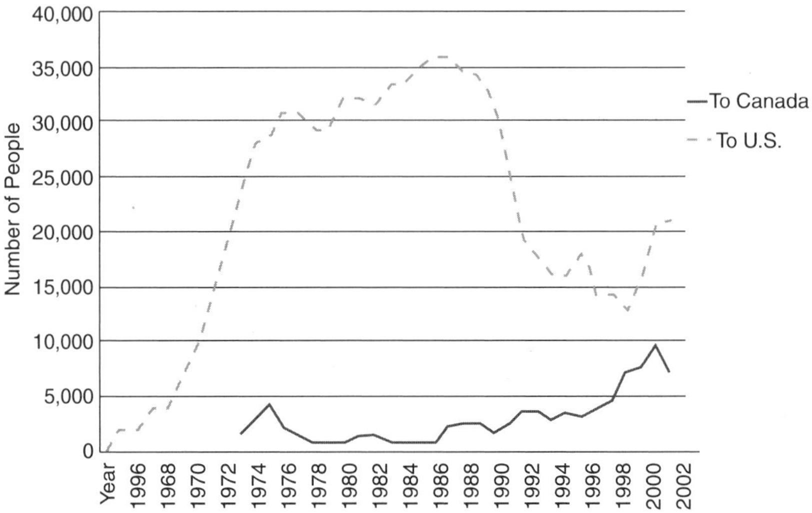

dictions about how increasing inequality in the destination country increases immigration of individuals with large human-capital endowments. Hatton (2003) uses the framework to show that an increase in the inequality in the destination country should increase the rate of flow of migrants. In short, income inequality may come with income opportunities for migrants with high levels of human capital.[3] The puzzle of the Korean immigration to North America is that while inequality rose in Canada, it rose more quickly in the United States (figure 4.3). Again, the expectation created by theory is that Korean migration to Canada should be declining and not rising.

The "new economics of migration" literature (Stark, 1991) has explored whether migration might usefully be examined as part of a portfolio investment decision of risk- diversifying families. Accordingly, the expectation is that families would choose to invest their human-capital assets (i.e., their children) over geographically dispersed and independent markets. Given the high level of integration of the Cana-

---

3 A fairly substantial literature, most recently in Hatton (2003), has demonstrated that the ratio of inequality of incomes also proxies for differences in the return to human capital, with more unequal countries delivering a higher (relative) return to human capital. We will be exploring this possibility in future research.

Figure 4.3. Theil Index of Wage Inequality

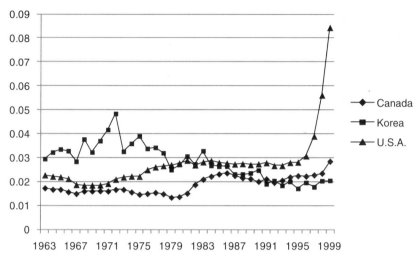

Source: University of Texas Inequality Project (UTIP) data.

dian and American economies, it seems unlikely that risk-diversifying family investors would have evaluated a Canadian-situated human-capital asset as being outside the efficient portfolio. Other economic models of migration have emphasized that search costs (Berninghaus & Seifert-Vogt, 1991; Maier, 1985), the option value of waiting (Burda, 1995), liquidity constraints (Ghatak & Levine, 1994; Hatton & William-son, 2002; Massey, 1988), and social network effects (Bauer & Zim-merman, 1995) do no better in explaining the observed rise in Korean migration to Canada.

When the economic models of migration are extended to exam-ine the impact of non-price factors such as political stability, politi-cal rights, and individual freedoms in the source country, economists have consistently found that these political factors are important determinants of observed migration patterns (Kamemera et al., 2000). Unfortunately these factors cannot explain the rapid increase in Korean migration to Canada as South Korean civil rights and political stability improved over the 1990s. Even if these "push" factors were important, the United States should have been the primary destina-tion for Korean migrants, as the "cultural distance" between South

Korea and the United States is smaller than between South Korea and Canada. By the beginning of the 1990s, large Korean communities were established in New York, Los Angeles, and Chicago. These communities provided a bridge for Koreans seeking to immigrate. Korean communities in Canada, at this time, were very small. Young people then growing up in South Korea could not avoid an overwhelming exposure to American culture through the presence of the U.S. Army in Korea, and through active bilateral trade that brought American movies and music to South Korea. In contrast, exposure to Canadian culture was much more limited. Thus, it is hard to understand why the early 1990s was a period in which Korean migrants began to substitute Canada for the United States as a destination for migration, educational attainment, and tourism.

An Extension of the Human-Capital Model

When families move, they do not just bring their human capital with them; many also bring substantial financial assets from the sale of their household physical capital (homes, businesses, and so on). The proceeds from these sales allow migrants to purchase the currency of their destination country and ultimately enable them to purchase a house and/or business in their new country. For Koreans and all migrants coming to Canada or the United States, the foreign exchange rate will determine how much physical household capital that they will be able to enjoy in their new home. As we will show, relative movements in exchange rates can cause Koreans to substitute Canada for the United States as a destination.

Economic studies of migration patterns have looked at how physical household capital can influence the migration decision. In Lucas's (1985) study of rural-urban migration in Botswana, a multinomial logit model confirmed the predictions of the Harris-Todaro model and indicated that the number of cattle owned played a role in the decision to migrate. In developed-country studies of internal migration, differences in housing costs were shown to strongly influence regional migration in Italy (Attanasio & Padoa Shioppa, 1991), Spain (Bentolila & Dolado, 1991), and the United States (Gabrel et al., 1992). These studies all indicate that households bring more than human capital with them, but none of these studies has examined how exchange-rate movements might cause international migrants to substitute one destination for another.

Consider the following model of a Korean migrant's decision to move to North America. Each family (i) is endowed with H_i units of human capital and K_i units of a physical household capital such as a house or business. This physical capital (with an appropriate choice of units) has a liquidation value of $P_k K_i$ won, where P_k is the price per unit of physical household capital in Korea. This could be converted into U.S. dollars to provide $e_{us} P_k K_i$ U.S. dollars of financial capital, where e_{us} is the number of U.S. dollars one Korean won will buy. With this financial capital, the family can buy $e_{us}(P_k/P_{us})K_i$ units of capital in the United States, where P_{us} is the U.S. price per unit of physical household capital in U.S. dollars. Similarly, the same family can purchase $e_c(P_k/P_c)$ K_i units of capital in Canada, where e_c is the number of Canadian dollars one Korean won will buy and where P_c is the Canadian price per unit of physical household capital in Canadian dollars.

For migrants to Canada, the ratio of household capital they can afford in Canada to the ratio of the household capital they can afford in the U.S. is $e_c(P_k/P_c)K_i / e_{us}(P_k/P_{us})K_i = (e_c/e_{us})(P_{us}/P_c) = X_t (P_{us}/P_c)$, where X_t is the number of Canadian dollars one U.S. dollar can buy. If the Canadian dollar depreciates in value, X_t rises, and the immigrant family will find that they can afford more physical household capital in Canada. Therefore, it follows that the probability that a family migrating to North America will choose Canada will tend to be increasing in X_t.[6]

If we look at the proportion of migrants to North America that choose Canada as a destination and compare this to the number of Canadian dollars one U.S. dollar buys (X_t), we see that the predicted relationship seems to exist (figure 4.4). The apparent correlation is not sufficient proof for the existence of such a relationship, as other factors must be accounted for before conclusions are drawn.

To account for the important factors influencing the pattern of Korean migration to Canada and the United States, we sought to estimate a simple economic model of migration that was capable of detecting substitution between destinations, and that could be easily extended to examine whether exchange-rate movements influenced destination choice. Baker and Benjamin's (1996) examination of migration from the Asia-Pacific region to Canada and the United States provided us with a useful Human-Capital Model of migration consistent with the direction of most of the empirical literature. Their results provided the usual strong evidence supporting standard economic models of migration. Their model also uniquely was extended to examine migrants

Figure 4.4. Korean Immigrants to Canada: The Exchange Rate Matters

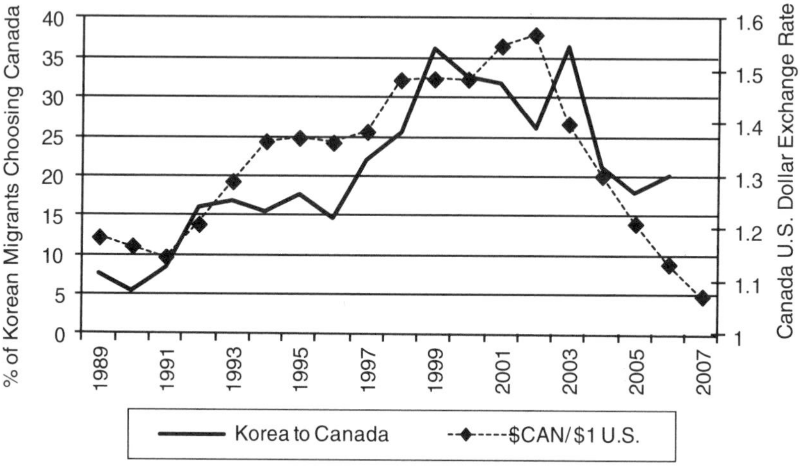

Source: Lawrence H. Officer, "Exchange Rates between the United States Dollar and Forty-one Currencies," *Measuring Worth, 2009*. Retrieved from http://www.measuringworth.org/exchangeglobal/, Citizenship and Immigration Canada; U.S. Department of Homeland Security.

substituting between Canada and the United States. When their model was extended in this way, the model no longer performed well at all, unless country dummy variables were added to the model. The fragility of their substitution finding to a small change in the specification caused them to conclude that "non-economic supply-side variables are the most important determinants of immigrant flows between the Asia Pacific countries and the United States and Canada" (p. 318).

One important objection to the Baker and Benjamin model is that it focuses exclusively on the supply of migrants and ignores the demand-side impact of immigration policies of the American and Canadian governments. DeVoretz (1995) points to evidence in Green and Green (1995) to suggest that Canadian tinkering with immigrant admissions criteria over their 1974–92 study period prevented Baker and Benjamin from identifying the supply relationship that they were attempting to estimate. Green and Green (1999) have, however, presented evidence showing that by the late 1980s the Canadian government abandoned its attempts to match inflows with domestic labour market conditions, "switching almost completely to long-term goals" (p. 447). With this switch to a policy of steady demand for immigrants, the identification problem recedes.

Given that the rapid growth in Korean migration to Canada occurred during a period of stable immigration policies, we have chosen to follow Baker and Benjamin by examining the economic factors behind the supply of Korean migrants to North America. Our point of departure is to look for a model that explains the rapid parallel growth in Korean visitors, Korean students, and Korean migrants choosing Canada as a destination. This parallel movement points to an important common cause that has not yet been identified in the migration literature.

The Baker and Benjamin (1996) model was developed to examine the patterns of Asia- Pacific immigration to Canada and the United States. They begin with log linear model in which the natural logarithm of Korean immigrants to Canada in *year t* ($\ln(IMM_{Ct})$) is a function of the natural logarithm of GDP in Korea in *year t* in constant U.S. dollars ($\ln(PCGDP_{Kt})$); the natural logarithm of GDP in Canada in *year t* in constant U.S. dollars ($\ln(PCGDP_{Ct})$); the unemployment rate in Canada in *year t* ($URATE_{Ct}$); and the natural logarithm of the population density in Korea in *year t* ($\ln(POPDEN_{Kt})$), which yields

$$\ln(IMM_{Ct}) = \beta_{C0} + \beta_{C1}\ln(PCGDP_{Kt}) + \beta_{C2}\ln(PCGDP_{Ct}) + \beta_{C3}URATE_{Ct}$$
$$\beta_{C4}\ln(POPDEN_{Kt}) + \varepsilon_{CKt} \tag{1}$$
$$\ln(IMM_{Ut}) = \beta_{U0} + \beta_{C1}\ln(PCGDP_{Kt}) + \beta_{U2}\ln(PCGDP_{Ut}) + \beta_{U3}URATE_{Ut}$$
$$\beta_{U4}\ln(POPDEN_{Kt}) + \varepsilon_{UKt} \tag{2}$$

A similar model can be constructed for Korean immigration to the United States, where the natural logarithm of Korean immigrants to the United States in *year t* ($\ln(IMM_{Ut})$) is a function of the natural logarithm of GDP in South Korea in *year t* in constant U.S. dollars ($\ln(PCGDP_{Kt})$); the natural logarithm of GDP in the United States in *year t* in constant U.S. dollars ($\ln(PCGDP_{Ut})$); the unemployment rate in the United States in *year t* ($URATE_{Ut}$); and the natural logarithm of the population density in South Korea in *year t* ($\ln(POPDEN_{Kt})$).

In Han and Ibbott (2005b), these two models were re-estimated using a longer time series. We discovered that the longer time series caused the estimates to become less statistically significant and seemed to contradict some important predictions of the economic model of migration. We explored many sensible extensions of the Baker and Benjamin model to see if the addition of plausible variables might deliver estimates that are more consistent with theory. By and large, the results were far from satisfactory. In all instances, a low Durban-Watson statistic indicated that autocorrelation was a problem. Attempts to correct for this using a Cochrane-Orcutt type procedure caused all the estimated parameters to become insignificant according to a standard t-test.

Rethinking the problem, we noted that Green and Green (1999) had identified a change in Canadian immigration policy in the late 1980s. The government abandoned fine-tuning the points system to match immigration flows to local labour market conditions. To capture the impact of these changes, we introduced a structural dummy variable for the years 1988 through to 2003. The dummy variable alone or interacting with the other variables did seem to improve the fit somewhat, but the model still showed the problems identified in the earlier specifications. Specifically, the parameter on $\ln(PCGDP_{Ct})$ was still negative, and the Durban-Watson statistic remained low. We concluded that there was a serious misspecification problem that was likely behind the poor fit and insignificant findings.

When we turned to the final model proposed by Baker and Benjamin (1996), we were surprised to find that many of the problems disappeared. They derived their final model by then differencing equations 1 and 2 and by assuming that $\beta_{C1} = \beta_{U1}$ and $\beta_{C4} = \beta_{U4}$. This, they argued, was equivalent to assuming that "from the individual migrant's perspective, a change in local income or local population density had the same impact on their propensity to migrate to either the United States or Canada, holding U.S. and Canadian opportunities constant" (p. 315). The result was the following estimating equation:

$$(\Delta\ln(IMM_t) = \beta'_0 + \beta'_1 \Delta\ln(PCGDT_t) + \beta'_2 \Delta URATE_t + \gamma_t \tag{3}$$

where $\Delta\ln(IMM_t)$ was $\ln(IMM_{Ct}) - \ln(IMM_{Ut})$, $\Delta\ln(PCGDT_t)$ was $\ln(PCGDT_{Ct}) - \ln(PCGDT_{Ut})$ and $\Delta\ln(URATE_t)$ was $\ln(URATE_{Ct}) - \ln(URATE_{Ut})$.

This empirical model implicitly assumes that the difference in the expected real returns to human capital that Korean immigrants can expect to earn in Canada, compared with the United States, can be proxied by the relative difference in real GDP per capita and differences in the unemployment rate. Building on the Baker and Benjamin model, we introduced the exchange rate to the model as a proxy for the impact of relative exchange rate movements on the relative affordability of physical household capital. The resulting model is:

Table 4.1. The Model with Substitution Performs Much Better

	Intercept	$\Delta ln(\text{PCGDP}_t)$	ΔURATE_t	R^2	DW
Baker and	−1.354*	4.178	−0.082	0.41	
Benjamin	(0.374)	(3.608)	(0.075)		
Equation 3	−6.0968*	−31.391*	−0.56962*	0.78	1.749
	(0.3915)	(3.325)	(0.09908)		

Notes: A parameter estimate with an asterisk indicates a significant t-statistic at the 5 per cent level.
The estimated standard errors are presented in parentheses below each parameter estimate.

$$\Delta\ln(IMM_t) = \beta'_0 + \beta'_1\Delta\ln(PCGDP_t) + \beta'_2\Delta URATE_t + \beta'_2\ln(X_t) + \gamma_t \qquad (4)$$

where $ln(X_t)$ is the natural logarithm of the Canada-U.S. exchange rate. The expectation is that depreciation in the Canadian currency relative to the U.S. currency (i.e., $ln(X_t)$ increasing) should cause some Korean migrants to consider substituting Canada for the United States as a destination. We were hopeful that the differencing in equation 4 might transform the data sufficiently to reduce the influence of auto-correlated errors on the estimation to allow us to examine whether exchange rate movements in the 1990s had caused Korean migrants to substitute Canada for the United States as their destination. The model in equation 4 allows testing for a substitution effect in a parsimonious manner.

Before estimating equation 4, we re-estimated equation 3 for Korean migration to North America. The results presented in table 4.1 are suggestive, as the estimates indicate a strongly significant negative parameter estimate for the difference in Canadian and American income. This should not be that surprising, as Baker and Benjamin found that the positive estimate quickly became negative with the addition of country dummy variables and a time trend. The results also show that the DW statistic does not support a conclusion of serial correlation in equation 3. Given all this, the evidence seems to point to Korean migrants' perplexingly choosing Canada over the United States when Canadian incomes fall relative to the United States.

While this choice might be explained by non-price political or sociological factors, there remains the possibility that other prices matter, and that the absence of these prices constitutes a specification problem. If our argument in the last section is correct, then it is likely that the exchange rate may be important. To investigate this, we estimated

Table 4.2. Principal Results

	Eqt. 3	Eqt. 4	Eqt. 4.1	Eqt. 4.2	Eqt. 4.3	Eqt. 4.4
Intercept	−6.0968*	−5.5411*	−1.7804	−1.5910	−5.2128	−5.7693
	(0.3915)	(0.497)	(3.437)	(3.295)	(0.348)	(0.395)
D			−2.8504	−3.4065	1.8443	0.2065
			(3.488)	(3.327)	(0.2175)	(8.574)
$\Delta ln(PCGDP_t)$	−31.391*	−26.827*	11.192	16.752		
	(3.325)	(3.084)	(24.78)	(23.93)		
$D^* \Delta ln(PCGDP_t)$			−27.104	−31.338		
			(24.82)	(23.76)		
$\Delta URATE_t$	−0.56962*	−0.60354*	−0.35131*	− 0.298*		
	(0.09908)	(0.125)	(0.1385)	(0.14)		
$ln(CXR)$		1.7915	3.5030 *		6.1322	
		(1.082)	(1.129)		(0.9674)	
$ln(WCXR)$				2.1275*		3.4781*
				(0.626)		(0.509)
R^2	0.78	0.88	0.93	0.93	0.87	0.88
DW	1.749	1.905	2.146	2.077	2.13	2.084

Notes: A parameter estimate with an asterisk indicates a significant t-statistic at the 5 per cent level.
The estimated standard errors are presented in parentheses below each parameter estimate.

equation 4 to see whether the addition of the Canadian dollar cost of U.S. dollars altered the estimates. The results, presented in table 4.2, do not provide as clear an adjudication of the issue as might be desired. The Durbin-Watson statistic and R squares improve greatly, but the sign of the income variable continues to suggest that Korean migrants make seemingly irrational choices. The exchange rate variable has the expected sign, but the t-statistic is low.

We argued earlier that there was reason to suspect a structural change in the late 1980s, and our regressions supported this view. Introducing a dummy variable to capture this structural change does alter the results in ways consistent with theoretical expectations. Presented in table 4.2 as equation 4.1, the estimated parameters on the extended model reveal a dramatically different picture. The negative parameter on the difference in GDP appears to be insignificantly different from zero, while the exchange rate parameter suggests a significant positive relationship. In other words, differences in Canadian and American GDP appear less important than the influence of the depreciation of the Canadian dollar in the rapid increase in Korean migration to Canada during the 1990s.

In equation 4.2, we examined whether replacing the nominal exchange rate with a real exchange rate weighted with a Canadian and American housing-price index changed the results. The estimates suggest that there is little reason to prefer either exchange rate. In equations 4.3 and 4.4, we examined the impact of dropping all the variables except the exchange rate and the dummy variable. The results are surprisingly strong, reinforcing our conclusion that migrants do substitute when prices change.

Conclusions

Our results do seem to solve the puzzle of why Korean immigrants substituted Canada for the United States as a destination despite the relatively lower returns to human capital in Canada. We find strong empirical support for our hypothesis that the depreciation of the Canadian dollar in the 1990s made Canada more attractive to Korean migrants to North America. More generally, our findings suggest that the impact of exchange-rate movements on migration flows deserves more attention. The empirical results also provide some surprises. It seems clear that differences in the unemployment rate between Canada and the United States do not have much influence in the destination choice of Korean migrants to North America. Finally, the regression estimates suggest that exchange-rate movements can be more powerful in influencing the direction of migration flows than household earnings opportunities. There are undoubtedly other groups of immigrants to Canada driven by economic factors other than wage differences.

When we look beyond the results reported here, we must concede there is much more to be understood in this price substitution story. The existing human capital theory of migration focuses on lifetime net returns to human capital. For many migrants, immigration is a much longer-term proposition where benefits can stretch over multiple generations. Complicating things further, immigration does not necessarily lead to permanent settlement. Over time, immigrants may return to South Korea or immigrate to other areas. We do not understand how these two factors influence the migration decision.

We also do not know how important the influence of education costs of children is to the destination decision of migrants. While Canada is attractive to Korean migrants because Canadian public education is perceived to be of high quality, there do remain substantial costs for parents who want to invest in their children's human capital. Supplementary academic classes, ESL education, extra-curricular activities, and university tuition must be met out of the limited financial resources of newly settled immigrant families. The rapid expansion of private academies and tutorial services catering to Korean families in Toronto and Vancouver suggests that such expense is not a trivial issue for recent Korean immigrants. Given that the household head often faces limited employment and income opportunities, additional financial obligation can create a liquidity constraint that forces the family to draw on savings and capital they bring from South Korea. For a family facing such liquidity constraints, depreciation in the Canadian dollar would increase the financial resources available for supporting these investments and thus increase the relative appeal of Canada as a preferred destination. If important, commitments of this nature would reinforce the influence of exchange-rate movements on the decision of where to migrate. Additional research should be done to explore the relative importance of these economic factors to those who immigrate to obtain a better education for their children.

At the very least, the evidence points to the need for further work in developing an empirical model capable of distinguishing how exchange-rate movements matter. In particular, the use of additional dummy variables to deal with regime shifts (i.e., the end of the cold war), and the level of development of the source country might prove helpful. Given the high level of uncertainty about the appropriate design of the empirical model, it would also be useful to estimate a random effects model, and explore more thoroughly the impact of heteroscedasticity and autocorrelation on the model.

Despite the weaknesses, the current study does provide a few innovations. First, there is the use of a sonnet in the introduction. Second, we have introduced the argument that foreign exchange rates matter in the migration decision. More generally, we have initiated an examination of migration flows in which migrants substitute destinations when prices change. The empirical and theoretical literature is virtually silent on this important aspect of economic choice.

While the focus of our study has been an examination of the economic forces behind the rapid rise in Korean immigration to Canada in the 1990s, it is certainly the case that social and political factors were also influential. The 1988 Seoul Summer Olympics was a watershed moment that ushered in profound changes to national governance and to the way South Korean society related to the world. Authoritarianism was replaced by liberal democracy, while the forty-year bilateral relationship with America had to contend with growing frictions. A rising tide of Korean national confidence ushered in a new ambitious foreign policy that had a more global outlook. The results included membership in the United Nations in 1991, membership in the OECD in 1996, and the development of new diplomatic partnerships aimed at diversifying Korea's economic and political ties.

One important result of this effort was the development of a much stronger diplomatic relationship between the Canadian and South Korean governments. The first notable outcome was the decision by the Canadian government to waive the visa requirement for Korean short-term visitors. This Canadian policy change did not directly apply to prospective immigrants, but it did send an effective signal of friendliness and goodwill to Koreans, narrowing the cultural gap between South Korea and Canada. The political momentum has more recently led the two governments to engage in negotiations toward a free-trade agreement.

Beyond the movement toward closer political ties between the two nations is a parallel movement of deepening personal ties between individual Canadians and Koreans. Over the past twenty years, young Canadians have been travelling to and working in South Korea in greater numbers. For instance, the number of Canadian teachers working in South Korea has grown so dramatically that Canadians have become the largest group of foreign teachers in South Korea (Han & Ibbott, 2005a). The combination of potent anti-Americanism and the growing number of personal connections to Canada through teachers might have played an influential role in the relative rise of Canada as a destination for Korean migration. At the very least, it certainly reduced the cultural distance between the two nations. There is a great deal yet to be learned. By pursuing interdisciplinary research into how sociopolitical events and institutional changes have affected the lives of Koreans in relation to international migration, we can attain a fuller understanding of the very unusual "Canada Boom" that began in the 1990s.

Data Appendix

In the following appendix, we provide details on the sources and manipulation of data used in the regressions.

IMM_{Ct} = Korean Immigration to Canada.
The annual flow of Korean immigrants to Canada was taken from a variety of Citizenship and Immigration Canada publications. Between 1973 and 1996, several different issues of "Citizenship and Immigration Statistics" were consulted. The data between 1997 and 2002 were obtained from several different issues of "Facts and Figures: Immigration Overview." The spring 2004 edition of "The Monitor" reported the number of Korean immigrants arriving in Canada in 2003. All these publications are available in pdf format at http://www.cic.gc.ca.

IMM_{Ut} = Korean Immigration to the United States
The annual flow of Korean immigrants to the United States was taken from various years of the "Yearbook of Immigration Statistics" published by the Office of Immigration Statistics of the U.S. Department of Homeland Security. This is available at http://uscis.gov/graphics/index.htm.

$PCGDP_{Kt}$ = Korean Per Capita Income in Constant (1992) U.S. dollars. For the years up to 2000, the GDP per capita data was collected from the Heston and Summers Penn World Tables, version 6.1. For the years 2001, 2002, and 2003, the series was extrapolated using the growth in the constant dollar series of GDP per capita. The source for this data was the KOSIS Statistical Database from Korean National Statistics Office (KNSO). This is available at http://www.nso.go.kr.

$PCGDP_{Ct}$ = Canadian Per Capita Income in Constant (1992) U. S. dollars
For the years up to 2000, the GDP per capita data was collected from the Heston and Summers Penn World Tables, version 6.1. For the years 2001, 2002, and 2003, the series was extrapolated using the growth in the constant dollar series of GDP per capita. The source for this data was the Statistics Canada CANSIM table 380-0002 (cat.# 13-001-XIB). This is available at http://www.statcan.ca/english/Pgdb/econ05.htm.

$PCGDP_{Ut}$ = American Per Capita Income in Constant (1992) U.S. dollars
For the years up to 2000, the GDP per capita data was collected from the Heston and Summers Penn World Tables, version 6.1. For the years 2001, 2002, and 2003, the series was extrapolated using the growth in the constant dollar series of GDP per capita. The source for this data was the NIPA tables at the U.S. Department of Commerce, Bureau of Economic Analysis. This is available at http://www.bea.doc.gov/bea/dn/nipaweb.

$URATE_{Ct}$ = Unemployment Rate in Canada
The Canadian unemployment rate series was constructed from Leacy (1983) and Statistics Canada's CANSIM II Series V2062815.

$URATE_{Ut}$ = Unemployment Rate in the United States
The unemployment rate series for the United States was taken from the U.S. Bureau of Labor Statistics Current Population Survey. The data are available at http://www.bls.gov/cps/home.htm#empstat.

$POPDEN_{Kt}$ = Population Density in Korea
The population density time series is from the World Bank's World Development Indicators.

U_t = $URATE_{Ut}$ / $URATE_{Ct}$

$W = w_{us}$ / w_c = The expected wage in the United States to the expected wage in Canada.
A proxy for this is the ratio of per capita GDP. The data for this variable came from the Centre for the Study of Living Standards (CSLS, 2007)

X_t = Cost of a U.S. Dollar in Canadian Dollars
The Penn World Tables, version 6.1, provided the exchange rates to 2000. The remaining years in the series were obtained from the Federal Reserve, Statistical Release G.5A.

$\Delta ln(IMM_t)$ = $ln(IMM_{Ct})$ – $ln(IMM_{Ct})$
$\Delta ln(PCGDP_t)$ = $ln(PCGDP_{Ct})$ - $ln(PCGDP_{Ut})$
$\Delta URATE_t$ = $URATE_{Ct}$ - $URATE_{Ut}$

REFERENCES

Attanasio, O.P., and Schioppa, F.P. (1991). Regional inequalities, migration and mismatch in Italy, 1960–86. In P. Schioppa (Ed.), *Mismatch and labour mobility* (pp. 237–320). Cambridge, UK: Cambridge University Press and CEPR.

Baker, M., and Benjamin, D. (1996). Asia Pacific immigration and the Canadian economy. In R. G. Harris (Ed.), *The Asia Pacific region in the global economy: A Canadian perspective* (pp. 303–56). Calgary: University of Calgary Press.

Bauer, T., & Zimmerman, K.F. (1995). Modeling international migration: Economic and econometric issues. In R. van der Erf and L. Heering (Eds.),

Causes of international migration. Proceedings of a workshop, Luxembourg, 14–16 December 1994 (pp. 95–115). Luxembourg: Eurostat.

Bentolila, S., and Dolado, J.J. (1991). Mismatch and internal migration in Spain, 1982–86. In F. Padoa-Schioppa (Ed.), *Mismatch and labour mobility*, (pp. 182–234). Cambridge: Cambridge University Press and CEPR.

Berninghaus, S., and Seifert-Vogt, H.G. (1991). *International migration under incomplete information.* Berlin, Germany: Springer-Verlag.

Borjas, G.J. (1987). Self selection and the earning of immigrants. *American Economic Review, 77,* 531–3.

———. (1989). Immigrant and emigrant earnings: A longitudinal study. *Economic Inquiry, 27,* 21–37.

———. (1994). The economics of immigration. *Journal of Economic Literature, 32,* 1667–717.

Burda, M.C. (1995). Migration and the option value of waiting. CEPR Discussion Paper No. 906. London: Centre for Economic Policy Research.

Chiswick, B.R. (2000). Are immigrants favorably self-selected? An economic analysis. In C.D. Brettell and J.F. Hollifield (Eds.), *Migration theory: Talking across disciplines* (pp. 61–76). New York: Routledge.

Clark, X., Hatton, T.J., and Williamson, J.G. (2002). Where do U.S. immigrants come from? Policy and sending country fundamentals. NBER Working Paper 8998. Cambridge, MA: National Bureau of Economic Research.

DeVoretz, D. (1995). *Diminishing returns: The economics of Canada's recent immigration policy.* Toronto: C.D. Howe Institute and the Laurier Institute.

Gabriel, S.A., Shack-Marquez, J., and Wascher, W.L. (1992). Regional house-price dispersion and interregional migration. *Journal of Housing Economics, 2,* 235–56.

Ghatak, S., and Levine, P.L. (1994). A note on migration with borrowing constraints. *Scandinavian Journal of Development Alternatives, 13*(4), 19–26.

Ghatak, S., Levine, P.L., and Price, S.W. (1996). Migration theories and evidence: An assessment. *Journal of Economic Surveys, 10,* 159–98.

Green, A.G., and Green, D.A. (1995). Canadian immigration policy: The effectiveness of the points system and other instruments. *Canadian Journal of Economics, 28,* 1006–1041.

———. (1999). The economic goals of Canada's immigration policy: Past and present. *Canadian Public Policy-Analyse de Politiques, 25,* 425–51.

Han, J.D., and Ibbott, P. (2005a). Economic impacts of international migration between Canada and Korea. *Korean Review of Canadian Studies, 11,* 47–77.

———. (2005b). Korean immigration to North America: Some prices that matter. *Canadian Studies in Population, 32*(2), 155–76.

Hatton, T.J. (2003). *Explaining trends in UK migration*. Working Paper, University of Essex.

Hatton, T.J., and Williamson, J.G. (2002). *What fundamentals drive world migration*. Working Paper, University of Essex.

Harris, J.R., and Todaro, M.P. (1970). Migration, unemployment and development: A two-sector analysis. *American Economic Review, 60*, 126–42.

Hicks, J. (1932). *The theory of wages*. London: MacMillan.

Kamemera, D., Oguledo, V.I, and Davis, B. (2000). A gravity model analysis of international migration to North America. *Applied Economics, 32*, 1745–55.

Lazarus, E. (1883). The New Colossus. In C.A. Sutherland (2003). *The Statue of Liberty: The museum of the City of New York*. New York: Barnes and Noble.

Leacy, F.H. (Ed.). (1983). *Historical statistics of Canada* (2nd ed.). Ottawa: Statistics Canada.

Lucas, R.E.B. (1985). Migration among the Botswana. *Economic Journal, 95*, 358–82.

Maier, G. (1985). Cumulative causation and selectivity in labor market oriented migration caused by imperfect information. *Regional Studies, 19*, 231–41.

Massey, D.S. (1988). Economic development and international migration in comparative perspective. *Population and Development Review, 14*(3), 383–413.

Padoa-Schioppa, F. (Ed.). (1991). *Mismatch and labour mobility*. Cambridge: Cambridge University Press and CEPR.

Park, J. (2012). A demographic profile of Koreans in Canada, chapter 2, this volume.

Rotte, R., and Vogler, M. (1998). *Determinants of international migration: Empirical evidence for migration from developing countries to Germany*. IZA Discussion Paper No. 12.

Sjaastad, L. (1962). The costs and returns of human migration. *Journal of Political Economy, 70*(5), S80–S93.

Stark, O. (1991). *The migration of labor*. Oxford: Blackwell.

Todaro, M.P. (1969). A model of labour migration and urban employment in less developed countries. *American Economic Review, 59*, 138–48.

Van der Erf, R., and Heering, L. (Eds.). (1994). *Causes of international migration. Proceedings of a workshop, Luxembourg, 14–16 December 1994* (pp. 95–115). Luxembourg: Eurostat.

5 Emerging Gateways in the Atlantic: The Institutional and Family Context of Korean Migration to New Brunswick[1]

ANN H. KIM AND CHEDLY BELKHODJA

Introduction

Federal and provincial governments have taken a more active approach to the dispersal of immigrants outside the traditional urban magnets of MTV (Montreal, Toronto, Vancouver). A Citizenship and Immigration Canada (CIC) report released in 2001 titled "Towards a more balanced geographic distribution of immigrants" argued that the regionalization of immigrants was a priority for places large and small. This argument has sparked increasing research and scholarly attention on the locational decisions and settlement and integration experiences of immigrants in smaller urban Canada, and we situate our study within this limited yet growing body of work. Using the case of Korean immigrants in New Brunswick (NB), we demonstrate that the regionalization of immigrants occurs within a broader institutional context that encompasses more than the individual traits of migrants and the social and economic conditions in places of destination.

We have begun to see new immigrant destinations emerge across Canada outside the traditional gateways within this relatively recent policy context, and recent Korean immigrants are a part of this new

1 This research was supported by the New Brunswick Population Growth Secretariat. The views and opinions reported here are not those of the New Brunswick Population Growth Secretariat, but are the sole responsibility of the authors. The authors would like to thank Sarah Choi, Jenna Im, David Lee, Cheon-Ae Park, and many others from the local New Brunswick communities and Korean Associations, Ashraf Ghanem, and Lizzie Cheng from the Population Growth Secretariat, and CERIS–The Ontario Metropolis Centre for access to the CIC Permanent Resident Data System (PRDS) 1980–2005.

wave of migrants. Part of the growth in the Korean population has appeared in the Atlantic region, where the rising presence and visibility of Korean immigrants has been palpable, and 2006 CIC figures reveal that South Korea is among the top three source countries of permanent residents to Saint John, Moncton, Fredericton, Halifax, and Charlottetown. While the other top source countries vary depending on the city, China, Iran, Taiwan, the United States, and the United Kingdom are commonly seen on the list (2007).

Many Korean immigrants arrive through the NB Provincial Nominee Program (NB PNP), and bring with them high levels of human and financial capital. The NB PNP program is one of many PNPs across Canada, and it adheres to this new policy of regionalization, which has as its goal the dispersal of immigrants away from the large centres to reduce the pressures of rapid population growth and to prevent further decline in low population areas (Carter et al., 2008). To date, all provinces and territories, with the exception of Quebec (which has a separate agreement with the federal government) and Nunavut, have an agreement with the federal government to run their immigration programs.[2] As priorities are identified by the region, the classes of entry vary widely, although all share an economic objective. The most common streams are the business class (also investor or entrepreneurial class) and skilled-worker class who are generally sponsored by employers. Some of the more comprehensive programs include streams for family, students, farm operators, and specified occupations. As of this writing, New Brunswick has two streams, a business class and a skilled-worker class, and most Koreans arrive through the business class.

In the recent past, various levels of government in New Brunswick have aggressively pursued immigrants from South Korea. For example, a local city councillor of Korean descent participated in a televised documentary about Saint John that was broadcast in South Korea (CBC News, 2007). For their efforts, then, the numbers arriving through this program and through the regular immigration program may continue.

While these streams may continue through aggressive recruitment schemes, taking into account the interests of the short- and long-term social, demographic, and economic well-being of New Brunswick, there is a need to understand the motivations for migration to smaller cities

---

2 Immigrants who have been nominated by a province or territory must still be approved by the federal government according to federal regulations. See http://www.cic.gc.ca/english/immigrate/provincial/index.asp.

and locational decisions, which would inform strategies for attracting and retaining future immigrants from South Korea and elsewhere.
With this objective, this chapter explores the reasons for recent Korean
migration to three cities in New Brunswick – Fredericton, Moncton, and
Saint John – places not historically or widely recognized as immigrant
destinations, nor places that are characterized as ethno-racially diverse
(Jabbra & Cosper, 1988). We first provide some background on these
issues by examining Korean migration flows to the Atlantic and the NB
PNP. Then we use focus group data from the *Study on Korean Immigrant
Settlement, Integration and Reception in New Brunswick* to consider questions on the move to smaller cities within an institutional context. We
find that family decisions to relocate from South Korea to New Brunswick often place children at the centre, and that the institutional contexts in places of origin and destination and the institutions that tie the
two places together are key to understanding these family decisions. By
institutional context, we refer to educational systems and the migration
industry, namely, immigration brokers and consultants.

Korean Migration Flows to Atlantic Canada

Very few Korean immigrants from the first wave of permanent migrants
to Canada indicated an Atlantic province as an intended destination of
settlement, but in absolute and relative terms, the flows to the Atlantic
region have increased over time (figure 5.1). During the period from
1973 to 1983, less than 1.0 per cent of immigrants (or 127) whose last
place of residence was South Korea intended to land in Nova Scotia,
New Brunswick, Newfoundland, or Prince Edward Island. For the more
recent period for which data are available (1995 to 2005), the percentage
of Korean immigrants to these four Maritime provinces increased to 2.3
per cent, or 1,535 immigrants, and consisted mostly of business, skilled,
or PNP-class migrants and their families. Many also came highly educated, with more than half of the adult immigrants having at least a
bachelor's degree.

    The increase to the Atlantic provinces coincides with a general dis-
persion of Korean migration away from Ontario. The decreasing importance of Ontario and the increasing importance of alternative places of
destination for newer migrants are clearly visible in figure 5.1. Given
that Winnipeg was the third top metropolitan destination in 2004 and
2005 for Korean immigrants, this trend toward increasing migration to
non-traditional gateways is likely to continue and suggests that immi-

Figure 5.1. Intended Place of Destination of Permanent Migrants from Korea[1] over Time[2]

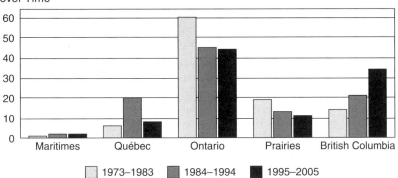

Notes:
1. Based on those who indicated North or South Korea as their country of last permanent residence.
2. Data were drawn from the Immigration Statistics Reports yearly from 1973 to 1980, and PRDS (formerly LIDS) 1980–2005.

grant settlement, incorporation, and retention will be key issues for these comparatively smaller places with significantly different social and economic contexts.

Despite the trends, however, the population of Korean immigrants settling outside of Ontario is still relatively low in size. Ethnic Koreans in Toronto and Vancouver number well over the 1,630 ethnic Koreans in the Atlantic (table 5.1). Yet for the Atlantic provinces, whose overall population sizes are also comparatively low, Korean immigration is having a significant impact on local communities. This is particularly true in New Brunswick, which was home to approximately 290 newcomers in 2006, compared with 205 in Nova Scotia, 55 in PEI, and 10 in Newfoundland.

More recent figures estimate that over 900 immigrants arrived from Korea in 2006 and 2007 alone, signalling a rapidly growing community. This rapid growth has raised concern among policymakers in New Brunswick about the short- and long-term changes that are needed to address the experiences of immigrant Koreans and other groups. As many of the immigrants have arrived under the PNP (nearly 1,200 Koreans from 2000 to 2008), policymakers have a vested interest in evaluating and understanding the effects of the program.

Table 5.1. Total Population and Korean Population in the Atlantic Provinces and Cities, 2006 Census

	Total Population	Ethnic Korean	Korean Immigrant		
			Permanent	Newcomer	Temporary
New Brunswick	729,997	635	370	290	75
Fredericton	85,688	170	160	160	0
Saint John	122,389	130	75	55	35
Moncton	126,424	60	30	20	30
Nova Scotia	913,462	845	430	205	265
Halifax	372,858	665	355	150	205
Newfoundland	505,469	70	10	10	40
St. John's	181,113	45	10	0	30
PEI	135,851	80	70	55	0
Charlottetown	58,625	80	65	55	0
Total Atlantic	2,284,779	1,630	880	560	380

Notes:
The numbers are based on the Korean single response to the ethnic ancestry question on the 2006 census.
Newcomers are defined as those who landed between 2001 and 2006.

The Provincial Nominee Program in New Brunswick

In the 1980s, the New Brunswick government began to recognize the importance of immigration for the economic and demographic development of the province. The McKenna years (1987–97) were marked by intense government activity focused on opening the province to the world, particularly to the international francophone community and through commercial relations with New England (Belkhodja & Ouellette, 2001). To be part of the new economic reality of globalization, the province felt it had to provide the necessary tools for promoting itself and attracting qualified immigrants. This goal was not insignificant for a small province with a population currently standing at three-quarters of a million inhabitants.

The 2007 report "Action Plan to be Self-Sufficient in New Brunswick" affirmed the conviction that international migration would lead to demographic growth in a province characterized by an aging population, low birth rate, and an exodus of its youth. In this context, immigration was a government priority. Thus, committed to attracting, integrating, and retaining qualified immigrants by supporting settlement agencies, the New Brunswick government created the Population Growth Secretariat that same year, which was charged with promoting immigration and diversity in the province.

Like others, the province of New Brunswick runs a PNP in agreement with the federal government. Signed in 1999, this agreement was renewed in 2004 allowing this provincial government to continue to select applicants who fulfil specific local economic needs. The nominees are grouped into two economically based categories: those with a job offer and those with the intention of establishing a business. Since the creation of the NB PNP, more than 2,000 applicants have been accepted, and it is mainly through this program's business stream that the province has attracted Korean immigrants.[3] Against this backdrop, we investigate the experiences of recently arrived Korean immigrants.

Korean Immigrant Settlement, Integration, and Reception in New Brunswick

The main purpose of the research study was to examine recent Korean migration to the province, and in particular to the three main cities of Fredericton, Saint John, and Moncton. The specific objectives were to study and understand the impact of the PNP on Korean immigrants and on local New Brunswick communities by investigating the motivations for migration to non-traditional gateways, and subsequent settlement and adaptation experiences. Through this project, we also hoped to highlight opportunities for ethnic community development for Koreans and to examine their reception by local institutions in the three sites.

To achieve these objectives, we relied primarily on semi-structured focus group and in-depth individual interviews, which took place between April and July 2009, and supplemented our understanding of the community with additional data sources. To ensure that our interpretation of the interview data resonated with immigrant experiences

---

3 As of this writing, the NB PNP business stream requires applicants to submit a business plan or proposal that will be of economic benefit to the province. According to the website of the New Brunswick Population Growth Secretariat <beinthisplace.ca/ImmigratingandSettling/Howtoimmigrate/NewBrunswickProvincialNomineeProgram/Businessapplicants.aspx>, applicants have to demonstrate management experience, their willingness to live in the province and manage the business, a monetary worth of at least $300,000, and an investment of $125,000. They must speak at least one of the official languages and place a refundable deposit of $75,000 as a guarantee of their commitment. The deposit, on which no interest will be paid, is made to the Government of New Brunswick after a business application is approved. The business must be established within two years of landing, as well as operated and actively managed by the applicant for one year before applying for a refund. Extensions may be considered.

and to follow up with some additional questions arising out of the focus groups, we invited key community leaders from the three cities to a consultation meeting in Fredericton in March 2010.

In this chapter, we draw from the focus group data to highlight the immigrants' shared experiences in the three sites. Altogether, four focus groups were held, one each in Moncton and Fredericton, and two in Saint John. Each group had seven to ten members who were recruited using purposive and snowball sampling techniques. While efforts were made to segment the groups by gender and immigrant entry class (i.e., PNP and independent), only one group consisted of all female members; all other groups were mixed gender and mixed immigrant entry class. The first author attended all four focus groups, which were co-facilitated by a research assistant in the Korean language. Each focus group interview was subsequently recorded, transcribed, and then translated into English.

There were a total of thirty-three participants in the four groups, twelve male and twenty-one female, with well over half the participants ranging in age from thirty-six to forty-eight years of age. All participants were married (some were couples in attendance), thirty had between one and three school-aged children, one participant did not have any children, and two participants had older children who had completed high school. Nearly 80 per cent had a bachelor's degree or higher, yet 75 per cent were unemployed. The vast majority landed as business-class immigrants under the PNP or as independent business-class immigrants, and of the thirty-one immigrants who arrived in New Brunswick after 2004, only one reported being self-employed, although during the interviews several participants mentioned that their spouses were self-employed.

The semi-structured group interviews were designed to elicit responses to three lines of questions: motivations for migration and locational decisions; settlement experiences; and future intentions. To enable a deeper understanding of the institutional factors that shape migration decisions, we limit our discussion to the first question in this chapter. We highlight the common responses across the three sites, namely, expectations of children within the educational system and the influence of players in the migration industry on migration flows. Differences in the urban contexts of Fredericton, Moncton, and Saint John might suggest that immigrant experiences should differ across the three cities; however, as the focus of this paper is on migration motivations and locational decisions, and not settlement experiences, we discuss the common themes that were raised in the three places.

Findings: Motivations for Migration and Locational Decisions

The demographic characteristics of places, namely, population size, as well as economic and educational opportunities, and social and familial connections are important factors in newcomer locational decisions and retention (Akbari & Harrington, 2007; Derwing & Krahn, 2008; Hou, 2007; Hyndman et al., 2006). Additional considerations are the quality of reception, housing issues, and climate (Derwing & Krahn, 2008; Krahn et al., 2005; Michalski & George, 1997). Thus, what draws immigrants to a place and keeps them there is its size (and by extension the quality of life), jobs, and other opportunities to upgrade skills, the presence of family and friends, appropriate housing, the friendliness of the people there, and a bearable climate. While some researchers point to the primacy of size (Akbari & Harrington, 2007; Hyndman et al., 2006), Hou (2007) argues that a location's overall attractiveness is what draws in (and retains) immigrants.

Demographic, economic, educational, and environmental factors also emerged as important for the Korean immigrants in our focus groups. Consistent with others (Di Biase & Bauder, 2005; Hou, 2007), participants mentioned the clean and quiet natural environment, access to a public education system, and quality of life. In addition, as in Lusis and Bauder's (2008) study, a few participants who had spent time in larger cities (i.e., Vancouver, Calgary, or Toronto) identified their drawbacks, characterizing them as "heartless" and suggesting that the existence of a large Korean community did not fit with their expectations of living in a foreign country. A small Korean community was appealing for the immigrants going to cities with smaller populations. Finally, the importance of the Internet as a medium for obtaining detailed information emerged in our discussions as it has in previous research (Lusis & Bauder, 2008). Immigrants used official and local sources of information, including the websites of local Korean associations.

The issues that have not widely surfaced in existing studies on smaller cities are some significant institutional and family factors. First, there is the primary role of children in shaping the migration decision in the context of the relative conditions in places of origin and destination. Second, there is the influence of private agents in the international migration industry, known as immigration brokers or consultants.

Both of these factors were salient features of Korean migration to New Brunswick.

A "Children's Paradise": Education in Canada versus Korea and the Migration Decision

Schooling is an all-consuming way of life for students in South Korea. They spend more hours in class than students in the West, and nearly every minute of their lives is organized around school and, in particular, examinations. Children are indoctrinated in their early days to believe that their ultimate goal in life is to enter top-class universities in Seoul. (Cho, 1995, p. 148)

Koreans seem still to be engaged in a battle over education ... We view the extreme demand for higher education in Korea and the accompanying social and psychological pressure on young people and their families as being analogous to a war for education. (Park & Weidman, 2000, p. 177)

These excerpts provide us with a sense of the intense educational environment that faces each child in South Korea, often referred to as a "battle" or "war," and the participants in the study corroborated this account. Parents emphasized the highly competitive nature of Korean society and its educational system, which made it extraordinarily stressful for children (and thus parents). Parents, particularly mothers, were under extreme pressure to pack their children's schedules with tutoring and lessons, and it was not uncommon to have children studying past midnight starting from elementary or middle school. This practice comes from an expectation not only to be the best but also to do everything well. "If a student can't do ten things, but can do one thing well, it's useless in Korea, but here, even though a student can't do everything, if that student does one thing well, they praise it" (female, Saint John).

It was recognized that this institutional environment would leave many children behind. "The education system is giving up on nine [students] for the one. This is the biggest problem in Korea." And in some cases, the push to move overseas came from the children themselves: "The school atmosphere is such that if you don't get good grades, they think you are stupid. My children dislike that." Children who rejected the Korean educational system were also likely to have studied abroad in other countries or in Canada. "After that [summer] program [in Canada], my children didn't want to come back to Korea. They liked the Canadian educational system very much. It was a very free atmosphere, and they were given lots of chances to express their opinions" (female, Saint John).

The less structured days of children in Canada gave parents the feeling that their children were "free" and perhaps bored. "Children are free and have lots of time to think. In Korea, they don't have free time" (female, Saint John). One parent enjoyed seeing her children voluntarily turn to playing the piano or reading books. In essence, this institutional context shaped Canada's appeal as a "children's paradise" for Korean immigrants, underscoring the central position of children in a family's decision to move. This circumstance is consistent with the literature on transnationalism, which recognizes the importance of the presence and participation of children in family migration decisions (Orellana et al., 2001). The presence of children means that decisions by parents are often taken with their children's interests and future in mind, and as is evident with the immigrants we interviewed in NB, migration decisions are made with their children's active involvement.

One woman in Moncton indicated that she had not thought about emigrating until she had children. Several also stated that they felt the pressure to move when their children were in elementary school, as competition in secondary school would become more intense. The desire to move to Canada from South Korea developed in light of relative differences in the educational environment and quality of life for children. "I didn't want to raise my children that way. I shouldn't raise them that way. Everybody has only one life; there is no reason to take the hard road" (female, Saint John).

While moving for the sake of the children's education was the reason most frequently cited by parents as motivating the migration, it was also harmonious with the desire for a better life for all members of the family. One woman expressed this thought, and she shared with us her husband's words prior to leaving South Korea: "Let's go somewhere else where we could have a family life and the children could have an education too."

Thus, the quality of life as a motivation extended to adults as well. As another mother in Fredericton elaborated, "Koreans compete with each other too much. They have lots of good qualities, but they love to compare everything, and you know what Koreans do to each other. I felt sick about those things. Here, we have the advantage of living an absolute life, not a relative one."

How she and other Korean immigrants found themselves in New Brunswick is the focus of the next section.

Voices of Influence: Immigration Brokers and Consultants

"Maybe the biggest part of the reason we came here was the immigration company's recommendation" (male, Fredericton). "Their [immigration broker's] recommendation is very powerful" (female, Saint John). In the scholarly literature on immigration and settlement in Canada's less-populated regions, the role of immigration brokers and how they facilitate migration streams has often been overlooked. Instead the emphasis has been on the characteristics of immigrants and places of destination. If the quality of life for children, and hence family, was one common thread tying together the immigrants in the focus groups across the three cities, another common connection was that most migrants used the services of an immigration company or broker. While not specifically asked about their experiences with immigration companies, most participants mentioned that they had contact with them, and based on the recommendations of immigration consultants they chose to apply to New Brunswick.

For the New Brunswick immigrants we interviewed, immigration brokers appeared to play several roles. First, they located potential families using local resources such as print and television media and information seminars. Second, they promoted New Brunswick as an attractive destination to families, situating the province on their map of Canada, which normally featured only Toronto and Vancouver. (And according to one respondent in Saint John, they had previously been promoting Winnipeg.) For their efforts, they were able to spread the word about New Brunswick to people who had never heard of the province and to persuade them to apply to a place they likely would have never considered. "I didn't know it [New Brunswick] before. I said I was interested in immigrating and they introduced it to me. That was the first time. In the east, close to Boston and other things, the environment" (male, Saint John). This attitude was confirmed by several other respondents, with one man in Moncton referring to the companies as "travel agencies," as they sold him and his spouse on the idea that Moncton was close to the sea.

Third, they facilitated the application process and in some cases even assisted applicants with their business plan. In doing so, they could also screen potential candidates and encourage those who fitted or could fit the criteria to apply, and then they would take an active approach, contacting the families after an immigration seminar. Their encouragement included touting the advantages of applying to the NB PNP relative to other programs in other regions of Canada and in other countries. "At that time my husband was checking around, and nearly all the immigration consultants recommended New Brunswick. The provincial government made it the easiest and fastest [migration process]. So when people said, 'Canada,' then immigration companies answered, 'New Brunswick'" (female, Saint John).

Many immigrants had heard that the NB PNP program was new, had no monetary deposit requirement, and that through this program they could obtain a Permanent Resident card very quickly, which would mean lower (or no) tuition fees for their children. All this was very appealing to the respondents and their families. Thus, the immigrants' exposure to and interactions with immigration consultants makes quite obvious that the consultants were very well positioned to recruit Korean families to smaller cities, and that they figured prominently in influencing and directing migration flows to New Brunswick.

Discussions

Korean immigrants have become increasingly attracted to smaller cities and towns outside the traditional immigrant urban agglomerations. In the recent period, cities in Atlantic Canada have seen increased flows, particularly in New Brunswick, owing to a large extent to the NB PNP. The success of efforts to attract Korean migrants to New Brunswick through the PNP or any other program depends on economic, demographic, social, and environmental factors.

In addition, the decision to migrate to a non-traditional gateway is shaped by the institutional context. The two key institutional factors in Korean immigrants' decisions to move to smaller cities in Canada that we have identified have not been widely examined previously: the first is the competitiveness of the educational system in South Korea and the pressure it places on children and their parents; the second is the active role that immigration consultants play in influencing the decisions of Korean migrants, particularly to smaller locales.

We learn that Korean migration to New Brunswick places children and children's education at the centre of the decision. Nearly all migrants in the focus group had children, and they indicated feeling more compelled to emigrate when their children were young. They were leaving not necessarily for a "better" education for their children but for a less competitive and stressful environment where their children could learn English and still have access to quality educational opportunities at the university level. In doing so, they hoped to improve their overall quality of life as a family. While the decision to migrate for a better life has always existed, Korean immigration is unique in that it occurs in the context of an extremely competitive and confining educational environment for children and parents and less as a result of better economic opportunities.

The gap between the education and lifestyle motivation of families and the economic basis of migration policies and programs, specifically the business-class program through which many Korean migrants arrive, is likely to raise challenges for both policymakers and immigrants. Although the objectives are not diametrically opposed or inconsistent – and in fact, most migrants indicated they would like to see themselves economically settled and integrated – many migrants who were approved under the PNP business program had no business experience in South Korea but appeared to be middle or top managers in corporate firms. Not only will they need additional support to establish and run their business, but also their settlement patterns will be determined by the schooling of their children, their children's experiences and future educational plans. For instance, many of them are aware that their children may leave for Canada's larger universities in several years and are cautious in their planning. In other words, the short-term nature of their children's education may not be congruent with investing in and establishing a business in Atlantic Canada.

With significant pressure to leave South Korea because of the highly competitive educational system, Korean migrants have myriad destinations from which to choose. In this sense, New Brunswick competes not only against other provinces but also other countries. Within this competition for immigrants with capital, the efforts of immigration consultants and brokers to some degree determine the direction of flows. To be sure, Korean migration to New Brunswick is shaped by the PNP and the opportunities it provides for Permanent Resident status relative to other provinces and countries. Yet, it is primarily through immigration brokers that potential applicants are persuaded to land in its towns and cities. Although the workings of immigration consultants, their influence and position in directing migration streams, and their effects on migration flows have been little discussed in the literature, there is recognition that they play a role in promoting linkages between places (Kukushin, 2009; Walton-Roberts, 2009). Clearly, greater attention is needed to understand the role and impact of brokers.

Two additional features of Korean migration to New Brunswick that were raised but not further explored in the focus groups were the use of the Internet to obtain information from earlier migrants on the immigration program and settlement, and exposure and contact with English-language teachers from New Brunswick in South Korea. These issues have been raised to a limited degree in previous research (Derwing & Krahn, 2008; Lusis & Bauder, 2008; M. Kwak, chapter 6, this volume), but there is more to be done. Specifically, the kind of information sought over the Internet should be investigated, as well as how the use of information obtained from the Internet shapes migration decisions and settlement experiences. With respect to the latter issue, with the increase in English-language programs in South Korea and elsewhere, and partnerships between school boards in Canada and South Korea, there is reason to expect that teachers have become the new "missionaries."

Based on these findings, the policy recommendations for New Brunswick's governments are obvious. It is clear that the regionalization of Korean migrant flows will depend mostly on provincial immigration regulations, on the perceptions of the quality of the educational system, and on the recommendations of immigration consultants. Hence, in order for Korean immigration to the region to continue or to rise, efforts must be made to, first, re-establish a no- or low-cost migration program (i.e., remove the $75,000 deposit required of business-class migrants that was added in February 2010 [see footnote 3 on page 77]); second, improve the quality of education in the province (and the perception of such); and third, work with immigration consultants to ensure that they have accurate and up-to-date information and that they are providing such information.

Finally, the issues raised above will help us to understand experiences beyond the migration and locational decisions of Korean immigrants, which can be explored in future work. Since, once again, immigration has become popularized as a way to improve a region's economic prospects (Florida, 2002), understanding the institutional context of international migration is important for appreciating the ebb and flow of population movements between particular places. Our next step is to examine issues related to settlement and integration and the future intentions of Korean immigrants in smaller places. New immigrant destinations are emerging across Canada, and cities in the Atlantic region are attracting increasing numbers of immigrants who are able to contribute to the social and economic vitality of their host communities. While part of the success of the PNP may lie in the numbers that flow across New Brunswick's borders, the true measure of success is the province's ability to foster immigrant integration and retention.

REFERENCES

Akbari, A.H., and Harrington, J.S. (2007). Initial location choice of new immigrants to Canada. Halifax: Atlantic Metropolis Centre.
Belkhodja, C., and Ouellette, R. (2001). L.J. Robichaud and F. McKenna: Deux axes de l'action du Nouveau-Brunswick au sein de la francophonie. *Actes du colloque* (pp. 115–26). Institut canadien de recherche sur le développement regional.
Carter, T., Morrish, M., and Amoyaw, B. (2008). Attracting immigrants to smaller urban and rural communities: Lessons learned from the Manitoba provincial nominee program. *Journal of International Migration and Integration, 9,* 161–83.
CBC News. (2007). *Korean Councillor hopes to woo immigrants to Saint John.* (January 8). Retrieved from http://www.cbc.ca/canada/new-brunswick/story/2007/01/08/nb-koreasj.html.
Cho, H.J. (1995). Children in the examination war in South Korea: A cultural analysis. In S. Stephens (Ed.), *Children and the politics of culture, Princeton studies in culture/power/history* (pp. 141–68). Princeton: Princeton University Press.
Citizenship and Immigration Canada (CIC). (2001). *Towards a more balanced geographic distribution of immigrants.* Ottawa: Strategic Policy, Planning and Research.
——. (2007). *Facts and figures 2006: Atlantic Canada supplement.* Ottawa: Strategic Policy, Planning and Research.
Derwing, T.M., and Krahn, H. (2008). Attracting and retaining immigrants outside the metropolis: Is the pie too small for everyone to have a piece? The case of Edmonton, Alberta. *Journal of International Migration and Integration, 9,* 185–202.
Di Biase, S., and Bauder, H. (2005). Immigrant settlement in Ontario: Location and local labour markets. *Canadian Ethnic Studies, 37,* 114–35.
Florida, R. (2002). The rise of the creative class. New York: Basic Books.
Hou, F. (2007). Changes in the initial destinations and redistribution of

Canada's major immigrant groups: Re-examining the role of group affinity. *International Migration Review, 41*, 680–705.

Hyndman, J., Schuurman, N., and Fiedler, R. (2006). Size matters: Attracting new immigrants to Canadian cities. *Journal of International Migration and Integration, 7*, 1–25.

Jabbra, N.W., and Cosper, R.L. (1988). Ethnicity in Atlantic Canada: A survey. *Canadian Ethnic Studies, 20*, 6–27.

Krahn, H., Derwing, T.M., and Baha, A.L. (2005). The retention of newcomers in second- and third-tier Canadian cities. *International Migration Review, 39*, 872–94.

Kukushkin, V. (2009). *Immigrant-friendly communities: Making immigration work for employers and other stakeholders in small-town Canada.* Report: The Conference Board of Canada.

Kwak, M.J. (2012). International student experiences of migration and consuming Canadian education, chapter 6, this volume.

Lusis, T., and Bauder, H. (2008). *"Provincial" immigrants: The social, economic, and transnational experiences of the Filipino Canadian community in three Ontario second-tier cities.* Toronto: CERIS – The Ontario Metropolis Centre.

Michalski, J.M., and George, G. (1997). *A snapshot of newcomers: Final report.* Toronto: Centre for Applied Social Research.

Orellana, M.F., Thorne, B., Chee, A., and Lam, W.S.E. (2001). Transnational childhoods: The participation of children in processes of family migration. *Social Problems, 48*, 572–91.

Park, N., and Weidman, J.C. (2000). Battlefield for higher education. In J.C. Weidman and N. Park (Eds.), *Higher education in Korea: Tradition and adaptation* (vol. 17), *Garland studies in higher education* (pp. 177–96). New York: Falmer Press.

Walton-Roberts, M. (2009). *India-Canada trade and immigration linkages: A case of regional (dis)advantage?* Vancouver: Metropolis British Columbia.

6 International Student Experiences of Migration and Consuming Canadian Education

MIN-JUNG KWAK

Introduction

Now we are living in a global world. Dealing with international markets, many Korean companies now want to hire workers with good communication skills. It has become very critical to understand the other's living culture as well as business culture. When the companies hire a person with experience studying abroad, I don't think they are expecting the person to be just a fluent English speaker. They'd like to see if the person has some understanding of the other culture. Thus, I think this kind of labour market atmosphere in Korea has made so many students take English programs overseas and pursue real living experiences there.

—Mr Chang,[1] a trading company marketing representative in Seoul

With the rise of the international education industry in Vancouver in recent years, the rapid growth of international students and visitors from South Korea has been phenomenal. While it has been one of the leading source countries of international students since the mid-1990s, little is known about their experiences. For Mr Chang, who was once an international student in Vancouver, learning English and obtaining knowledge of Western culture in Canada were necessary steps to take for his career. He now works for an international trading company and frequently travels between the United States and South Korea. After one year of study in Vancouver, he did not consider himself to be a fluent English speaker, but the experience gave him some confi-

---

1 Names have been replaced with pseudonyms.

dence to face foreigners without anxiety. As Mr Chang noted, many Korean companies now think that learning English means more than their capacity to speak another language; it means gaining the ability to understand other cultures. His experience explicitly illustrates how achieving a form of human capital (studying English) can be coupled with cultural capital gain (knowing Western culture). International students believe they will accumulate cultural capital through consuming Western education. Their expectation is that this capital gain will eventually benefit South Korean companies in the increasingly competitive international market.

I argue, however, that this seemingly simple objective of international students is accompanied by a complex process of production, consumption, and reproduction of cultural capital. For some time, the acculturation process was typically described as a linear model in which ethnic minorities absorb local Western culture. In the process, migrants from Eastern countries have been often viewed as powerless and passive cultural minorities. I contend, however, that with their significant financial resources and selective consumption practices, the human agency of Korean international students needs to be reconsidered. In the context of global capitalism, their identity will be explored not only as a source of global capital that vitalizes the Canadian education industry but also as a confident bearer of competitive capitalist ideology. For example, we need to ask why Korean students specifically choose Canada rather than another Western country as the destination for their studies. In that regard, why has Vancouver been more attractive to them? Are they merely passive learners of "superior" Western culture, or do they carry significant agency as powerful global capitalists? How do they utilize their cultural capital? What kinds of roles do international students and their families play in shaping and reshaping the Canadian education industry? I probe these questions by exploring identity formation of international students through their everyday activities. I also consider how the process of consuming Canadian education is spatially bound and shaped by social networks.

Drawing on interview data with nineteen international students and six of their mothers, I explore the transnational experiences of students between two politico-cultural societies. This chapter consists of four sections. First, I provide an overview of Korean student migration to Canada. Second, by probing the reasons for studying abroad, I explore the cultural logic of consuming Canadian education. This investigation involves considering why the commodification of education and culture is seen as necessary, and how its usage has become more important than ever in a newly emerging global economy. In the third section, I examine the ways in which Canadian education has become institutionalized and embodied as "cultural capital" by Korean students and their parents. I am particularly interested in how their transnational identity formations cross multiple boundaries of place, ethnicity, and culture. Finally, by reflecting on the narratives of migration provided by both international students and their parents, I consider the policy implications for these questions: how can we improve the welfare of international students and families, and how can we further improve the industry and make it more beneficial to Canadian society?

Research Background

In addition to the rapidly growing number of Korean immigrants, many Koreans come to Canada to pursue their educational and career objectives with temporary permits. The rapid growth in number of international students and visitors from South Korea has been phenomenal since a visa exemption was granted to Koreans in 1994. Under this agreement between South Korea and Canada, Korean visitors can enter and stay in Canada for up to six months without a visa.

In the late 1990s, South Korea was the leading source of international student inflows to Canada (CIC, 2003; CIC Facts and Figures, 1998–2008a). The inflow dropped temporarily in 1998 as a result of the Asian financial crisis; however, the number fully recovered in 1999 and kept increasing until 2003. There were 13,941 Korean students who received study permits to enter Canada in 2008.[2] The number of Korean students accounted for about 18 per cent of total foreign student inflows to Canada in that year. An additional data source from CIC identified more than 100,000 Korean students who applied for or renewed their study permit for the five-year period from 1998 to 2003.[3]

While these numbers are already substantial, it is important to note that CIC reports do not take into account the number of students on tourist (visitor) visas. In 2007, for example, more than 200,000 Koreans

---

2 To measure "flows," the CIC special report counted only the number of students entering the CIC system (presumably the country) for the first time. Thus, the number does not include those students who renewed their visas in that particular year (CIC, 2003).

3 Data source: FOSS Data Warehouse Cubes (27 May 2003). This information has been provided courtesy of T. Vermette, a program specialist at CIC Pacific Regional Office.

visited Canada, and more than 60 per cent of the inflow came through British Columbia customs.[4] According to Tourism British Columbia, South Korea was the sixth- largest source of visitors to Canada and the fifth-largest to the province in 2007. In addition, it is tacitly known that extending the tourist visa period is not too onerous for Korean students as long as they prove their student status and financial stability. In my previous research on the international education industry, agency operators often agree that the average annual share of students with tourist visas would account for about 40 to 50 per cent of the total student inflow from South Korea (Kwak & Hiebert, 2010). It can therefore be estimated that in 2008, the actual number of Korean students who came to Canada could have been nearly 30,000.

The Cultural Logic of Consuming Global Education, Cultural Capital, and Spatial Mobility

With the advance of global capitalism, we have witnessed the intensified commodification of nearly every form of good and service in recent years (Nash, 2000). Especially in the most advanced post-industrial economies, cultural competence has taken on significance as an economic resource. From high culture to ethnic cuisine, cultural products are invested in, developed, and put on the market for sale just like any other consumer good. As I argued elsewhere (Kwak & Hiebert, 2007, 2010), education has become a commodity, and Canadian educational programs (products) are widely sold on the international market. I emphasized that the developmental process of the Canadian education industry is in fact a form of globalization and highlights the often hidden roles of different players in the market. Turning the analytical focus on the consumption side of the process, I find that it is important to examine the ways in which Canadian education is selected, consumed, and reproduced by international students and their families. This set of inquiries necessitates critical assessment of migration and living experiences that are bound to specific conditions of mobility and spatiality.

According to Bourdieu (1984), the *culture of consumption* is closely related to the process of social reproduction. What you consume is what you are, Bourdieu claims, and is often what you will become. In the process of learning and practicing culture, cultural resources are

---

4 This number does not include immigrants and temporary visa holders (e.g., international students and temporary workers).

therefore consumed, invested, and accumulated. Zukin (1990) and Ong (1999) argue that in certain contexts, cultural capital becomes *elastic* and *flexible* as resources are negotiated and reproduced involving different actors. Then immigrants, international students, and temporary visitors can be viewed as flexible consumers/capitalists who actively seek out and learn other experiences from a foreign culture and use them, mixing them with their own knowledge base.

In Waters's (2006) reading of Bourdieu, cultural capital exists in three forms: first, academic institutions grant diplomas and degrees that can be seen as *institutionalized* capital; second, capital is *embodied* through the process of being obtained, attributed, and characterized by individuals; and last, such capital can also be *objectified* in material forms (e.g., books, music, and art forms). In her case study of Hong Kong migrant students, Waters (2006) demonstrated how Asian middle-class families were able to accumulate a more valuable form of cultural capital by obtaining a Western university degree. On their return to Hong Kong, graduates were able to gain easier access to good jobs. Their skills and qualifications were well received not only because they were competitive but also because they carried the symbolic value of cultural capital (a Western university degree). Their transnational social networks also played an important role. This example shows how the hegemony of social-class relations can be reproduced through cultural capital.

Focusing solely on the social reproduction of cultural capital easily demonstrates the rigid quality of a Western degree as a more valuable form of cultural capital. It is equally important, however, to scrutinize the process of "embodiment" and "reproduction" of a Canadian degree. The hierarchical relationship between the assumed superior Western cultural resources and inferior cultural resources of Asian migrants needs to be deconstructed through the agency of migrants who are spatially conscious and network driven. In that regard, Waters (2006) highlights the importance of place-based transnational social networks in this process. This chapter adds to her discussion of a geographically sensitive account of cultural capital by examining the case of Korean students and their families who choose to consume overseas education for specific purposes and within changing political-economic contexts. I also explore the ways, beyond their consumer roles, in which international students and families have come to play an important role in reshaping the Canadian education industry.

Why Study Abroad? Three Stages of the Decision-Making Process

Between Seoul and Vancouver, I interviewed a total of nineteen Korean international students, consisting of ten short-term ESL program students, six full-time undergraduate students, and three graduate students, as well as six of their mothers (two in Korea and four *kirogi* mothers in Vancouver).[5] All ESL students were interviewed in Seoul, recollecting their experiences of short-term study (three months to one year) in Vancouver. All nine university students were interviewed in Vancouver between 2005 and 2006. The six undergraduate students first came to Vancouver as high school students and were enrolled in programs ranging between three and eleven years in length, and in many cases this included several programs taken sequentially. The graduate students who participated in my study had spent much less time in Canada, typically two years. Two mothers whom I met in Seoul sent their children to Vancouver for short-term programs (three months and six months). The other four *kirogi* mothers living with their children in Vancouver had various plans for a longer stay, i.e., for more than two years.

When they were asked why they decided to study abroad and in Vancouver, the interviewees' answers were largely structured around a traditional model of migration that concerned "push" and "pull" factors. The push factors focused on the negative aspects of Korean society and its educational system, and the pull factors involved considering Canada as a good destination for international education. Neoclassical economic approaches assert that international students actively weigh the pros and cons of studying abroad, and the possible return of the human capital they acquire (e.g., Borjas, 1989; Chen, 2006). However, this binary approach conceals the complex process of their decision making. Analysing their responses, I could see how social networks and cultural linkages work together as another set of important determining factors that are often transnational, involving various linkages between Seoul and Vancouver. In weighing the negative aspects of being educated in South Korea and the positive return of study-

5 In the context of education migration and transnational family organization, the term *kirogi* mothers refers to mothers who are living with, and primarily responsible for, taking care of children in the absence of fathers who work and live in another country. The term is similar to the "lone mother" of an astronaut family for Hong Kong Chinese migrants (Waters, 2002).

ing abroad, Korean students and their parents in my study narrowed their choice to Vancouver, relying on their social networks and cultural linkages. The role of mediators becomes critical, as many informants choose Vancouver because someone they knew provided credible information and/or helped them settle. For those who did not have close social networks, Korean-Canadian agents played similar roles, negotiating cultural understanding with students and their families from South Korea. Considering these factors, I identified three stages of the decision-making process: the decision to leave (push); the decision to choose Vancouver (pull); and the decision to utilize and rely on transnational social networks.

Similar to most East Asian countries, South Korea is known to have a highly competitive and stressful educational system. In South Korea, education is believed to be the only way to elevate one's social status. Reflecting this popular belief, the number of young people attending university has climbed from 40 to 86 per cent in the past two decades (*Wall Street Journal*, 2005). In South Korea, there are over 350 universities and colleges. To be regarded as successful, however, students need to excel in standardized tests and enter one of the top three universities, known as SKY (acronyms for Seoul National University, Korea University, and Yonsei University). As one parent interviewee noted, "reaching SKY" is not that easy. To enter these schools, students need to be ranked in the top 5 per cent of their cohort. Evaluating students for university entrance has been highly controversial, and the South Korean Ministry of Education has frequently changed the method of evaluation. Most parents who had enrolled their children in elementary or high schools in Vancouver at the time of the interview mentioned that this was an important push factor in their decision to leave South Korea. Because the cost of private education is climbing, some mothers argued that sending their children abroad was considered to be a cost-effective option as well. With the growing need for early English education, the highly stressful school environment in South Korea was another reason for seeking overseas education. Mrs Jung, who accompanied her Grade 12 son and Grade 10 daughter to Vancouver two years ago, spoke of her son's experience: "My son really didn't like the standardized and highly competitive education system in Korea. In his first year of high school, he had to study till three or four o'clock in the morning. The result wasn't rewarding either. So my son wanted to leave Korea and study abroad. Respecting my son's decision, my husband and I began to talk about where to send him" (female, Vancouver).

Two broad pull factors of Canada as a study destination were mentioned. First, my informants recognized that Canada has many general advantages. It is known to be a beautiful and safe country. Located geopolitically close to the United States, Canada is believed to share many cultural traits with American society. In Canada, Vancouver is preferred because of its natural beauty and geographical proximity to Korea. For many students, Vancouver is a great place to live and enjoy many natural amenities. For those who were considering the "*kirogi* family option," which requires at least one parent to travel frequently between South Korea and Canada, Vancouver is a particularly attractive city to send their children. Mrs Jung's remark illustrates the positive pull factors of Vancouver as a destination city: "Comparing the U.S. and Canada, we thought that the U.S. is far more dangerous to educate our son in. Vancouver seemed safer. Since there is no visa requirement for Koreans, I can spend several months here with my kids and travel back and forth. The weather is nicer than other parts of Canada. So after long contemplation with my husband, we decided Vancouver would be the location. Since we didn't have anybody here, we had to rely on an education agency's service. Through an Internet search, I got some more information about Vancouver, and I found one local agency in Vancouver, one that has a branch office in Korea. We paid everything in Korea" (female, Vancouver).

Second, Canada was chosen because of its good reputation for educational programs. However, it is interesting, after close examination, to see that Korean families value international education differently depending on its geographical location and level of study. For example, while obtaining English skills and other academic credentials from a Western country is generally well regarded back in South Korea, Korean families value American accents more than British ones. In Vancouver, different school districts are compared with those of Seoul, and the west side of Vancouver has long been considered the "eighth school district" in Seoul. Many informants pointed out that Canada is particularly popular because of the higher standard of educational programs for younger (K–12) students.

On the other hand, university students and postgraduate students had a different perspective. Most university students agreed that Canadian universities offer good programs with excellent scholarships; however, many of them complained that Canadian universities are undervalued among the general public and employers in South Korea, where a second-tier state university in the United States is often regarded more highly than a top Canadian university. The quality of institutions and possible return value of international education are largely shaped by existing social networks, educational agents, and returned students who provide information to potential international students.

Social networks, education agents, and other information providers proved to be important mediating factors. While most Korean students and parents recognized Canada as a good destination country, oftentimes social networks played a key role in settling on a destination city. Many mentioned that they had friends, relatives, and/or acquaintances in Vancouver, and the parents of younger students rely on these networks for information about the city, schools, and the settlement process. As Mrs Jung's above remark hinted, those who do not have personal contacts typically hire an agent to help them. In many cases, parents use existing social networks in addition to hiring the professional services of an educational agency. Ms Ahn, an international educational agent who helps place students in Canadian destinations, emphasized this point: "Dealing with my clients, I have hardly seen people who do not know anyone there in Vancouver. Usually they have someone who can help them. That is especially the case for younger students' families. So, we process visas for them. Then, the family utilizes their personal network to enrol children in school and look for home-stay or a place to stay. That is so typical."

While close social networks are always helpful for Korean students, weak ties are also helpful. All the university students who took ESL programs in Vancouver were able to establish some contacts prior to leaving South Korea for Vancouver. Although several students did not have any contacts prior to coming to Canada, they stated that it was easy to find someone who could share information about schools and accommodation, mainly through referrals and/or Internet forums. In South Korea, the latter form of social networking has become increasingly popular, and a large number of returned students have begun to work as pseudo educational agents steering others toward Vancouver, which imparts an important structural advantage for the international education industry in Vancouver.

In the virtual space of Internet forums, former and potential international students gather and exchange hands-on information about schools, accommodation, and travel. In addition to relying on educational agents, many students and parents indicated that they obtained useful information through such Internet forums. For those students and parents who lack a direct social network in Vancouver, Internet forums play an indirect, but seemingly unbiased, mediating role in their decision making. In the case of postgraduate students who pursue master's or doctoral degrees, this role was often played by their Korean university alumni association and/or faculty members. Jessica, a PhD student at the University of British Columbia (UBC), relayed that her experience of coming to Vancouver was rather unusual because many Korean students choose to go to an American university where strong Korean social networks have been established. "Usually you get to choose a school where your friends were and are attending. Most of my friends go to a certain school in the U.S. [where there is a well-established Korean alumni association]. I was almost convinced to go there. As you have to consider the career path after graduation, you can't ignore the power of social networks. It is very important in Korea. But I was a bit tired of studying the same subject for so long. I did my BA and MA in education engineering, but I wanted to study something different. While searching, I got to know about this UBC program and corresponded with a faculty member here. So, that's how I applied here. It was a new opportunity for me but also a risky choice too because I had no one here."

The Geographically Specific Value of International Education

In her discussion of the geographies of cultural capital, Waters (2006) demonstrated how a Western degree is recognized and utilized as cultural capital for Hong Kong graduates when they search for jobs on their return. She examines the ways in which employers in the Hong Kong financial services industry valued the UBC degree and how this value was mediated through transnational social networks like the UBC alumni association. The role of social networks can be significant, as they influence the hiring process and further disseminate the reputation of certain institutions. In the case of Korean students, it is too early to see this kind of effect. The number of Korean students at UBC began to rise only in recent years, and its transnational alumni association has not been as firmly established as that of Hong Kong students. We may see a different picture in the near future, but so far American degrees have carried a higher value for Korean employers, leading Korean parents to highly regard Canadian education for their elementary- and secondary-school-aged children, but to send them to an American university. For Korean students and parents, the value of international education is geographically specific depending on the level of study.

Because of a long political-economic relationship with the United States, South Korea has maintained strong academic linkages with American institutions. Since the 1960s, the United States has been the primary destination for Korean emigrants and international students. In South Korea, the most well known and valued degrees are usually from American universities. The faculty lists of Korean universities are often dominated by American degree holders. When I interviewed UBC students and mothers of younger students, their expectations of a Canadian education were limited. For them, Canada is a good place to learn English and enjoy a pleasant natural environment. Canada is known for decent public education programs for elementary and secondary students; however, higher education in Canada is undervalued. The myth of the superiority of an American degree was so prevalent in the minds of my interviewees that it affected their strategy of cultural capital accumulation. For example, making the decisions regarding when and where to send their children centred on how they used their education and financial capital, and eventually turned them into a form of cultural capital.

According to a South Korean newspaper article, the pattern of international education has become more transnational, involving several countries for study destination (*Vancouver Chosun Ilbo*, 2004). If students are capable, the ideal academic track would be to spend a year or two of elementary school in an English-speaking country, return to South Korea for three years of junior high school to enter the most competitive private high schools in South Korea, and then apply to renowned universities in the United States for undergraduate and graduate degrees. The eventual terminus of this transnational circuit of international education is most likely to be in South Korea, where this type of mixed educational cultural capital can yield maximum returns. The following comment from Ms Moon, an international education agent in Seoul, also testifies to the nationally specific nature of cultural capital and the transnational circuit of Korean consumption of international education: "Most elementary students who accompany their mother spend about a year or two in Vancouver. When teenaged students decide to go to Canada, they are aiming to finish university there. In most cases, however, Korean students want to go to U.S. universities. You see, if you can't get in to UBC or U of T, the most famous ones in Canada, it is better for them to go to U.S. universities because of their name value back in Korea" (female, South Korea).

The Transnational Space of International Education Students

The students and the mothers of young international students gave mixed responses when asked about their experiences of studying and living in Vancouver. Some described their time in Vancouver positively and with great enthusiasm, whereas others recollected it with disappointment. Those who were interviewed in Vancouver also gave mixed responses. In many ways, preconceived notions about studying abroad and the lifestyle in Vancouver seem to greatly affect the ways in which students enjoyed their new opportunities as well as coped with unexpected challenges. The varying objectives, levels, and durations of their study were also important ingredients in their assessment. For example, younger students who took a shorter program at the elementary level enjoyed their time in Vancouver the most. Without particularly high expectations, younger students were expected to enjoy the atmosphere of Canadian schooling and the friendship of local students. Back in South Korea, the parents of the children often stated that their child(ren) easily blended into the new environment and came back with enjoyable memories. Mrs Paek, a mother of two elementary school students, sent both of her children to the United States and Canada at different times. Using summer and winter programs, she wanted her children to experience different school environments and cultures. Even though she did not accompany her children, she could sense how much they enjoyed the experience. She spoke of her eleven-year-old son, who initially planned a three-month stay but later extended his stay for another three months in Vancouver. "He just loved the school [in Vancouver]. He didn't want to come back to Korea, spending six months there. My son asked me to come to live in Canada [smiles]. I think he liked the school system, which is very understandable. He didn't have to go to *hakwon* [after-school programs]. He didn't have much homework to do. He could go to bed earlier. No wonder he liked the system a lot better than here" (female, South Korea).

On the other hand, the students who attended private ESL schools and expected to improve their English skills within a short period of time were the ones who often expressed various levels of disappointment. Their negative comments about Vancouver as a study destination were threefold: first, Vancouver turned out to be not Western enough; second, they did not have enough interactions with "real Canadians"; third, the quality of private ESL education and other international education–related services were below their expectations. These resentments were largely expressed about the unsettling gaps between imagination and reality as well as higher expectations and dis-appointment. Their imagination about a superior Western society and expectations of effortless gain in cultural capital did not match real-ity. Interestingly, their frustrations were explicitly expressed with their socio-economic position as global consumers. When asked about his first impression of Vancouver, Mr Han, a former ESL student in Van-couver who is now working in the film industry in South Korea, openly expressed his disappointment. His idea of Vancouver as a Western city was shattered when he walked around downtown one day. He recalled, "At first, I thought that it [Vancouver] was good in a way. But once I walked around the streets of downtown, I realized that Vancouver is not really that glamorous. It wasn't the Western city that I have long dreamed of. What I saw were so many Asians on the street. I should admit that I was a bit disappointed" (male, South Korea).

Mr Han's remarks reveal his imaginings of Vancouver as a West-ern city and a white society. The reality differed from the expectation because of the arrival of many international students from Asia. Some ESL student interviewees acknowledged that they tried to avoid enroll-ing in schools with a large proportion of co-ethnic students because they believed that such an environment would not be helpful for improving their English skills. This preference for diversity has made some school coordinators pay a higher commission to European agencies for bring-ing more "white students" into their classrooms. Anthony, an interna-tional program coordinator of a well-known ESL school in Vancouver admitted such a practice: "Well, we have a mix. As my staff probably told you, there are commissioned and non-commissioned agents, and in Korea, mostly non-commissioned. We would not pay money to peo-ple for students who are going to come here anyway. We would like to see a lot more students from Europe, for example, so there we may pay commissions" (male, Vancouver).

The disappointment of ESL students was also strongly expressed when they emphasized their role as consumers of Canadian educa-tion. With the influx of international students to British Columbia since the mid-1990s and their significant economic contribution to the local economy, the quality of private ESL education, private career-train-ing institutions, and related services for international students have drawn heightened attention from both the media and policymakers. While discussing the problem of Vancouver's "fly-by-night schools" with Chinese consular officials, the former Immigration minister Judy Sgro emphasized that "Canada has to do more to guarantee international students get the education they are paying for if Canada wants to continue attracting more of them" (Sutherland, 2004, p. 1). Despite this apparent commitment at the federal level, there was little evidence that all levels of government were working together to ensure a high quality of private ESL education and career training for international students. Instead, the British Columbia government decided in 2004 to release about two hundred private ESL schools in the province from the control of the Private Career Training Institutions Agency (PCTIA). The PCTIA, which oversees about six hundred career-training institutions in British Columbia, has limited capacity. With a number of overnight failures of Vancouver's private business colleges, for example, there have been many complaints from affected international students (*Globe and Mail*, 2005).

The most typical complaints about private ESL schools and trade schools in Vancouver focused on the unsatisfactory quality of the programs. For most Korean international students, admission is guaranteed with tuition payment, and earning program certificates is relatively easy. Mr Chang told me that they were "all meaningless certificates" that no one really regards seriously even back in South Korea. Mr Kwon recollected that he was taught like an elementary school student in his English communication class at a private ESL school in Vancouver. Their complaints extended to the housing issues and public attitude toward international students as well. Despite her own positive experiences of studying and living in Vancouver, Ms Kang summarized the major issues that Korean students often faced: "I was so lucky to meet such a good home-stay family. But I have seen so many friends suffer from bad home-stay experiences. In general, we Korean students are not that fussy. Not enough food and no communication at all is a common story. The main problem is many Vancouver homeowners do home-stay for a living or to make extra money. The business is usually not documented. Since it is mostly an under-market operation, there is no proof or record. With a lack of English proficiency, many students can't even complain. That is why, after a month or two, so many Korean students instead choose to rent their own place and share the place with other friends" (female, South Korea).

While many ESL students complained about limited contacts with "real Canadian culture," their negative assessments of studying and living experiences in Vancouver were often balanced by new friendships built within the social circle of Korean students. Returning from Vancouver, most students said that they maintained close contacts with

Korean friends they had met during their study. Mr Chang told me that he and six friends who returned from Vancouver have been meeting regularly and socializing over drinks in Seoul. Some of them were maintaining transnational networks with those who are still studying in Vancouver, or decided to stay permanently in Canada. Such transnational social networks are often easily extended to the Korean-Canadian community in Vancouver as well. Knowing someone in Vancouver is useful when other friends and relatives inquire about studying in Vancouver and need someone who can assist. As I discussed elsewhere (Kwak & Hiebert, 2010), this kind of transnational social network was also essential for establishing business partnerships for agency operations between Seoul and Vancouver. International students are not only consumers of Canadian education but also mediators for and contributors to the production side of the industry.

The Transnational Space of Identity Formation

In the previous literature on international migration and ethnic studies, immigrant identities have often been studied within a binary and linear framework. The identities of migrants are believed to be spatially bound to one place, and their experiences are examined within either the context of their origin country or that of their destination. For example, people who live in South Korea are believed to be Korean and imagined to have a Korean identity. In the same vein, "Canada" or "Canadian identity" are often used with a lack of specificity or appropriate caution. Rouse (1995) problematizes the concept of collective identity, which ignores individuality and represents hegemonic cultural identity. He further claims that the identities of migrants should be examined on the basis of multi-local and transnational affiliations. Gupta and Ferguson (1992) similarly argue that the spatial assumptions embedded in "culture," "society," "community," and "nation" should be reconsidered when theorizing increasingly fragmented and hybridized cultural identities in the modern world. Instead, they adopt the metaphorical spatial concept of "borderlands" for hybrid identities. In the borderlands, seemingly separated and distant identities overlap and are infused and redefined. Thus, transnational space is where a new identity is formulated and isomorphic representation is contested.

In this section, I discuss how the identities of international students and temporary visitors should be reconsidered in the context of transnational migration. While analysing their experiences as consumers of international education and temporary migrants to Canada, I find that three realms of identities are blurring, thereby challenging the existing views on the binary divisions of culture/economy, production/consumption, and temporary/permanent migration.

First, it is interesting to examine how cultural and economic identities intersect. Are international students a cultural minority or powerful global capitalists? As I discussed earlier, my informants told me that they had certain ways of imagining Canadian education and the living environment as a white Western society. They often viewed themselves as a cultural minority whose cosmopolitan desire was fulfilled by obtaining globally competitive language skills and cultural understanding in Canada. However, their vision of consuming Canadian education was not only based on this cultural desire but also derived from strategic objectives. Canadian education is a commodity (institutionalized cultural capital) for international students, and learning is investing in a form of cultural capital. Immersing themselves in a Western environment and acquiring a better understanding of Western culture are acts of cultural-capital embodiment. Observing the relationships between white English tutors and Korean students, Michelle, an international graduate student at UBC, pointed out this blurring of identities: "Some of my Canadian friends are teaching English for international students. It is good that they make extra money, but sometimes I feel that they simply consider Korean students as a cash cow. It is also true that Korean students prefer white Canadian tutors to other ethnic-minority tutors. Probably that's why those white English teachers think that Korean students are easy. But I don't know. I don't think it is right" (female, Vancouver).

In her statement, Korean international students are described as cash cows as well as an "easy cultural minority." At the same time, however, the capitalist identity of international students is often explicitly declared when they negotiate for their rights as consumers. In the rapidly growing global market of international education, Korean international students are not only significant sources of global capital but also strategic consumers whose objective and decision making are largely shaped by capitalist ideology. They hardly view themselves as merely passive absorbers of Western culture but rather as confident middle-class consumers of cultural capital. Recalling an unpleasant encounter with customs officials at Vancouver's airport, Mr Chang complained, "Even at the airport, the immigration officials treated me like an illegal immigrant. It was not a pleasant experience at all. At one point, I was thinking, Why on earth am I here spending so much money, while they treat me as a criminal? I heard similar experiences from many other friends."

According to Helen, a fourth-year university student in Vancouver, "There are not enough job opportunities here. Especially for international students, it is really hard. I have spent $13,000 a year in high school. And now I am paying $14,000 a year for university tuition. I heard that UBC charges much more, about $18,000 a year for international science students. But what do we get after all? If you are lucky, you get a co-op opportunity. But, most job openings are directed to local students, so you are most likely to return to Korea. I think I should get some return from what I have spent" (female, Vancouver).

Second, my previous research (Kwak & Hiebert, 2007) indicates that the consuming role of international students is not limited to educational products. These students are everyday consumers at local stores and restaurants, and of housing and public transit. They are also tourists. Furthermore, the roles of international students and their families are not confined to consumer activities. They actively make choices and often relay their consumption experiences to other potential consumers in South Korea. In so doing, they play an important role in shaping and reshaping the production system. According to an international education director of one of Vancouver's local colleges, word of mouth is noted as an important advertising tool for Canadian education. In the virtual world of the Internet, information about studying abroad in general, the educational programs, and the living environment of Canada in particular are freely exchanged. International students and their families are major contributors to these indirect forms of advertisement: Mr Chin, a former international student in Vancouver, says, "I registered through an education agency. But I should say that I mostly relied on the information given by other students. If you go to any Internet forums created by Korean international students, there is lots of information available. The students provide information based on their own experiences without any profit. So I think that it is a quite reliable source of information. After collecting information from the forums, I chose about three schools and went to an agency to register" (male, South Korea).

The international students who studied in Vancouver, and those who are currently studying there, exercise agency in influencing the decisions of potential consumers. Most private ESL school coordinators and educational agency operators agreed that they pay close attention to assessments of their programs posted on the web. Ms Oh, the Korean coordinator of a private ESL school, stated, "It is very hard to satisfy the needs of every student. You can't neglect any student because it will appear on the Internet forums the very next day and hurt our business" (female, South Korea). These Internet forums, created by international students familiar with local settings, have become an important structural advantage for the Canadian education industry. Some of the former international students have become engaged with transnational businesses operating between Seoul and Vancouver. The role of international students and their families in the industry of international education is much more complex than once imagined.

The third form of blurring identity I noticed among international students probably requires the most imminent attention from policymakers. Among international students and their families, there is strong interest in permanent migration. The graduate students who are pursuing higher education with families in Vancouver tend to consider permanent migration more positively. In these families, children have become an important indicator of whether the family will permanently immigrate. Michelle, the graduate student at UBC, for example, told me that it is hard to imagine raising her American-born children in Seoul. During her studies in Vancouver, her children became accustomed to a more relaxed educational and living environment. At the time of the interview, Michelle was planning to return to South Korea after earning the degree. However, considering the cultural shock and different degree of pressure that her children would face in Seoul, she told me that it would not be an easy decision to make. Michelle also told me that she has seen many other Korean student families with children applying for immigration to Canada.

Kirogi families constitute another group that seriously considers permanent immigration. Facing many difficulties of raising and educating their children in the absence of one parent, the *kirogi* mothers in the study told me that they considered the possibility of permanently migrating with their husbands. Dealing with her son's disorderly behaviour by herself, Mrs Chun, the mother of two international students in Vancouver, persuaded her husband to immigrate to Canada in order to end his absence in the household: "There have been many cases that we need his father's presence. As my son gets older, the need becomes greater, I find. My son listens to his father better. For my son, his father's discipline has worked a lot better than mine. After two years, I heard that everyone considers immigration. I think we have to consider that too. We were thinking of going to the U.S. But things were not that easy. Canada is not too bad either. In fact, these days, we are looking for a way to apply for immigration to Canada and reunite our family here. The kids are very happy about the decision. One concern is getting a job here once we move. But, yeah, I guess that is the problem to worry about later" (female, Vancouver).

Despite strong interest in permanent migration, Korean immigration to Canada has drastically decreased in recent years. As is hinted in Mrs Chun's comment, many people in Korea now realize that successful application does not guarantee smooth settlement in Canada. The hardship in the Canadian labour market was identified as a major reason to reverse their decision to apply for permanent residency. Many international students have changed their minds once they faced the reality of the Canadian job market. Mr Han, a former ESL student in Vancouver who is working as an accountant in Seoul, stated, "I thought about immigration before. But I changed my mind. My Korean CPA credential is hardly useful there. In order to get the certificate again, it will take a lot of time and energy for me. It is especially difficult for immigrants. So to live there permanently? I don't know. I have seen many young Korean Canadians working in Vancouver. It seemed to me that they don't have equal opportunities as white Canadians. I understand, though. If foreign migrant workers took our jobs here in Korea, I wouldn't be so happy about it. So I don't know. I don't think I will live there [Canada] permanently" (male, South Korea).

Witnessing the economic struggles of recent immigrants to Canada, federal and provincial governments in Canada are increasingly viewing international students as a potential source of skilled labour. After spending several years in Canada, international students are believed to integrate better, since they have gained facility in one or both official languages and possess domestic educational credentials. The emerging desire to persuade international students to become permanent residents intersects with another objective of government, generating a more regionally dispersed pattern of immigrant settlement. Pilot projects to encourage "regionalization" have been established, such as the Off-Campus Work Permit (OCWP) and Post-Graduation Work Programs (PGWP) for post-secondary international students, which were pilot tested and proven successful in the Prairie and Atlantic regions between 2003 and 2005 (British Columbia Ministry of Advanced Education, 2006). Both programs allow international students to gain Canadian work experience and thus encourage them to remain in Canada. The programs are now being fully implemented nationwide.

The political and demographic vision has become even clearer with the implementation of a new immigration program called the Canadian Experience Class (CEC), first announced in the annual report to Parliament on immigration in 2007 and implemented in 2008 (CIC, 2008b). Under the program, qualified skilled temporary workers and international students are now able to apply for permanent resident status while they are in Canada.

So far, however, the transition from temporary to permanent migration has not been easy for everyone. In the case of recent graduates from university, it is nearly impossible to apply to immigrate in their own capacity. Ms Kang, who spent two years as an ESL student and is currently working as an education agency operator in Seoul, told me what she observed in Vancouver: "I have seen many mature students who were interested in immigration. Most of them have some work experience in Korea, but not extensive. They don't see a good future in Korea, so they want to settle in Canada. But, as you know, things are not that easy. Even getting a work permit in Canada is difficult. I heard that some travel agencies and education agencies are hiring people who are willing to pay the cost of applying and paying extra tax for a work permit up front, like $10,000. That's how desperate some students are" (female, South Korea).

The implementation of the CEC program may ease such difficult situations faced by some international students. For successful implementation of the program, the Ministry of Citizenship and Immigration has changed the two existing work permit programs for international students. Under the new PGWP program, international students who graduate from eligible programs at certain post-secondary institutions are able to acquire an open work permit without restrictions on the types and places of employment (CIC, 2008c). Qualified individuals can apply for a work permit without a job offer, and once they obtain a job, they can work for up to three years.[6] With a minimum of one year of Canadian work experience in a managerial, professional, or technical position, international students can apply for permanent residency rights through the CEC program.

---

6 The previous PGWP allowed only a maximum of two-year work permit depending on location. With a federal vision of regionalization, the program gave a longer work permit to those who find employment outside Montreal, Vancouver, and Toronto. In addition, the job needed to be matched with the area of their education in Canada.

Working together with the provincial government of British Colum-bia, the ministry also announced a pilot expansion of the existing OCWP (CIC, 2008a).[7] While the previous OCWP program benefited only inter-national students who studied at public universities and colleges in the province, the new program has expanded to private institutions. This four-year pilot project will be tested and analysed at the provincial level. All these changes are believed to enable more international stu-dents to obtain Canadian work experience easily and eventually choose to stay in Canada permanently.

This kind of political response follows precedents by the Australian and New Zealand governments (Ho & Bedford, 2008). It seems appar-ent that researchers now need to consider the two seemingly separate categories of "temporary" and "permanent" migration more in connec-tion to each other.

Discussion and Policy Recommendations

> It [the government] will also position Canada as a destination of choice for talented foreign students and skilled workers by more aggressively selecting and recruiting through universities and in key embassies abroad.
> —Governor General Adrienne Clarkson,
> reading the Speech from the Throne, 2002

Accepting about 60,000 international students annually, Canada has become a popular study destination (CIC, 2008a). Business leaders and policymakers in many English-speaking countries have begun to pay close attention to the temporary movement of international stu-dents. The 2002 Speech from the Throne confirms this point in the Canadian context. International students and their families are wel-come in Canada because they can contribute to revenue generation for school boards and enrich cultural diversity in our classrooms. Poli-cymakers in major immigrant-receiving countries have come to con-sider the transition from international students to permanent residents more seriously (Ho & Bedford, 2008). If the international education industry is beneficial to the national and local economies, and if inter-national students are considered an important source of future immi-grants, what can be done to promote the industry and attract more talented international students to Canada? Drawing on everyday

---

7 The provinces of Manitoba and Alberta also agreed to participate in the pilot project.

experiences of international students and their families, I recommend the following.

First, it is important to maintain high-quality educational programs and service provisions for all levels of international students. Weak regulations in the educational industry in general have been pointed out as the key problem. As noted earlier, many career-training institutions and in particular private language schools in Vancouver were typical targets of student complaints. With the rise of neoliberal governance, the regulatory system of these private schools has become relaxed and privatized. Inconsistent policy approaches between education (provincial and municipal) versus immigration policies (federal) of Canada have also worked as a disadvantage for global market promotion. In countries like Australia and New Zealand, international education has been developed, regulated, and promoted at the national level. The future success of the industry as a whole will most importantly depend on a more integrated approach between education, migration, and international trade.

Second, the well-being of international students needs to be considered more seriously. Many students and families felt they were only seen as cash cows and that their basic rights were largely neglected. As temporary migrants, international students have limited access to social services. In school, there has been a significant lack of educational and emotional support. With drastic budget cutting in British Columbia public schools, ESL classes have been disappearing. Where classes are available, international students are often placed in the same classroom regardless of their different language and learning capacities. It is essential to hire more counsellors who actually work on behalf of international students in schools.

Third, there has been an increasing political consensus that talented international students should be a potential source of immigrants to Canada. However, most international students and industry workers argued that there are many barriers to prevent them from applying for permanent residency. Limited work and educational opportunities for international students are noted as the most significant issues. The implementation of the CEC program with these experiences in mind will shed new light on Canadian immigration as a whole. As designed, this plan should make Canada a more attractive place for international students and potential immigrants, though now it is too early to tell. Later on, more potential immigrants will consider the path of obtaining Canadian education first and then applying for permanent residency. The CEC program will certainly benefit a small proportion of international students in the short term, but it will entail many challenges as well. First, all levels of educational institutions in Canada, especially those at the secondary and post-secondary levels, need to respond well to the growing interest of international students in Canadian education and to their different needs. Second, will Canadian employers and foreign students understand and work well with the program? Who is more willing to work with the program? In the early stage, there could be many misuses of the program and labour disputes between Canadian employers and international student workers. Third, what does this program mean to existing immigrant populations and the general public in the Canadian labour market? If it were successful, how would the program change the public attitude to international students and temporary foreign workers? Fourth, in relation to the previous question, the government needs to work harder to provide more efficient economic integration programs for recent immigrant populations. Finally, for researchers, all these questions warrant more investigation into the program and its future impacts on international students, the immigrant community, and the broader Canadian society.

In this chapter, I have examined the consumption side of the international education industry. Everyday experiences of international students and their families reveal that they are not passive cultural minorities but rather active agents of transnational migration. Using strong social and cultural networks, they pursue a strategic economic decision to consume Canadian education. Their everyday experiences of studying and living in Vancouver demonstrate a blurring transnational space of multiple identity formations. The suggested policy recommendations urge policymakers, business professionals, and the local community to approach international students and their hardships with more consistent and egalitarian attitudes. The reputation of the city as a place for international students depends on the provision of adequate housing, health services, and the creation of a safe study and living environment. It is equally important for policymakers to pay close attention to the successful integration of incoming immigrant populations as well. Temporary migrants often envisage their future in terms of the socio-economic status of permanent migrants, and this perception will affect their vision of Canada as a place to work and live.

REFERENCES

Borjas, G. (1989). Economic theory and international migration. *International Migration Review, 23,* 457–85.

Bourdieu, P. (1984). *Distinction: A social critique of the judgement of taste.* Cambridge, MA: Harvard University Press.

British Columbia Ministry of Advanced Education (27 April 2006). *Off-campus work permit program launched in BC.* BC Government News Release 2006AE0016-000504.

Chen, L.H. (2006). Attracting East Asian students to Canadian graduate schools. *Canadian Journal of Higher Education, 36*(2), 77–106.

Citizenship and Immigration Canada (CIC) (1998–2008a). *Facts and figures: Immigration overview.* Ottawa: Strategic Policy, Planning and Research.

———. (2003). *Foreign students in Canada 1980–2001.* Ottawa: Strategic Research and Statistics.

———. (2008b). *Government of Canada introduces changes to work permits for international students, making Canada more attractive for skilled individuals.* CIC News Release: 21 April 2008. Retrieved from http://www.cic.gc.ca/english/department/media/releases/2008/2008-04-21.asp.

———. (2008c). *Government of Canada extends off-campus work program to international students in private institutions.* CIC News Release: 20 May 2008. Retrieved from http://www.cic.gc.ca/english/department/media/releases/2008/2008-05-20.asp.

Clarkson, A. (2002). *The 2002 Speech from the Throne: The Canada we want.* Ottawa: Public Service Canada.

Globe and Mail (Toronto) (21 June 2005). Corporate college's closing leaves foreign students looking for tuition refunds. S1.

Gupta, A., and Ferguson, J. (1992). Beyond culture: Space, identity, and the politics of difference. *Cultural Anthropology, 7*(1), 6–23.

Ho, E., and Bedford, R. (2008). Asian transnational families in New Zealand: Dynamics and challenges, *International Migration, 46*(4), 41–62.

Kwak, M.J., and Hiebert, D. (2007). *Immigrant entrepreneurship and the role of non-government organizations in an era of neo-liberal governance.* Metropolis British Columbia (MBC) working paper series #07–05.

———. (2010). Globalizing Canadian education from below: A case study of transnational immigrant entrepreneurship between Seoul, Korea and Vancouver, Canada. *Journal of International Migration and Integration, 11*(2): 131–53.

Nash, J. (2000). Global integration and the commodification of culture. *Ethnology, 39*(2), 129–31.

Ong, A. (1999). *Flexible citizenship: The cultural logic of transnationality*. New York: Routledge.

Rouse, R. (1995). Questions of identity: Personhood and collectivity in transnational migration to the United States. *Critique of Anthropology, 15*(4), 351–80.

Sutherland, S. (22 January 2004). Immigration ministers discuss fly by night language schools. *Canada.com News*. Victoria: The Canadian Press.

Vancouver Chosun Ilbo (3 August 2004). Changes in the pattern of early overseas education for Korean students (in Korean). A3.

Wall Street Journal (29 July 2005). Bucking the class system: As school pressure mount on kids in South Korea, some families are taking drastic steps by leaving the country. Retrieved from http://onlilne.wsj.com/article/0,,SB112258803643499167,00.html.

Waters, J. (2002). Flexible Families?: Astronaut households and the experiences of lone mothers in Vancouver, BC. *Social and Cultural Geography, 3*, 117–34.

———. (2006). Geographies of cultural capital: Education, international migration and family strategies between Hong Kong and Canada. *Royal Geographical Society, 31*, 179–92.

Yeoh, B., M.W. Charney, and C.K. Tong (Eds.). (2003). *Chinese migrants abroad: Cultural educational and social dimensions of the Chinese Diaspora*. Singapore: Singapore University Press.

Zukin, S. (1990). Socio-spatial prototypes of a new organization of consumption: The role of real cultural capital. *Sociology, 24*(1), 37–56.

PART II

Immigrant Socio-economic and Social-Psychological Integration

7 Social, Economic, and Demographic Characteristics of Korean Self-Employment in Canada

ELIC CHAN AND ERIC FONG

Introduction

In recent decades, ethnic entrepreneurship has been a major topic in the study of immigrant adaptation and ethnic relations. Ethnic entrepreneurship is important to immigrants' economic livelihood, and some studies have even suggested that ethnic entrepreneurship serves as an alternative path to economic achievement among ethnic members and to generate jobs for co-ethnic members (Nee et al., 1994; Portes & Bach, 1985; Sanders & Nee, 1987). Studies have also indicated that large numbers of successful co-ethnic entrepreneurs are important for the development of ethnic communities (W. Li, 1998). They provide financial support for various activities for their communities (Fong, 1994; Min, 2008).

Reasons for Participating in Ethnic Entrepreneurship

The literature has suggested various reasons why ethnic members become involved in ethnic businesses. The explanations can be grouped into three categories: supply-side, demand-side, and the glass ceiling. The *supply-side* explanation contends that entrepreneurship depends on the availability of individuals who have the skills, experience, and motivation to undertake self-employment (Light & Gold, 2000; Light & Rosenstein, 1995). These qualities can be approximated by examining the demographic and social characteristics that are traditionally associated with business ownership. The main factors associated with the supply-side explanation include gender, age, education, and marital status (Waldinger, 1994; Waldinger et al., 1990). Differences in these factors explain differentials in resources, i.e., in the availability of individuals suitable for entrepreneurship. For example, one type of resource is human capital. Because of the wide range of responsibilities entailed in entrepreneurship, individuals require an adequate level of education and work experience to operate a successful business. Thus, people who possess more education and work experience are more likely to be self-employed than those with less education and work experience (Sanders & Nee, 1996; Waldinger et al., 1990). Another resource is access to labour. Since most businesses require assistance, labour recruitment becomes crucial. Given that most ethnic businesses are small in size (Min & Mozorgmehr, 2003), they usually rely on family labour in their operations. In this light, individuals who are married are more likely than those who are not married to have access to family labour, and are therefore more likely to engage in self-employment (Sanders & Nee, 1996).

In contrast to examining group characteristics, the *demand-side* explains ethnic entrepreneurship as a result of market conditions (Light & Rosenstein, 1995; Waldinger et al., 1990). This perspective concentrates less on the characteristics of the pool of potential business owners and emphasizes the characteristics of the opportunity structure. There are several types of demand that encourage ethnic entrepreneurial activities. The first is consumer demand (Light & Gold, 2000). A sizeable ethnic community creates a demand for ethnic goods, which is often high among immigrants and co-ethnic members with difficulty in the official language. Therefore, the main demand factors associated with this perspective include size of ethnic community and proportion of members with low language proficiency. The second type of demand is characterized by the industrial structure (Light & Rosenstein, 1995). Industries such as retail trade, finance, insurance, real estate, and professional and personal services are traditionally associated with a high proportion of self-employment. Market conditions that favour the existence of these industries are indicative of a demand for entrepreneurship.

The last factor is rooted in theories of disadvantage. Rather than focusing on the availability of resources or opportunities, *the glass ceiling* effect presents self-employment as a solution to blocked mobility in the labour market (Light & Bonacich, 1988; Light & Rosenstein, 1995; Yoon, 1997). Owing to immigrants' exclusion from mainstream occupations in professional and managerial positions, as well as in large formal organizations, most resort to poor-paying jobs with low prestige and little chance of advancement (Fernandez & Kim, 1998). Those who are able to secure white-collar jobs are skeptical of further advancement because of their perception of discrimination in the workplace (Min, 1984).

Past research confirms the disadvantage of minorities, including Koreans, in the workplace. Despite Korean immigrants' relatively high levels of education and rate of employment, they typically earn less than the native-born population (Iceland, 1999). Recognizing the threshold of achievement in working for someone else, they enter self-employment in the hope of achieving greater success (Min, 1984). Yoon's (1997) study of Korean businesses in Chicago showed that close to half of Korean business owners entered self-employment to improve their financial situations and their autonomy on the job. Assuming that mobility to high-paying and/or prestigious occupations will be blocked, Korean immigrants use self-employment as a means to economic success. For this perspective, income and occupational distribution are used to evaluate the advantages of entrepreneurship over wage and salary employment.

The factors highlighted in the three perspectives are not mutually exclusive. Together, they provide theoretical frameworks in which to interpret the data on self-employment among Koreans. In the following sections, we present results drawn from the 2006 Canadian census to explain Korean self-employment patterns.

Korean Entrepreneurship in Canada

Despite their increasing numbers in the past decade, Koreans in Canada have not been given much attention in the literature. Research on Korean entrepreneurship has been quite active in the United States but almost non-existent in Canada. Since Koreans in Canada have a different migration history from Koreans in the United States and face a different multicultural environment, their road to integration, including participation in ethnic businesses, takes a unique trajectory.

In this chapter, we will look at Korean ethnic businesses. To begin the exploration of the reasons for Koreans participating in ethnic businesses, we provide an overview of the demographic, social, and economic characteristics of Korean entrepreneurs in Canada. To fully appreciate the unique background of Korean entrepreneurs, our discussion will compare and contrast Korean entrepreneurs and wage earners. We also provide information on entrepreneurs in Canada overall in order to highlight some similarities and differences between them and Korean entrepreneurs.

Data

The data in this chapter are derived from the 2006 Canadian Census Individual Public Use Microdata File. To examine the characteristics of Korean entrepreneurs, we created a subsample from the data to high-light the Korean population in Canada. We first used the ethnic-origin variable to categorize those who identified themselves as Korean. Since most Korean immigrants have settled in the urban gateway cities in Canada (see J. Park, chapter 2, this volume), we selected respondents residing in Toronto and Vancouver.

The census variable "class of worker" was used to operationalize self-employment. For our analysis, we selected respondents over fifteen years of age who worked mainly for wages, salaries, commissions, tips, piece rates, or other forms of payment. Self-employed respondents are those whose job consisted mainly of operating a business (either incorporated or unincorporated) or professional practice, with or without paid help. Those who were not considered self-employed were defined as wage and salary earners. It is important to be aware that the definition of self-employed does not exclude self-employed persons who may also earn a salary. It is also noteworthy that the 2006 Canadian Census Individual Public Use Microdata File does not allow us to identify the customer background and the location of individual businesses to examine the middleman theory, a theory has been applied to understand Korean businesses in the United States.

Demographic Background of Korean Entrepreneurs

Studies consistently show that Koreans in the United States exhibit high levels of entrepreneurship (Fernandez & Kim, 1998). The trend is similar in Canada. One in every four Koreans in Toronto and Vancouver are self-employed. More than 75 per cent of those engaged in self-employment are over forty years of age (see table 7.1). In contrast, Korean wage and salary earners are more evenly distributed across all age groups. The pattern reflects that, as suggested by the supply-side explanation of participation in entrepreneurship, starting a business requires capital and work experience. Older individuals are more likely to have greater access to capital and to have more work expe-

Table 7.1. Demographic Characteristics of Koreans and the General Population by Employment Status in Canada, 2006

| | Korean | | | | General Population | | | |
| | Self-Employed | | Wage/Salary Earners | | Self-Employed | | Wage/Salary Earners | |
	N	(%)	N	(%)	N	(%)	N	(%)
Gender								
Male	188	(57.8)	414	(47.9)	8,868	(65.4)	49,801	(49.7)
Female	137	(42.2)	450	(52.1)	4,688	(34.6)	50,419	(50.3)
Total	325		864		13,556		100,220	
Age								
Under 18	0	(0.0)	18	(2.1)	70	(0.5)	3,137	(3.1)
18–24	6	(1.8)	179	(20.7)	410	(3.0)	14,498	(14.5)
25–29	11	(3.4)	134	(15.5)	678	(5.0)	10,863	(10.8)
30–39	53	(16.3)	225	(26.0)	2,799	(20.6)	23,277	(23.2)
40–49	122	(37.5)	183	(21.2)	4,101	(30.3)	24,632	(24.6)
50–59	112	(34.5)	92	(10.6)	3,401	(25.1)	17,359	(17.3)
60 and over	21	(6.5)	33	(3.8)	2,097	(15.5)	6,454	(6.4)
Total	325		864		13,556		100,220	
Marital Status								
Divorced	5	(1.5)	12	(1.4)	1,128	(8.3)	6,557	(6.5)
Married	297	(91.4)	456	(52.8)	9,075	(66.9)	50,955	(50.8)
Separated	0	(0.0)	17	(2.0)	470	(3.5)	3,306	(3.3)
Never Married	22	(6.8)	378	(43.8)	2,625	(19.4)	38,186	(38.1)
Widowed	1	(0.3)	1	(0.1)	258	(1.9)	1,216	(1.2)
Total	325		864		13,556		100,220	

Source: 2006 Canadian Census Individual Public Use Microdata File.

rience. Therefore, this trend is also found among the general population, where more than 60 per cent of self-employed persons are over forty years old.

Past research suggests that immigrant entrepreneurship involves family members, particularly the assistance of a spouse (Yoon, 1991). Sanders and Nee (1996) showed that most immigrant entrepreneurs are married. This pattern suggests that since immigrant businesses are typically small scale, with limited resources, immigrant entrepreneurs have to rely on family members who work for low pay, or quite often without pay. Our data show that more than 90 per cent of Korean entrepreneurs are married, much higher than among the wage-earning Koreans (53 per cent). Although it is not directly shown here, the reliance on spousal assistance may have contributed to the gender balance found in Korean entrepreneurship compared with the general population. Self-employment among the general population is mostly dominated by men (65 per cent), whereas it is roughly equal between men and women among Koreans.

Immigration Characteristics of Korean Entrepreneurs

Koreans in Canada are a new immigrant group. Immigrants from Korea did not gain entry on a large scale prior to the implementation of the point system in 1967, and have only begun entering Canada in significant numbers in the past twenty years. Table 7.2 shows that nearly all Koreans (over 95 per cent) immigrated to Canada after 1970, and about one-third arrived between 2000 and 2006. The slight difference in the period of migration between self-employed Koreans and Koreans who earn wages and salaries suggests that there has been no specific period when large numbers of entrepreneurs immigrated to Canada. Among other groups, such as Chinese from Hong Kong, a large number of entrepreneurs entered the country after the implementation of Canada's Business Immigration Program (P. Li, 1998).

However, the patterns of age at migration of Korean entrepreneurs and wage and salary earners are considerably different. Korean wage and salary earners tend to have immigrated at a younger age. Table 7.2 illustrates that over 60 per cent of Korean wage and salary workers immigrated before the age of thirty, compared with only 27 per cent of Korean entrepreneurs. Immigrating past the age of thirty seems likely to result in self-employment for Koreans. The difference in age at migration may reflect a difference in adaptability to the labour market.

Immigrating at a younger age allows more opportunities for re-socialization (e.g., at school). Younger migrants are also more adaptable when it comes to learning a new culture. Koreans arriving in Canada at an older age may have difficulty finding jobs comparable to their jobs in Korea before immigration. Limited opportunities in the labour market may push them to seek self-employment. This relationship between age at migration and entrepreneurship is markedly different for non-Korean immigrants. Table 7.2 shows that non-Korean immigrant entrepreneurs are generally younger when they first immigrated, as more than half of them immigrated under the age of thirty. In addition, the distribution is less pronounced and more evenly distributed across age groups.

Owing to the relatively recent arrival of Koreans in Canada, it is not surprising to find a large proportion of them to be foreign-born. Despite the high proportion of immigrants among the Korean population, it is still astonishing to find that self-employment is almost exclusive to Koreans who were born outside Canada. Table 7.2 reports that over 97 per cent of self-employed Koreans are foreign-born, while Canadian-born Koreans are almost all wage and salary earners. In this light, it is clear that Korean entrepreneurship is solely an immigrant experience. Although not all Korean immigrants participate in entrepreneurial activities, self-employment seems to be a popular strategy among Korean immigrants for adapting to the Canadian labour market. The pattern seems to be different from the general population. For the general population, self-employment is evenly split between native-born and foreign-born.

Educational Characteristics of Korean Entrepreneurs

Table 7.3 describes the educational attainments of Koreans and of the general population according to employment status. Overall, Koreans in Canada have a high level of education. Whether or not self-employed, over 45 per cent have obtained a bachelor's degree or higher. Koreans who are self-employed do not differ drastically from Korean wage and salary earners in this regard.

Examination of the major fields of study among Koreans reveals that there is little distinction between the self-employed and the wage earners. The majority of both groups concentrated their studies in the humanities, the arts, engineering, or business-related fields. In the general population, there are not great differences between the self-

Table 7.2. Immigration Characteristics of Koreans and the General Population by Employment Status in Canada, 2006

| | Korean | | | | General Population | | | |
| | Self-Employed | | Wage/Salary Earners | | Self-Employed | | Wage/Salary Earners | |
	N	(%)	N	(%)	N	(%)	N	(%)
Year of Immigration								
Before 1960	0	(0.0)	0	(0.0)	441	(6.7)	1,393	(3.1)
1960–1969	1	(0.3)	19	(2.9)	768	(11.6)	3,179	(7.0)
1970–1979	38	(12.4)	64	(9.8)	1,277	(19.3)	6,994	(15.4)
1980–1989	39	(12.7)	94	(14.4)	1,139	(17.2)	8,357	(18.4)
1990–1999	125	(40.8)	282	(43.1)	2,049	(31.0)	15,807	(34.8)
2000–2006	103	(33.7)	196	(29.9)	931	(14.1)	9,722	(21.4)
Total	306		655		6,605		45,452	
Age at Migration								
Under 10	7	(2.3)	89	(13.5)	792	(11.4)	6,923	(14.9)
10–14	5	(1.6)	92	(13.9)	470	(6.8)	4,404	(9.5)
15–19	10	(3.3)	94	(14.2)	698	(10.0)	5,344	(11.5)
20–29	61	(19.9)	126	(19.1)	2,317	(33.3)	14,453	(31)
30–39	101	(33.0)	148	(22.4)	1,733	(24.9)	10,387	(22.3)
40–49	111	(36.3)	104	(15.8)	747	(10.7)	3,996	(8.6)
50–59	11	(3.6)	5	(0.8)	163	(2.3)	864	(1.9)
60 and over	0	(0.0)	2	(0.3)	38	(0.5)	220	(0.5)
Total	306		660		6,958		46,591	
Place of Birth								
In Canada	7	(2.2)	144	(16.7)	6,440	(47.5)	51,988	(51.9)
Outside of Canada	318	(97.8)	720	(83.3)	7,116	(52.5)	48,232	(48.1)
Total	325		864		13,556		100,220	

Source: 2006 Canadian Census Individual Public Use Microdata File.

Table 7.3. Educational Characteristics of Koreans and the General Population by Employment Status in Canada, 2006

	Korean				General Population			
	Self-Employed		Wage/Salary Earners		Self-Employed		Wage/Salary Earners	
	N	(%)	N	(%)	N	(%)	N	(%)
Highest Level of Education								
No Degree	8	(2.5)	40	(4.6)	1,412	(10.4)	12,090	(12.1)
High School	68	(20.9)	191	(22.1)	2,890	(21.4)	26,651	(26.6)
Trade, College, Below Bachelor	77	(23.7)	207	(24.0)	4,442	(32.9)	31,639	(31.6)
Bachelor and Above	172	(52.9)	426	(49.3)	4,775	(35.3)	29,750	(29.7)
Total	325		864		13,519		100,130	
Major Field of Studies								
Educational Services	11	(4.4)	48	(7.6)	431	(4.7)	5,245	(8.5)
Fine, Applied Arts and Humanities	45	(18.1)	137	(21.6)	1,644	(17.8)	8,420	(13.7)
Social Science	31	(12.4)	69	(10.9)	1,145	(12.4)	7,353	(12.0)
Business Related Fields	50	(20.1)	98	(15.5)	1,905	(20.6)	14,586	(23.7)
Agricultural and Food Science	20	(8.0)	35	(5.5)	297	(3.2)	2,281	(3.7)
Engineering and Technology	54	(21.7)	120	(19.0)	2,341	(25.3)	13,688	(22.3)
Health and Medical	23	(9.2)	60	(9.5)	952	(10.3)	5,775	(9.4)
Mathematics and Others	15	(6.0)	66	(10.4)	538	(5.8)	4,102	(6.7)
Total	249		633		9,253		61,450	

Source: 2006 Canadian Census Individual Public Use Microdata File.

employed and wage earners in relation to field of study. Most of the differences do not fall beyond the range of 5 percentage points across all major fields, including subjects related to health and medicine. However, it is worth mentioning that there are differences between the general population and Koreans in the areas studied in university. For the general population (both self-employed and wage and salary workers), engineering and technology, as well as business and related fields, account for the highest proportion of areas studied. Canadians who majored in these two areas represent nearly 45 per cent of the general workforce. Although studies in engineering and business are also popular among Koreans, a substantial proportion majored in the humanities and the arts. This pattern may reflect the educational emphases in Korea and Canada, and may explain why immigrants who arrive at an older age have more difficulty securing jobs. People with university credentials, especially training in the humanities and the arts, acquired from abroad may encounter difficulty being recognized in Canada. It is also worth noting that the percentage of self-employed Koreans who studied business and related fields is comparable to those in the general population. This similarity illustrates that Koreans are drawn to entrepreneurial activities not necessarily because of their educational background in business or related fields, but rather, as suggested earlier, as a strategy for economic survival when facing limited opportunities in the labour market.

Language Characteristics of Korean Entrepreneurs

Running a business requires knowledge of at least one official language, in order to handle documentation, communicate with governments, and sometimes to establish client networks. Knowledge of the official languages in Canada among Korean entrepreneurs is similar to that of Korean wage and salary earners. Table 7.4 shows that more than 85 per cent of both groups have knowledge of one official language, and more than 75 per cent use at least one official language at work. Although both groups are just as likely to have knowledge of English, the self-employed Koreans are less likely to be bilingual in English and French. At the same time, self-employed Koreans are more likely to use a non-official language in their workplace than their wage-earning counterparts, which suggests that self-employed persons are more likely to be working in a co-ethnic environment. The findings also seem to suggest

Table 7.4. Language Characteristics of Koreans and the General Population by Employment Status in Canada, 2006

	Korean				General Population			
	Self-Employed		Wage/Salary Earners		Self-Employed		Wage/Salary Earners	
	N	(%)	N	(%)	N	(%)	N	(%)
Knowledge of Official Language								
English Only	279	(85.9)	774	(89.6)	11,910	(87.9)	89,053	(88.9)
French Only	2	(0.6)	1	(0.1)	9	(0.1)	33	(0.0)
Both English and French	2	(0.6)	51	(5.9)	1,353	(10.0)	9,149	(9.1)
Neither English nor French	42	(12.9)	38	(4.4)	284	(2.1)	1,985	(2.0)
Total	325		864		13,556		100,220	
Language Often Used at Work								
Official Langaage	249	(76.6)	701	(81.1)	12,493	(92.2)	95,800	(95.6)
Non Official Language	76	(23.4)	163	(18.9)	1,063	(7.8)	4,420	(4.4)
Total	325		864		13,556		100,220	

Source: 2006 Canadian Census Individual Public Use Microdata File.

that Korean businesses generate a considerable number of jobs for their co-ethnic members.

For the general population, there are no differences in language ability between self-employed and wage and salary earners. The two groups are just as likely to have bilingual speakers, as well as those who have knowledge of neither English nor French. However, differences can be observed when examining language usage at work. Although the differences are small, it is noteworthy that the self-employed in the general population are less likely to use English or French at work and, at the same time, are more likely to use a non-official language. The patterns suggest that there are ethnic groups other than Koreans that resort to self-employment when language proficiency is an issue.

Despite Koreans' familiarity with English, limitation in communication is evident. Table 7.4 reveals that close to 12 per cent of self-employed Koreans, and 4 per cent of Korean wage and salary earners, have no knowledge of either official language. This lack of knowledge translates into language use in the workplace. Our data show that a fair proportion (more than 18 per cent) of Koreans use a non-official language (presumably Korean) at work. This percentage is about three times higher than that of entrepreneurs in Canada overall, and four times higher than that of wage and salary earners overall.

Language use at work is important. It facilitates opportunities for social interaction with the dominant group. Since Korean-speaking business people have low English- or French-language proficiency, they are restricted to serving only their co-ethnic market, and/or to working alongside other co-ethnics. This circumstance limits their social interaction with the wider society, which may delay their course of social integration over time. Although working in the ethnic economy may provide an alternative to unemployment, those who lack language skills may find themselves limited to poorly paying jobs that yield low economic returns.

Earnings of Korean Entrepreneurs

Understanding the earnings of Korean entrepreneurs helps us to explore their economic well-being. Table 7.5 compares the earnings of Koreans and the general population by employment status. Koreans who are wage earners seem to be able to garner higher earnings, as 25 per cent earn more than $40,000, while only 12 per cent of Korean entre-

Table 7.5. Earnings of Koreans and the General Population by Employment Status in Canada, 2006

	Korean				General Population			
	Self-Employed		Wage/Salary Earners		Self-Employed		Wage/Salary Earners	
	N	(%)	N	(%)	N	(%)	N	(%)
Total Income								
Under $20,000	202	(63.3)	452	(52.6)	5,536	(41.3)	31,695	(31.7)
$20,000–$29,999	51	(16.0)	104	(12.1)	1,885	(14.1)	13,295	(13.3)
$30,000–$39,999	26	(8.2)	96	(11.2)	1,334	(10.0)	13,798	(13.8)
$40,000–$49,999	10	(3.1)	75	(8.7)	983	(7.3)	11,395	(11.4)
$50,000–$59,999	8	(2.5)	32	(3.7)	729	(5.4)	8,429	(8.4)
$60,000–$69,999	7	(2.2)	23	(2.7)	552	(4.1)	6,171	(6.2)
$70,000–$79,999	4	(1.3)	25	(2.9)	379	(2.8)	4,461	(4.5)
$80,000–$89,999	3	(0.9)	15	(1.7)	274	(2.0)	2,980	(3.0)
$90,000–$99,999	1	(0.3)	10	(1.2)	223	(1.7)	1,941	(1.9)
$100,000 and over	7	(2.2)	28	(3.3)	1,498	(11.2)	5,972	(6.0)
Total	319		860		13,393		100,137	

Source: 2006 Canadian Census Individual Public Use Microdata File.

preneurs achieve similar income levels. The findings are unexpected, as previous studies suggest that immigrant entrepreneurs earn more than employees (Logan et al., 2002; Sanders & Nee, 1987). However, it is important to point out that the percentage of persons earning higher income, $100,000 or above, is marginal for both entrepreneurs and employees. In the general population, the percentage of entrepreneurs who earn more than $100,000 is much higher than the percentage of employees who do. It seems that among average Canadians, not only is self-employment an alternative for economic achievement, but it also provides opportunities for a higher percentage of entrepreneurs than employees to achieve high incomes.

Despite their high level of schooling, Koreans in general do not achieve the same level of economic success compared with the general population of Canada. Close to half of Koreans in Canada earn less than $20,000 a year. For Koreans, self-employment is not a better alternative; it does not seem to offer an economic advantage over working for someone else.

Industrial Distribution among Korean Entrepreneurs

Data on the distribution of self-employed Koreans by industry reveal a strong contrast with Korean wage earners. When compared with Korean wage and salary earners, self-employed Koreans are highly concentrated in the retail trade (26 per cent), where their proportion is double that of Korean wage and salary earners. At the same time, compared with their employed counterparts, self-employed Koreans are less likely to be in industries such as construction and manufacturing, or in professional and technical services.

Compared with the general Canadian population, Korean entrepreneurs are involved in different industries. In particular, Korean entrepreneurs are less likely than the general population to be employed in industries related to construction and manufacturing (4.3 per cent versus 17.9 per cent), or professional services (4.9 per cent versus 21 percent). Yet they are more likely to be involved in retail trade (26.5 per cent versus 7.8 per cent) and hospitality services (21.9 per cent versus 3.7 per cent). The high concentration in certain industries signifies the development of ethnic industrial niches among Koreans. These differences also highlight that Korean entrepreneurs do not compete in the same industries as non-Korean businesses.

Table 7.6. Labour Force Characteristics by Industry of Koreans and the General Population by Employment Status in Canada, 2006

	Korean				General Population			
	Self-Employed		Wage/Salary Earners		Self-Employed		Wage/Salary Earners	
	N	(%)	N	(%)	N	(%)	N	(%)
Industries								
Primary Industries	2	(0.6)	6	(0.7)	202	(1.5)	1,406	(1.4)
Construction and Manufacturing	14	(4.3)	84	(9.7)	2,420	(17.9)	17,327	(17.3)
Wholesale Trade	22	(6.8)	42	(4.9)	581	(4.3)	5,950	(5.9)
Retail Trade	86	(26.5)	115	(13.3)	1,052	(7.8)	11,407	(11.4)
Transportation and Warehousing	3	(0.9)	34	(3.9)	701	(5.2)	5,082	(5.1)
Information and Cultural Industries	1	(0.3)	30	(3.5)	399	(2.9)	3,746	(3.7)
Finance, Insurance, and Real Estate	15	(4.6)	74	(8.6)	889	(6.6)	8,952	(8.9)
Professional, Scientific, and Technical Service	16	(4.9)	75	(8.7)	2,840	(21.0)	7,915	(7.9)
Management, Admin, and Support	8	(2.5)	34	(3.9)	894	(6.6)	5,219	(5.2)
Educational Services	19	(5.9)	85	(9.8)	376	(2.8)	7,175	(7.2)
Health Care and Social Assistance	13	(4.0)	73	(8.5)	1,125	(8.3)	8,493	(8.5)
Arts, Entertainment, and Recreation	6	(1.9)	21	(2.4)	593	(4.4)	2,032	(2.0)
Accommodation and Food Services	71	(21.9)	124	(14.4)	496	(3.7)	6,968	(7.0)
Other Services	48	(14.8)	50	(5.8)	959	(7.1)	4,403	(4.4)
Public Administration	0	(0.0)	16	(1.9)	0	(0.0)	4,021	(4.0)
Total	324		863		13,527		100,096	

Source: 2006 Canadian Census Individual Public Use Microdata File.

Conclusions

This chapter has explored the key demographic and social characteristics in explaining the trends observed regarding the labour-force participation of Koreans in Canada. Koreans in the United States exhibit high levels of entrepreneurship; they are no different in Canada. Our descriptive analysis of census data showed that Koreans who are self-employed are generally older and married. They are also often foreign-born persons who immigrated beyond the age of thirty. Though the demand of the growing Korean community can partly explain the high rate of entrepreneurship, it cannot explain why entrepreneurs are generally older and married. The demographic patterns of Korean entrepreneurs also support the supply-side explanation that older persons are more likely able to access financial resources, and may also have experience running businesses.

As found in previous studies, the majority of Korean entrepreneurs are university educated and proficient in the English language. Since Koreans in Canada earn less than the average Canadian despite their high level of education, it may be argued that their involvement in entrepreneurship illustrates a turn to self-employment as an alternative avenue to economic achievement. This argument, however, is not supported by the fact that self-employed Koreans earn less than their wage and salary earning counterparts. Another possible explanation may be that Koreans become entrepreneurs in response to blocked career mobility; subsequently, they choose industries strategically and develop ethnic niches that are not in direct competition with the general population of entrepreneurs. Although it is beyond the scope of this study to contrast the different types of self-employment (e.g., unincorporated versus incorporated businesses) or explore the application of middleman theory to Korean businesses in Canada, future research should consider these forms of self-employment in order to fully evaluate the earnings of self-employment compared with those of wage earners.

The Korean experience in Canada is relatively new compared with other groups. Their labour-market participation reveals much about their economic integration into Canadian society. Their propensity toward self-employment plays an important role in the development of their community. Our study has taken a first step in painting a general picture of this new immigrant group. However, more attention is needed to evaluate the effects of such a prevalent phenomenon among the Korean community and in Canadian society at large.

REFERENCES

Fernandez, M., and Kim, K.C. (1998). Self-employment rates of Asian immigrant groups: An analysis of intragroup and intergroup differences. International Migration Review, 32(3), 654–81.

Fong, T.P. (1994). The first suburban Chinatown: The remaking of Monterey Park, California. Philadelphia: Temple University Press.

Iceland, J. (1999). Earnings returns to occupational status: Are Asian Americans disadvantaged? Social Science Research, 28(1), 45–65.

Li, P. (1998). Chinese in Canada. Don Mills, ON: Oxford University Press.

Li, W. (1998). Los Angeles' Chinese ethnoburb: From ethnic service center to global economy outpost. Urban Geography, 19(6), 502–17.

Light, I. H., and Bonacich, E. (1988). Immigrant entrepreneurs: Koreans in Los Angeles, 1965 1982. Berkeley: University of California Press.

Light, I.H., and Gold, S.J. (2000). Ethnic economies. San Diego: Academic Press.

Light, I.H., and Rosenstein, C.N. (1995). Race, ethnicity, and entrepreneurship in urban America. New York: Aldine de Gruyter.

Logan, J.R., Zhang, W., and Alba, R.D. (2002). Immigrant enclaves and ethnic communities in New York and Los Angeles. American Sociological Review, 67(2), 299–322.

Min, P.G. (1984). From white-collar occupations to small business: Korean immigrants' occupational adjustment. Sociological Quarterly, 25(3), 333–52.

———. (2008). Ethnic solidarity for economic survival: Korean greengrocers in New York. New York: Russell Sage Foundation.

Min, P.G., and Mozorgmehr, M. (2003). The United States: The entrepreneurial cutting edge. In R. Kloosterman, A. Russell, and J. Rath (Eds.), Immigrant entrepreneurs: Venturing abroad in the age of globalization (pp. 17-37). Oxford: Berg.

Nee, V., Sanders, J.M., and Sernau, S. (1994). Job transitions in an immigrant metropolis: Ethnic boundaries and the mixed economy. American Sociological Review, 59(6), 849–72.

Portes, A., and Bach, R. (1985). Latin journey: Cuban and Mexican immigrants in the United States. Berkeley: University of California Press.

Sanders, J.M., and Nee, V. (1987). Limits of ethnic solidarity in the enclave economy. American Sociological Review, 52(6), 745–67.

———. (1996). Immigrant self-employment: The family as social capital and the value of human capital. American Sociological Review, 61(2), 231–49.

Waldinger, R. (1994). The making of an immigrant niche. International Migration Review, 28(1), 3–30.

132   Elic Chan and Eric Fong

Waldinger, R., Aldrich, H., and Ward, R. (1990). *Ethnic entrepreneurs: Immigrant business in industrial societies*. Newbury Park, CA: Sage.

Yoon, I.J. (1991). The changing significance of ethnic and class resources in immigrant businesses: The case of Korean immigrant businesses in Chicago. *International Migration Review*, 25(2), 303–32.

———. (1997). On my own: Korean businesses and race relations in America. Chicago: University of Chicago Press.

8 Acculturative Stress among Korean Immigrants

SAMUEL NOH AND MIEA MOON

Introduction

Immigrants and refugees are at risk of experiencing psychological distress due to heightened exposure to various stressful events in the country of settlement, including poor labour-market integration, poverty, identity crisis, social stigma, and racial discrimination (Dean & Wilson, 2009; Fitinger & Schwartz, 1981; Fleury, 2007; Kuo, 1984; Hull, 1979; Sue & Morishima, 1982). Acculturative stress refers to perceived internal strain resulting from repeated exposure to stressful events occurring during the transition from one's culture of origin to a new culture (Berry, 1998; Joiner & Walker, 2002). Acculturative stress has been examined among diverse racial and ethnic groups as well as different types of migrants, including immigrants, refugees, sojourners (e.g., international students), and native-born descendants of migrants. In these studies, acculturative stress has been linked to a host of negative outcomes, including depression, anxiety, and suicidal ideation (Crockett et al., 2007; Hovey, 2000; Joiner & Walker, 2002; Salgado de Snyder, 1987). Among Korean immigrants in the United States, higher scores for depression have been attributed to acculturative stress (Hurh & Kim, 1990). Furthermore, acculturative stress has been associated with depressive symptoms among Korean-American immigrants at various stages of the life course, including adolescents and the elderly (Cho & Haslam, 2010; Han et al., 2006; Oh et al., 2002; Park, 2009).

Measuring acculturative stress in immigrants provides a deeper understanding of immigrants' shared experiences, as well as their challenges and accomplishments in various aspects of life in the country of settlement. For example, a comparison of relative levels of stress in different parts of daily life can provide an empirical basis on which to judge the particular areas of difficulties experienced among members within an immigrant community (e.g., Korean immigrants in Vancouver). Empirical data on acculturative stress also facilitate a comparison of diverse immigrant groups to evaluate and identify groups at most need for assistance. Moreover, identifying areas of the acculturation or settlement process that are particularly challenging to an immigrant allows mental health professionals or immigrant case workers to better target resources toward an immigrant's specific areas of difficulty.

Although research on Korean-American immigrants has grown recently, there is a paucity of studies on the experience of acculturative stress among Korean immigrants in Canada. In addition, while a large number of studies have examined the association of various health outcomes with acculturative stress, few studies have examined socio-economic and demographic predictors of acculturative stress. Furthermore, there is little descriptive information about the ways in which Koreans immigrants experience acculturation and settlement processes. Thus, this chapter describes the experience of acculturative stress among Korean immigrants in Toronto, and explores selected socio-economic and demographic predictors of acculturative stress. This chapter will also introduce a multidimensional measure of acculturative stress that was originally developed for Korean immigrants in Canada.

Acculturative Stress

Although research on acculturative stress has been growing rapidly, there have been challenges in regard to the conceptualization and measurement of the construct. For example, some studies confound cause and effect variables by using mental health measures, such as depression scales or psychosomatic checklists as indictors of acculturative stress (see Rudmin, 2009, for a review). Other studies have confounded acculturation and acculturative stress by treating acculturative stress as a component of acculturation. Such studies will regard the variance in mental health accounted for by the level of acculturation as the impact of acculturation stress (see Berry et al., 1987; Dona & Berry, 1994; Liebkind, 1996; Zamanian et al., 1992).

Several direct and multidimensional measures of acculturative stress have been developed to more adequately assess the experience of stress arising from the acculturation process. From a pool of 125 items derived from the recurrent themes of adjustment difficulties found among international students, Sandhu and Asrabadi (1994) distinguished six major components or sources of acculturative stress: perceived discrimination, homesickness, perceived rejection, sense of insecurity, stress due to change or culture shock, guilt about leaving family behind, and betrayal of one's own culture. Some multidimensional measures of acculturative stress found in the literature include the Acculturative Stress Scale for international students (Sandhu & Asrabadi, 1994), the Social Attitudinal Familial Environmental Scale (SAFE) (Mena et al., 1987; Padilla et al., 1985), and the Multidimensional Acculturative Stress Inventory for adults of Mexican origin (MASI) (Rodriguez et al., 2002). Some limitations of current acculturative stress measures include inadequate coverage of areas in which immigrants are likely to experience stress from the acculturation process. For example, since the MASI was designed for both first-generation immigrants and native-born descendants of immigrants, it lacks sources of stress that are relevant specifically among first-generation immigrants or foreign-born migrants, including feelings of homesickness or intensive longing for one's home country. Other measures do not clearly distinguish acculturative stress from general sources of life stress that are not specifically related to the process of acculturation. For example, loss of job is a significant stressor for both immigrants and non-immigrants.

Researchers have recently underscored the importance of considering the role of context of reception in the acculturation process (Schwartz et al., 2010). The experience of acculturative stress will likely differ according to whether an immigrant perceives the context of reception in the settlement country to be negative or positive. As such, comprehensive acculturative stress measures may incorporate items that assess perceived stress due to an unfavourable context of reception, including experiences of discrimination and marginalization.

Acculturative Stress Index

The multidimensional Acculturative Stress Index (ASI) was devised for the Korean Mental Health Study (KMHS), a study of the mental health of Korean immigrants living in Toronto, Canada, in 1990 (Noh & Avison, 1996; Noh & Kaspar, 2003; Noh et al., 1992a, 1992b). The ASI is a twenty-four-item scale consisting of six areas or domains in which immigrants tend to experience the most difficulties: (1) *homesickness* (i.e., feelings of longing or nostalgia due to the separation from one's home country); (2) *social isolation* (i.e., lack of supportive social relations in Canada); (3) *discrimination* (i.e., experiences of discrimination at work or school); (4) *marginalization* (i.e., a sense of being excluded from social and political opportunities); (5) *socio-economic adjustment* (i.e., experiences of economic and financial strain in the settlement country); and (6) *family relations* (i.e., changes and/or problems in family relations). On a four-point Likert scale ranging from *never* (1) to *always* (4), respondents are asked to report how often they experience stress due to the circumstances described in each item of the ASI. Respondents may also indicate if the circumstances described in an item are not applicable. As such, the ASI assesses information on the frequency and degree of perceived stress experienced as a result of the acculturation process. It is operationally separate from acculturation, as it does not include indicators of acculturation such as familiarity with or preference for various cultural aspects of the country of settlement and country of origin.

Research on acculturative stress among immigrants of diverse racial and ethnic groups has grown rapidly; however, there are few studies on the experience of acculturative stress among Korean immigrants in Canada. Furthermore, while studies have examined the relationship of acculturative stress to physical and mental health outcomes, there is relatively little research on the socio-economic and demographic predictors of acculturative stress. Thus, the current study examines the experience of acculturative stress among Korean immigrants in Toronto, and explores socio-economic and demographic predictors of six domains of acculturative stress encompassed by the ASI.

Sample and Data

Data for this study were drawn from the KMHS conducted in the early 1990s. The Directory of the Korean Society of Toronto (KST), which listed over 4,100 households and an estimated 8,000 adults, was used as a sampling frame. A random number table was used to select a representative sample composed of a total of 1,039 households (about 25 per cent of the KST). An information letter explaining the purpose and nature of the study was mailed to each household. One adult (age eighteen or older) was randomly selected from each household. Those who immigrated before the age of sixteen were excluded, since their migratory experiences were likely to be substantially different from those of older immigrants. Interviews were conducted by bilingual interviewers following a structured schedule that contained an array of psychosocial measures. A total of 860 adults completed interviews, with each interview lasting approximately ninety minutes.

Sample Demographic Characteristics

Females represented 47 per cent of the total sample (860 respondents). The mean age of the sample was forty-five years, with the majority of respondents within the age range of thirty-six to forty-five; less than 20 per cent were older than fifty-five. The vast majority of respondents were currently married at the time of interview (82.6 per cent). A significantly lower (p <.01) percentage of males were divorced or separated compared with females (0.9 per cent versus 4.2 per cent).

More than half (52.6 per cent) of the sample completed education in South Korea at a level beyond high school. The completion of a university degree was significantly higher (p <.01) among the male respondents; nearly 50 per cent of the male respondents completed university degree(s), compared with 30 per cent of female respondents. While most men (80.5 per cent) and women (67.6 per cent) reported that they were employed, men were significantly more likely to work (p <.01). Female respondents were significantly more likely to report higher household income than men (p <.05).

Overall, the respondents were largely middle-aged and currently married. Compared with the general population of Toronto at the time of interview, Korean immigrants had a lower divorce rate and were more likely to have a post-secondary education. Most men and women in the current sample were actively engaged in the labour market and appeared to earn as much as other residents of Toronto.

Migration Experiences

Over 40 per cent of adult immigrants migrated in their early adulthood (twenty-six to thirty-five years of age). On average, the respondents had been living in Canada for twelve years. Although over 50 per cent of the sample had been in Canada for twelve years or more, only a small percentage (19 per cent) received formal education in Canada. Over 75 per cent of men and 85 per cent of women received no formal education in Canada.

More than 75 per cent of the sample emigrated from the metropolitan area of Seoul. Another 13 per cent of the sample emigrated from other large cities or urban areas (containing a population of a million or more) in South Korea; the remaining 11 per cent were from small cities or rural towns in South Korea.

Most respondents (80.7 per cent) had relatives or friends present in Canada when they arrived, indicating a pattern of chain migration.

When respondents were asked if they received any support from these friends and relatives and, if so, whether the support was helpful, over 30 per cent of the total sample reported that they received "very helpful" support. Twenty-two per cent, however, had no support available or did not find the support they received to be helpful. Another 20 per cent felt the support they received was "not very helpful." The respondents were also asked if they plan to return to South Korea. While the majority (63 per cent) said that they were not planning to return, a considerable minority (37 per cent) were either contemplating or definitely planning to return to South Korea.

Measuring Acculturative Stress

The central construct of this paper, acculturative stress, was measured by the Acculturative Stress Index, as described previously. Item scores were summed to compute the six subscale or domain scores and total scale score. Means scores for each acculturative stress domain were computed by dividing the domain score by the number of items in the domain. Cronbach's alpha (α) for the six acculturative stress domains ranged from .72 to .82. Cronbach's alpha for the total twenty-four-item scale was .92.

Socio-economic and Demographic Variables

Seven socio-economic predictors were included in the analyses: age, sex, marital status, length of residence in Canada, Korean education level, Canadian education level, and annual household income. Age was measured by year of chronological age. Sex was measured as a binary variable with *females* coded *1* and *males* coded *0*. Marital status was measured as a binary variable with *currently married* coded *1* and *not currently married* coded *0*. Length of residence was measured by the number of years lived in Canada. Annual household income was measured using eleven categories ranging from *less than $10,000* to *more than $60,000*.

The level of education completed in South Korea (Korean Education) was measured using six levels: *elementary school or less* (1); *middle school* (2); *high school* (3); *community college* (4); *university degree* (5); and *graduate/professional school degree* (6). The level of education completed in Canada (Canadian Education) was measured using four levels: *none* (1); *high school* (2); *college or university* (3); and *graduate school* (4).

Figure 8.1. Mean and Standard Deviations of ASI Domains

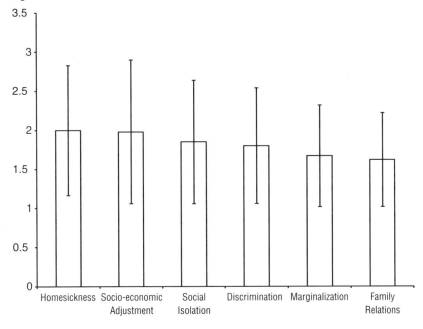

Note: Respondents were asked to indicate how often they experience stress due to the circumstances described in each item of the ASI using a four-point Likert scale.

Findings

Acculturative Stress Domains

As immigrants may be exposed to diverse forms of acculturation and adjustment needs, acculturative stress is best conceived and measured as a multidimensional construct. Accordingly, the measure employed in the present study, the ASI, consists of six domains. As illustrated in figure 8.1, a pattern of three clusters, based on mean levels of acculturative stress reported for each ASI domain, emerged in the data. Specifically, the average level of stress reported for the homesickness and socio-economic adjustment domains was significantly higher than that reported for the discrimination and social isolation domains (p <.001).

In turn, the average level of stress reported for the discrimination and social isolations domains was significantly higher than that reported for the family relations and marginalization domains (p <.001). Although differences between each cluster of domains were statistically significantly (p <.001), the differences between the domains within each cluster were not.

It is reasonable to anticipate that Korean immigrants would report the most acculturative stress from homesickness (e.g., living away from family and friends), especially during the initial phase of settlement. New immigrants experience sudden disruptions of extended family and social networks, and experience linguistic and cultural changes that may hinder them from enjoying the same activities they enjoyed in their home country. The emergence of socio-economic adjustment difficulties as a salient source of acculturative stress is consistent with previous research findings. For example, a qualitative research study of skilled immigrants in Canada found that lack of income, loss of employment-related skills, and loss of social status were among the most frequently cited reasons for poorer health (Dean & Wilson, 2009).

Korean immigrants reported the least acculturative stress from changes in family relations (e.g., family members losing cohesion with each other) and marginalization (e.g., not understanding the political or educational system in Canada). Given that a considerable proportion of the Korean immigrants participating in the study were either not married or did not have children, it seems reasonable to find relatively infrequent reports of stress from family-related conflicts.

Socio-economic Background and Acculturative Stress

Who is more likely to experience stress from the acculturation process, and who is more protected from the stressors? As indicated previously, there is little research on the socio-economic determinants or predictors of acculturative stress among Korean immigrants. Table 8.1 summarizes the results from regression models of the six domains of the ASI and total ASI scale scores. The reported values are standardized regression coefficients (or partial correlations) of selected socioeconomic and demographic factors. We found that overall acculturative stress was independent of respondents' sex and household income level, as shown in the first column of the table. However, there was a significant relationship between acculturative stress and age, such that acculturative stress was significantly higher among younger respondents

Table 8.1. Standardized Regression Coefficients of Socio-economic Background

Predictors	Total (I)	Home-sickness (II)	Socio-economic Adjustment (III)	Acculturative Stress Domains Discrimination (IV)	Social Isolation (V)	Marginality (VI)	Family Problems (VII)
Female sex	.003	.109**	-.032	-.047	.022	.001	.016
Age (years)	-.189***	-.105*	-.239***	-.137**	-.158***	-.195***	-.143***
Marital status	.093*	.025	.019	.024	-.029	.069	.150***
Korean Education	.163***	.046	.130***	.201***	.093*	.114**	.082*
Years in Canada	-.119**	-.300***	-.160***	-.146**	-.167***	-.038	.044
Canadian Education	-.141*	-.124**	-.107**	-.078*	-.060	-.125**	-.135**
Household Income	-.075	-.052	-.101*	-.104*	-.061	-.017	-.013
R Square	.128	.167	.147	.119		.077	

*$p < .05$; **$p < .01$; ***$p < .001$

compared with older respondents. Interestingly, the level of education received in South Korea prior to immigration was significantly associated with acculturative stress, such that higher levels of acculturative stress were found among more highly educated immigrants.

This finding may suggest that immigrants with higher levels of education may have immigrated to Canada with greater or unmet expectations about their quality of life and ability to succeed in reset-. tlement relative to those with lower levels of education. However, with increased length of residence and education in Canada, immigrants appear to experience lower levels of stress from the acculturation process. In addition, overall acculturative stress level was higher among married immigrants. Finally, as illustrated in the first column of the table, we find that among all variables considered, age exerted the largest protective influence on the level of reported acculturative stress. In addition, the adverse effect of pre-migration educational background was larger than the effects of most predictors included in the analysis. The results in columns (II) through (VII), which report the relationships of the selected socio-economic and demographic variables with the six domains of acculturative stress, provide insight into the associations reported in regard to the overall or total level of acculturative stress. By examining the values reported across each row of table 8.1, we find that more women than men reported stress due to homesickness or nostalgia. However, homesickness was the only domain in which men and women differed in regard to acculturative stress. Similarly, the influence of marital status on acculturative stress seemed to be confined to the domain of family relations, which include relationships with parents-in-law and children. Thus, the influences of sex and marital status were fairly limited and content specific. In contrast, the stress-suppressing effect of (older) age on acculturative stress was the most consistent, showing significance across all the domains included in the ASI.

Relatively consistent effects were also noted in regard to the education received in South Korea prior to immigration. Pre-migration educational background was related to an increase in acculturative stress in all domains with the exception of homesickness. The effect of the Korean education level on acculturative stress was most salient for the discrimination domain. That is, given an equal level of education attained in Canada, those with higher Korean education, compared with lower Korean education, were more vulnerable to the experience of stress due to social stigma and discrimination ($\beta = .201$, $p < .001$). On the other hand, educational attainment in Canada was associated with a decrease in acculturative stress in all domains, with the exception of stress due to social isolation.

Increased length of residence in Canada was associated with lower levels of acculturative stress among Korean immigrants, especially in the domain of homesickness. The strong negative association ($\beta = -.300$, $p < .001$) found between length of residence in Canada and stress from homesickness is unsurprising, as immigrants are likely to experience more intense longing for home during the initial phase of settlement. In addition, it seems that as Koreans reside longer in Canada, they experience less stress from socio-economic strain, discrimination, and social isolation. Finally, income was largely independent of acculturative stress. However, higher income was associated with lower acculturative stress in two specific domains: socio-economic adjustment and discrimination. This pattern of findings is not surprising since these domains include stress from circumstances directly related to income level, such as underemployment, low standard of living, and loss of social status.

Overall, our data revealed that Korean immigrants in Toronto experienced stress most frequently due to missing family and social networks in Korea, and from difficulties in socio-economic adjustment. They tended to feel stress least frequently from experiences of social marginalization and family problems. Our findings indicate that the level of acculturative stress among Korean immigrants in Toronto was independent of sex, marital status, and household income level. Indeed, the experiences of acculturative stress seemed to be a function of pre-migration expectations of the acculturation and settlement process, which may be related to education in Korea and the degree of acculturation, as indicated by length of residence and educational attainment in Canada. In addition, age appeared to have consistently significant effects in reducing all domains of acculturative stress. Thus, it seems reasonable to assume that although Korean immigrants expressed modest levels of acculturative stress, such stressful life experiences tend to diminish as they get older and live longer in Canada. The present study, therefore, is consistent with the proposition that acculturation (e.g., increase in Canadian education) may reduce acculturative stress.

Discussions

The study examined the experience of acculturative stress, as well as the socio-economic and demographic antecedents of acculturative stress, among Korean immigrants in Canada using a multidimensional measure of acculturative stress. Among the current sample, immigrants experienced the most acculturative stress in the domains of homesickness and socio-economic adjustment, and the least amount of acculturative stress in the domains of family relations and marginalization. The emergence of homesickness as a major source of acculturative stress among immigrants underscores the importance of identifying sources of acculturative stress that are unique to first-generation immigrants or foreign-born individuals residing in the host or settlement country (e.g., international students). Furthermore, the emergence of socio-economic adjustment difficulties as a salient source of acculturative stress highlights the need to identify and remove barriers to immigrants' successful social and economic integration. This finding is especially critical given the growing contribution of immigrants to the Canadian population as well as the increasing shortage in the local labour market due to a declining birth rate and an aging population.

Results of the current study demonstrated that overall, age, length of residence, and educational attainment in Canada were inversely related to acculturative stress. Pre-migration educational level, however, was related to higher scores on the ASI. The adverse effects of pre-migration education on acculturative stress levels may be explained by the concept of *relative deprivation.* Immigrants with high levels of formal education often immigrate with significant occupational or professional qualifications and experiences. Compared with the less well educated, they tend to make an easier transition during the initial stage of settlement because of their superior language proficiency and familiarity with, or preference for, Western culture and values. However, they also come with higher expectations of socio-economic attainment in the country of settlement. Higher expectations may result in greater disappointment and frustration if their expectations remain unmet for an extended period of time.

Relative deprivation is more likely to be experienced by well-prepared immigrants from non-traditional source countries. Among adult Korean immigrants, English proficiency tends to reach a plateau very quickly, normally after the first few years of settlement. The social and cultural advantages due to pre-migration education seem to decrease over time, which may lead to greater stress among all immigrants, but perhaps particularly among those who are better educated prior to immigration. Moreover, many professionals from the non-traditional source countries experience structural and systemic barriers to receiving social recognition of their professional qualifications and experiences (Uba, 1994). Portes, Parker, and Cobas (1980) suggested that the accumulation of resources, and incorporation of dominant society values that accompany acculturation, lead to an increase in perceptions of power imbalances and socio-economic inequality along racial and ethnic lines. Thus, greater familiarity with the dominant culture may lead to heightened perceptions and experiences of discrimination.

One of the most important limitations of the present study is the use of cross-sectional data. Future research could examine relationship patterns between acculturative stress domains and social, psychological, and economic variables using a longitudinal research design. The long-term health impact of the various sources of acculturative stress could also be examined. Another limitation of the present study is in regard to the composition of the sample: since the sample was composed only of first-generation Korean immigrants, the generalizability of the current findings is limited. In addition, since data were derived from a survey conducted twenty years ago, the sample may not reflect the composition of the current Korean-Canadian community in Toronto. Since the experience of acculturative stress varies across individual characteristics, circumstances, and immigrant communities, data collected from more recent samples are likely to yield findings different from those presented in this chapter. For example, levels of acculturative stress from homesickness may not be as high today as they were twenty years ago. Indeed, given the ease of transnational communication, frequency of international travel, and the growing number of transnational migrants (see chapters 1, 2, 6, and 14, this volume), physical separation from one's homeland may not necessarily induce homesickness. The validity of the acculturative stress measure employed in the current study, as well as the importance of acculturative stress as a social psychological construct, will be verified only through continued scrutiny and by employing a diverse range of populations. Despite the limitations of the study, the findings presented in this chapter demonstrate the importance of examining acculturative stress in the study and understanding of the immigrant experience.

REFERENCES

Berry, J.W. (1998). Acculturative stress. In P.B. Organista, K.M. Chun, and G. Marin (Eds.), *Readings in ethnic psychology* (pp. 117–22). NewYork: Routledge.

Berry, J.W., Kim, U., Minde, T., and Mok, D. (1987). Comparative studies of acculturative stress. *International Migration Review, 21*, 491–511.

Cho, Y.B., and Haslam, N. (2010). Suicidal ideation and distress among immigrant adolescents: The role of acculturation, life stress, and social support. *Journal of Youth and Adolescence, 39*, 370–9.

Crockett, L.J., Iturbide, M.I., Torres Stone, R.A., McGinley, M., Raffaelli, M., and Carlo, G. (2007). Acculturative stress, social support, and coping: Relations to psychological adjustment among Mexican American college students. *Cultural Diversity & Ethnic Minority Psychology, 13*(4), 347–55.

Dean, J.A., and Wilson, K. (2009). "Education? It is irrelevant to my job now. It makes me very depressed…": Exploring the health impacts of under/unemployment among highly skilled recent immigrants in Canada. *Ethnicity & Health, 14*(2), 185–204.

Dona, G., and Berry, J.W. (1994). Acculturation attitudes and acculturative stress of Central American refugees in Canada. *International Journal of Psychology, 29*, 57–70.

Fitinger, L., and Schwartz, D. (1981). *Strangers in the world.* Bern: Hans Huber.

Fleury, D. (2007). *A study of poverty and working poverty among recent immigrants to Canada.* Ottawa: Human Resources and Social Development Canada.

Han, H.R., Kim, M., Lee, H.B., Pistulka, G., and Kim, K.B. (2007). Correlates of depression in the Korean American elderly: Focusing on personal resources of social support. *Journal of Cross-Cultural Gerontology, 22*(1), 115–27.

Hovey, J.D. (2000). Acculturative stress, depression, and suicidal ideation in Mexican immigrants. *Cultural Diversity & Ethnic Minority Psychology, 6*, 134–51.

Hull, D. (1979). Migration, adaptation, and illness: A review. *Social Science and Medicine, 13*, 25–36.

Hurh, W.M., and Kim, K. (1990). Adaptation stages and mental health of Korean male immigrants in the United States. *International Migration Review, 24*, 456–79.

Joiner, T., and Walker, R. (2002). Construct validity of a measure of acculturative stress in African-Americans. *Psychological Assessment, 14*, 462–6.

Kuo, W.H. (1984). Prevalence of depression among Asian-Americans. *Journal of Nervous Mental Disease, 172*, 449–57.

Liebkind, K. (1996). Acculturation and stress: Vietnamese refugees in Finland. *Journal of Cross-Cultural Psychology, 27*(2), 161–80.

Mena, F.J., Padilla, A.M., and Maldonado, M. (1987). Acculturative stress and specific coping strategies among immigrant and later generations of college students. *Hispanic Journal of Behavioural Sciences, 9*(2), 207–25.

Noh, S., and Avison, W.R. (1996). Asian immigrants and the stress process: A study of Koreans in Canada. *Journal of Health and Social Behavior, 37*(2), 192–206.

Noh, S., and Kaspar, V. (2003). Perceived discrimination: Moderating effects of coping, acculturation, and ethnic support. *American Journal of Public Health, 93*, 232–8.

Noh, S., Speechley, M., Kaspar, V., and Wu, Z. (1992a). Depression in Korean immigrants in Canada: I. Method of the study and prevalence. *Journal of Nervous and Mental Disease, 180*, 573–7.

———. Depression in Korean immigrants in Canada: II. Effects of gender, work, and marriage. *Journal of Nervous and Mental Disease, 180*, 578–82.

Oh, Y., Koeske, G.F., and E. Sales. (2002). Acculturation, stress, and depressive symptoms among Korean immigrants in the United States. *Journal of Social Psychology, 142*(4), 511–26.

Padilla, A.M., Wagatsuma, Y., and Lindholm, K.J. (1985). Acculturation and personality as predictors of stress in Japanese and Japanese-Americans. *Journal of Social Psychology, 125*, 295–305.

Park, W. (2009). Acculturative stress and mental health factors Korean adolescents in the United States. *Journal of Human Behavior in the Social Environment, 19*(5), 626–34.

Portes, A., Parker, R.N. and Cobas, J.A. (1980). Assimilation or consciousness – perceptions of United States society among recent Latin-American immigrants to the United States. *Social Forces, 59*, 200–24.

Rodriguez, N., Myers, H.F., Mira, C.B., Flores, T., and Garcia-Hernandez, L. (2002). Development of the multidimensional acculturative stress inventory for adults of Mexican origin. *Psychological Assessment, 14*, 451–61.

Rudmin, F.W. (2009). Constructs, measurements and models of acculturation and acculturative stress. *International Journal of Intercultural Relations, 33*, 106–23.

Salgado de Snyder, S.N. (1987). Factors associated with acculturative stress and depressive symptomatology among married Mexican immigrant women. *Psychology of Women Quarterly, 11*, 457–88.

Sandhu, D.S., and Asrabadi, B.R. (1994). Development of an acculturative stress scale for international students: Preliminary findings. *Psychological Reports, 75*, 435–48.

Schwartz, S.J., Unger, J.B., Zamboanga, B.L., and Szapocznik, J. (2010). Rethinking the concept of acculturation: Implications for theory and research. *American Psychologist, 65*(4), 237–51.

Sue, S., and Morishima, J. (1982). *The mental health of Asian Americans*. San Francisco: Jossey-Bass.

Uba, L. (1994). *Asian-Americans: Personality patterns, identity, and mental health.* New York: Guilford.

Zamanian, K., Thackery, M., Starrett, R. A., Brown, L.G., Lassman, D.K., and Blanchard, A. (1992). Acculturation and depression in Mexican American elderly. *Clinical Gerontologist*, 11, 109–21.

9 Korean-Language Maintenance in Canada

MIHYON JEON

Introduction

One of the major challenges for immigrant minorities is the maintenance of their heritage language and culture. Immigrant communities often encounter subtractive bilingualism within families and schools (Duff & Li, 2009), which leads to language shifts from heritage languages to dominant languages. Immigrant communities in Canada are no exception, although Canada is well known for its multiculturalism and the multiethnic foundation of its population, and also for its proactive policies and initiatives to deliver heritage-language instruction and encourage the maintenance of diverse cultures.

This chapter discusses the Korean-Canadian community in the Greater Toronto Area, by examining the practices of language use and education of 137 Korean Canadians. Koreans are one of the fastest-growing visible-minority groups in Canada. In 2006, the visible-minority population of Canada was more than 5 million, and accounted for 16.2 per cent of the total Canadian population (Statistics Canada, 2006). Korean Canadians are also among the more recent immigrant groups to enter Canadian society. In 2006, 141,895 Koreans resided in Canada, 34 per cent of whom arrived between 2000 and 2006. In 2006, 90 per cent of Koreans were first-generation immigrants; only 8.3 per cent were Canadian-born second generation; and 0.8 per cent were third generation. These figures do contrast with the overall generational breakdown for the total population in Canada of ethnic origin, which is 23.9 per cent first generation, 15.6 per cent second generation, and 60.5 per cent third generation.

Because of the relatively short immigration history of Koreans to

Canada, there have been only a handful of studies on Korean Canadians (e.g., Hong, 2008; Kwak, 2004; Noh, 2009, 2012). There has also been a lack of systematic investigation of Korean Canadians' language maintenance and shift to English, with the exception of two studies completed by Kim (1992), and Park and Sarka (2007). They will be reviewed in the following section. The current study, therefore, seeks to fill this gap by exploring the patterns of Korean- and English-language learning and usage among Korean-Canadian youth.

The Ecology of Language Maintenance and Shift for Immigrants

In exploring Korean-Canadian language maintenance and shift, the paradigm called "the ecology of language" is adopted here as a theoretical framework. Haugen (1972) defines language ecology as the study of interactions between any given language and its environment, including both psychological and sociological. Haugen (1972) emphasizes the reciprocity that exists between language and environment, calling for a need not only to describe the social and psychological situation of each language but also to examine closely the effect of this reciprocity on the language.

Following Haugen, Mühlhäusler (1996) regards "the well-being of individual languages or communication networks as dependent on a range of language-external factors as well as the presence of other languages" (p. 49). Furthermore, Mühlhäusler (1996) argues for applying ecological theory to the goal of language maintenance (pp. 311–24) so as to count the decline and loss of linguistic heterogeneity in the world. In her synthesis of the ecology of language, Hornberger (2002) draws on three principles: language evolution, language environment, and language endangerment. Following the principles of language evolution and language environment, Hornberger suggests that "languages, like living species, evolve, grow, change, live, and die in relation to other languages and also in relation to their environment" (2002, p. 33). The endangerment principle refers to "the notion that some languages, like some species and environments, may be endangered and that the ecology movement is about not only studying and describing those potential losses, but also counteracting them" (Hornberger, 2002, p. 33).

Such an ecological approach to language shift explores the "interrelated sequences of causes and effects [that are] producing changes in the traditional language behavior of one group under the influence of another, resulting in a switch in the language of one of the groups" (Mackey, 2001, p. 68). Mackey (2001) also notes that a language shift will involve at least two languages, some contact between those people speaking them, and a period of time for the change to take place. The general pattern for the direction of language shift is almost always toward dominant languages that offer economic, practical, and physiological rewards. For example, parents in many parts of the world prefer to educate their children in dominant languages (e.g., majority languages in multiethnic countries that also have immigrants, or former colonial languages such as English, French, or Spanish in post-colonial societies) (Mackey, 2001). Language shifts to dominant languages often involve both constant outside pressures on the language minority community and internal pressures within the members of the same community, based on what the people in that community want most and what assets are valued most by its members (Mackey, 2001).

Fishman (1989) observed a general trend of a complete language shift within three generations. The first generation speaks the native language, while the bilingual second generation appears between the first generation and the majority-language-speaking third generation. The bilingual second generation delineates an intergenerational period of transitional bilingualism that defines the process of language shift. However, recently, more and more language-minority communities have been undergoing a complete shift in language within just two generations (Wiley, 2001). Language shift creates communication problems because of a lack of a common language for parents and children, a circumstance that can lead to alienation of children from their parents over time (Shin, 2005). Moreover, the failure of the intergenerational transmission of the minority language means a loss of language resources not only to those family individuals but also to communities and the nation where immigrants must integrate as a whole (Krashen et al., 1998). This overwhelming trend toward faster language shift is present in many language-minority communities worldwide, even with the benefits of minority-language maintenance, which also includes higher majority-language proficiency and literacy (Cummins, 1996); more positive self-concept; cognitive flexibility (Hamers & Blanc, 2000); strengthening of communication between family members; and contribution to community maintenance.

In the context of countries where speaking the dominant language is essential for full participation in society, it is crucial for minority children to develop bilingual proficiency in both the dominant and the minority languages. There are indeed multiple and interacting factors that create and sustain bilingual development of such language-minority groups. Along with Hamers and Blanc (2000) and Allard and Landry (1994), Gibbons and Ramirez (2004) categorize these factors into three groups: societal, contact, and attitudinal. The societal factor refers to a broad socio-structural area manifested via the existence of both majority and minority social institutions and media. The contact factor refers to individuals' daily interactions with language, including interpersonal contact and non-interactive contact through media. The attitudinal factor refers to individual beliefs about language that are then socially constructed and shared with other members in a society.

The current study investigates how these factors are linked to heritage-language maintenance among Korean Canadians by exploring the relationship between these factors and language proficiency in Korean as well as English. In such a language-ecological study of Korean-language maintenance in the Canadian context, it will be necessary to explore how Korean and English are both learned, used, and valued by Korean Canadians, since English occupies the dominant language position in the ecology of language in Canada.

The Canadian Context: Heritage-Language Maintenance versus Language Loss

The language ecology of Canada is as diverse as those in other multiethnic and multicultural nations. According to the 2006 census data (Statistics Canada, 2006), English is the mother tongue of 58 per cent of Canadians, while French is the mother tongue of approximately 22 per cent, which makes Francophones the largest linguistic minority nationally. The remainder of Canadians (approximately 20 per cent of the total of just over 31 million) speak neither English nor French as their mother tongue (Statistics Canada, 2006). These speakers of other than English or French are speakers of indigenous languages and speakers of heritage languages. Of one million self-identified indigenous persons (less than 4 per cent of the total population), under 30 per cent reported having conversational skills in an indigenous language (Statistics Canada, 2006). The speakers of a "heritage language" (HL) are speakers of languages other than the official ones (English and French) or indigenous languages (Cummins, 1992). More recent immigrants to Canada from countries where languages other than English or French are spoken belong to the group known as heritage-language speakers. The Korean language in the Canadian context is thus classified as a heritage language. Canada has a national commitment to sustaining the diversity of its own language ecology, namely, the protection and promotion of Canada's two official languages, English and French, as well as since the late 1960s ongoing legislative support for non-official languages (see Burnaby, 2008, and Duff, 2008, for recent reviews of language policies and trends in Canada).

While a significant number of studies that have documented the language shift among immigrant groups have focused on the American context (Fishman, 1989, 1991, 2001; Wong Fillmore, 1991; Young & Tran, 1999; among many others), a handful of studies have examined the same issue in the Canadian context. In her study of Spanish-speaking, female-headed families who came to Canada in the late1980s and early 1990s, Baergen (2008) argued that the most significant consequence of the loss of an immigrant heritage language is a loss of family communication and family relationships. Canagarajah's (2008) study of the Sri Lankan Tamil immigrant communities in Canada, the United Kingdom, and the United States documented a rapid shift toward English among immigrant children across three generations. He reported that in Toronto, 82.1 per cent of the sixty-four children studied said they used English, or English mixed with Tamil, to talk to each other, while their parents mostly used Tamil to communicate to each other. Subhan's (2007) study of Bangladeshi immigrants in Toronto found that language maintenance is not noticeable within these families in significant ways, and there is a general lack of awareness among the families about the importance of heritage-language maintenance. Li (2006), using a case study of three Chinese-Canadian families, argues that helping immigrant children become multilingual is a challenging task that requires a concerted effort between parents, public schools, and community organizations.

In his 1992 study of ninety-two Korean students in Toronto, Kim found that Korean-Canadian students' attitudes and motivation toward learning and maintaining the Korean language were significantly associated with their own Korean-language-use patterns and the degree of the Korean proficiency that they already attained or held. He also found that parents' attitudes influenced these students' attitudes and motivation in learning the Korean language. Park and Sarkar (2007) explored the attitudes of Korean immigrant parents toward heritage-language maintenance for their children in Montreal. According to the study, Korean parents held very positive attitudes toward maintaining the Korean language. They perceived that Korean-language maintenance would be beneficial for their children's cultural identity formation as Koreans; would provide their children with better economic opportunities; and would facilitate better communication among family members.

The Current Study

A survey was administered to 137 second-generation or 1.5-generation Korean Canadians in the Greater Toronto Area. The mean age of the survey respondents was 18.15 (from twelve to twenty-nine years old). Fifty-four male and 54 female Korean Canadians participated (29 respondents did not specify their sex).[1] Out of 116 respondents who identified their birthplaces, 50 were born in Canada (second generation); 64 were born in Korea and had moved to Canada (1.5 generation); and 2 were born in a third country. There were no third-generation participants. The average length of stay for 1.5-generation Korean Canadians was ten years.

Three undergraduate research assistants served as focal contacts and assisted in the distribution and collection of the survey between September 2007 and February 2008. The survey was distributed among the research assistants' social networks of family, friends, and acquaintances in the Greater Toronto Area. The same research assistants coded and input the survey results into a database for statistical analysis.

The survey contained six sections that elicited the following information: (1) English- and Korean-language proficiency; (2) demographic details; (3) parent and children's use of Korean and English in different domains; (4) media and literacy exposure; (5) Korean-language education; and (6) language attitudes toward Korean, English, and bilingualism. Of the three factors related to bilingual development and heritage-language maintenance by Korean Canadians, the data about "societal factors" were elicited from sections (2) and (5); the "contact factor" from sections (3) and (4); and the "attitudinal factors" from section (6). However, this categorization is not clear-cut, since the three factors do interrelate and overlap. For example, media exposure in section (4), although categorized under "contact factors," shows that

---

1 It is unknown why a high number of the survey participants did not specify their sex.

accessibility of the Korean language in media within Canada is part of the societal factors, since that factor is manifested through the existence of social media.

To examine the relationship between language proficiency and the factors for language development, English and Korean proficiencies were measured through self-assessment and cloze tests, respectively. The self-assessment section included two sets of four questions designed using a five-point Likert scale format (1 for *not very well* and 5 for *very well*). The four questions on Korean-language proficiency asked the following questions: (1) how well do you understand Korean?; (2) how well do you speak Korean?; (3) how well do you read Korean?; and (4) how well do you write in Korean? The cloze test section also had two sets of questions, i.e., one for Korean and the other for English. In each set with ten questions, a passage with ten blanks was presented with four answer keys for each question. The Korean passage consisted of fifty-six words and the English passage had sixty-three words.

The second section on the demographic details had the following five sub-sections: (1) family members living in the household; (2) birth order of the respondent; (3) family members' gender, age, birthplace, current residence, first language, and other languages spoken by family members; (4) parents' education levels; and (5) parents' occupations. The third section on language use had two sets of questions: one for language use among family members and the other for language use in other domains, such as relatives, friends, neighbours, and so on. All these questions were designed to use a seven-point Likert scale with values ranging from 1 to 7: *exclusively English*; *almost always English*; *mostly English*; *Korean and English equally*; *mostly Korean*; *almost always Korean*; and exclusively *Korean*. The fourth section consisted of fifteen questions about media and literacy exposure using a seven-point Likert scale with the same values as those offered above. The categories for media and literacy exposure included TV, radio, movies, music, the Internet, magazines/newspapers, non-fiction books, novels, dictionaries, and textbooks. The fifth section had two sets of questions about Korean-language-education practice, the first set on Korean-language education within the family and the second set for educational practices in a Korean-language school/class. The last section consisted of twenty-seven questions about attitudes toward Korean, English, and bilingualism. Some of these sample statements included *Korean is important for academic success*; *I feel comfortable when I speak English*; and *becoming bilingual is beneficial for me*. A five-point Likert scale had values ranging from 1 to 5, namely, *strongly disagree, somewhat agree, neutral, somewhat agree*, and *strongly agree*.

Study Findings

Korean and English Proficiency

The self-assessment section included four questions on Korean and for English, respectively: (1) *how well do you understand Korean/English when your hear it?*; (2) *how well do you speak Korean/English?*; (3) *how well do you read Korean/English?*; (4) *how well do you write in English?* A five-option Likert scale was used, ranging from 1 for *not well at all*, to 5 *for very well*. The results indicated that the survey respondents evaluated their own English proficiency higher than they did their own Korean proficiency. The mean score for the self-assessed Korean listening skills (N=123) was 3.94 (SD=1.096); for speaking skills, 3.37 (SD=1.270); for reading skills, 3.21 (SD=1.439); and for writing skills, 2.93 (SD=1.492). The mean score for the self-assessed English listening skills (N=122) was 4.68 (SD=.564); for speaking skills, 4.58 (SD=.748); for reading skills, 4.58 (SD=.678); and for writing skills, 4.52 (SD=.730). The mean scores for the English-language skills were higher than those for Korean: the mean score for Korean was 3.36, and that for English was 4.59.

The high standard deviation scores for the Korean skills suggest that there was a great range of variation in the self-assessed Korean proficiency of the survey participants. Among the four language skills, listening scored highest, followed by speaking, reading, and writing, which indicates that Korean-Canadian children find writing most difficult. In contrast, self-reported English proficiency showed little differences in the four language skills. The results of the cloze tests in Korean and in English also revealed that Korean-Canadian children's English proficiency is higher than that for their Korean proficiency. The cloze tests contained ten questions in Korean and ten questions in English. The mean score for Korean was 2.20 (SD=2.495), and the score for English was 5.95 (SD=2.879) out of a possible 10.

Parental Educational Level and Occupation

The majority of Korean-Canadian immigrant parents had post-secondary education. The fathers' education level was higher than the mothers' education level. Of the survey respondents' fathers, 27.5 per cent

(28 out of 102) had postgraduate degrees; 46 per cent (47) had bachelor's degrees; 13.9 per cent (14) had associate degrees; 9.9 per cent (10) had high-school diplomas; and 1 per cent (1) had a middle-school diploma. Of the survey respondents' mothers, 14.7 per cent (15 out of 102) had postgraduate degrees; 52.9 per cent (54) had bachelor's degrees; 14.7 per cent (15) had associate degrees; and 17.7 per cent (18) had high-school diplomas. This data indicate a weak, but positive, correlation between parental educational levels and students' Korean proficiency. The fathers' education level in particular showed a higher level of correlation with their children's Korean-language proficiency (Pearson correlation= .290, p < 0.01) than did the mothers' education level (Pearson correlation = .248, p < 0.01). This result may indicate that immigrant parents' educational attainment is one of the likely determinants of Korean immigrant maintenance of the Korean language, although the reasons can only be speculated here (e.g., higher educational attainments of parents may enable children to access more resources in the Korean language).

Of the fathers, 62.4 per cent (68 out of 109) were white-collar workers or owned small businesses, followed by 15 in professional fields, such as doctors, teachers, and accountants (13.8 per cent); 12 skilled manual workers (11 per cent); 4 unskilled manual workers (3.7 per cent); and 2 retired or doing home duties (1.8 per cent). Of the mothers, 44 (43.6 per cent) were white-collar workers or owned small business, followed by 14 professionals, such as doctors, teachers, and accountants (13.9 per cent); 10 skilled manual workers (9.9 per cent); 7 unskilled manual workers (6.9 per cent); and 25 retired or doing home duties (24.3 per cent).

Language-Use Practice

A seven-point Likert scale question was used to elicit information from the participants about language use within Korean-Canadian immigrant families with 1 representing *exclusively English*; 2, *almost always English*; 3, *mostly English*; 4, *Korean and English equally*; 5, *mostly Korean*; 6, *almost always Korean*; and 7, *exclusively Korean*. Table 9.1 shows those results. The language-use pattern indicates that language shift is indeed under way in the Korean-Canadian family. There were clear differences in language-use patterns, as exhibited by first-generation immigrant parents and second- or 1.5-generation children. The grandparents spoke exclusively Korean. The immigrant parents almost exclusively used Korean with their own parents. The immigrant parents also used mostly Korean and English with their spouses and used the highest amount of English with their children. The immigrant parents used Korean most with their first-born child (mother to the first-born was 5.54 and father to the first-born 5.53 on the scale from 1 for *exclusively English* to 7 for *exclusively Korean*), followed by the second-born (mother to the second-born 5.40; father to the second-born 5.36), and then the third-born (mother to the third-born 4.75; father to the third-born 5.00). Later-born children used less Korean with their parents than did earlier-born children (e.g., the first-born child to mother was 4.96; the second-born to mother, 4.77; and the third-born to mother, 4.03).

Among siblings, immigrant children used more English than they did Korean. Third-born children used mostly English, followed by second-born and first-born. Later-born children generally learn English at an earlier age than do first-born children through exposure to English brought home by the first-borns. Similar patterns among Spanish-speaking Mexican immigrants in the United States have been reported by Hakuta and D'Adrea (1992), and among Korean American children by Shin (2005).

Other than in the common domain of family, Korean is mainly used in the domain of relatives (mean=4.53; SD=2.04). The domain of church (mean=2.96; SD=1.79) showed a less exclusive use of English, but still mostly English. Even in the domain of friends (mean=2.00; SD=1.60), Korean-Canadian youths almost exclusively use English. The mean scores in other domains were 2.14 doctor's office (SD=1.61); 1.89 restaurants (SD=1.24); 1.78 schoolmates (SD=1.32); 1.57 shops (SD=1.01); 1.54 teachers (SD=1.19); and 1.27 neighbours (SD=1.10). These results also point to a language shift occurring from Korean to English.

This section suggests that there is a pattern of language shift among Koreans in Canada, as both second- and 1.5-generation Koreans almost exclusively use English when they interact with siblings and friends. The same pattern of language shift is also evident in that Korean is used only in the domains of family and relatives, while English is used in most other domains. However, the results also point to the importance of using Korean at home, since the Korean proficiency of children was highly related to the use of Korean between parents and their children, and the use of Korean among siblings.

Media and Literacy Exposure

As Korean Canadians grow up, their exposure to media in Korean

Table 9.1. Language Use at Home and the Correlation between Family Language Use and Korean-Language Proficiency

The speaker		The person spoken to						
		Mother	Father	Child 1	Child 2	Child 3	Grandmother	Grandfather
Mother	Mean (SD)		6.5 (0.99)	5.54 (1.67)	5.40 (1.73)	4.75 (1.78)	6.86 (0.6)	6.92 (0.40)
	Corr.		.283**	.591**	.651**	.697**	0.074	.153
	N		119	117	103	29	32	22
Father	Mean (SD)	6.48 (1.05)		5.53 (1.61)	5.36 (1.71)	5.00 (1.68)	6.96 (0.18)	6.91 (0.41)
	Corr.	.323**		.584**	.629**	.557**	.046	.145
	N	116		116	103	29	31	21
Child 1	Mean (SD)	4.96 (2.02)	5.02 (2.02)		3.19 (2.26)	2.69 (2.21)	6.18 (1.72)	6.00 (1.96)
	Corr.	.605**	.614**		.654**	.693**	.356*	.551*
	N	119	117		103	29	32	21
Child 2	Mean (SD)	4.77 (2.13)	4.81 (2.17)	3.09 (2.26)		2.65 (2.19)	6.00 (1.94)	5.92 (2.14)
	Corr.	.627**	.600**	.627**		.674**	.357*	.498*
	N	102	101	101		29	32	21
Child 3	Mean (SD)	4.03 (2.15)	4.00 (2.17)	2.84 (2.38)	2.81 (2.4)		5.52 (2.26)	5.16 (2.58)
	Corr.	.639**	.587**	.600**	.603**		.306	.562
	N	30	30	30	30		16	9
Grandmother	Mean (SD)	6.90 (0.54)	6.90 (0.54)	6.83 (0.58)	6.83 (0.58)	6.94 (0.24)		7.00 (0.00)
	Corr.	.045	.045	.131	.131	.138		
	N	27	27	27	27	14		17
Grandfather	Mean (SD)	7.00 (0.00)	7.00 (0.00)	6.85 (0.36)	6.85 (0.36)	6.60 (0.95)	7.00 (0.00)	
	Corr.			.413	.413	.165		
	N	17	17	16	16	9	17	

Exclusively English=1; exclusively Korean=7
** Correlation is significant at the 0.01 level (2-tailed).
* Correlation is significant at the 0.05 level (2-tailed).

declines, while their exposure to media in English increases. The exposure to media like TV, radio, movies, and music was measured before, during, and after primary school years using a seven-point Likert scale that ranged from 1, *exclusively English* to 7, *exclusively Korean*. In all four categories, there was a pattern of decrease of exposure to Korean. For example, for TV, the mean score for each period was 4.36 before; 3.86 during; and 2.82 after primary school. These results complement prior studies that have found that language shift is often initiated or facilitated when immigrant children begin attending schools that have a medium of instruction in languages other than their mother tongue (Richard & Yamada-Yamamoto, 1998; Tuominen, 1999; Wong Fillmore, 1991). Furthermore, the correlation between exposure to media in Korean and actual Korean proficiency showed a strong relationship. For example, the correlation between exposure to television in Korean before primary school and Korean-language proficiency is very high (Pearson correlation= .689, p < 0.01); the correlation between exposure to television in Korean during primary school and Korean-language proficiency is also very high (Pearson correlation= .739, p < 0.01). However, the correlation between media exposure to Korean after primary school and Korean proficiency is lower but still significant (Pearson correlation= .4809, p < 0.01). The same pattern of the correlations is also found in the genres of radio and music, except for movies. The exposure to media in Korean before and during primary school provides more of a positive impact on Korean-language proficiency than does that exposure after primary school.

The survey results demonstrate that English is more dominantly used than is Korean in most literacy practices. Of the genres of literacy practice, Korean Canadians use the least amount of English when they use the Internet, although that genre still scored 3.00 (*mostly English*). The use of Korean appears to be extremely low in the categories of textbooks and written homework, which points to the dominance of English in the school domain. The predominant use of English over Korean in most literacy practices is also a clear indicator of the language shift from Korean to English. The next table summarizes the findings.

The use of Korean in literacy practices is of course highly associated with Korean proficiency. The use of Korean in such literacy practices as diaries, the Internet, letters/cards, and messages/e-mails/MSN appears to have an overwhelmingly positive correlation with Korean proficiency. However, the use of Korean in textbooks and written homework shows a weak correlation with Korean proficiency, which

Table 9.2. Language Choice for Literacy Practices and the Correlation between Literacy Practice and Korean-Language Proficiency

		Language choice for literacy practices		Correlation between literacy practice and Korean-language proficiency
	N	Mean	SD	Corr.
Internet	118	3.00	1.94	.663**
Magazines/newspapers	119	2.79	1.77	.611**
Non-fiction books	119	2.64	1.85	.597**
Novels	118	2.57	1.86	.590**
Dictionaries	119	2.28	1.67	.474**
Textbooks	119	1.82	1.47	.323**
Religious texts	119	2.32	1.88	.550**
Letters/cards	118	2.78	1.83	.663**
Diaries	117	2.29	2.07	.672**
Written homework	119	1.89	1.62	.368**
Messages/e-mails/MSN	119	2.57	1.76	.617**

Exclusively English=1; almost always English=2; mostly English=3; Korean and English equally=4; exclusively Korean=7
Range: Min=1; Max=7
** Correlation is significant at the 0.01 level (2-tailed).

may indicate a general lack of Korean use in those literacy practices that are more relevant to formal schooling in Canada.

In summary, Korean Canadians are exposed to English media more than they are to Korean media, and they also use more English than Korean in their literacy practices. However, there remains a strong link between Korean proficiency and Korean media exposure and Korean literacy practices. The findings in this section provide concrete evidence that enhancing the exposure of immigrant children to media in their heritage language and encouraging their literacy practices in that language will contribute to further development of that heritage language.

Korean-Language Education at Home and in Korean-Language Schools

Of the respondents, 71.3 per cent (92 out of 129) reported that their parents taught them Korean. In an open-ended question on their parents' rationale for teaching them Korean, the majority (over 90 per cent) answered that teaching Korean helps in the formation of a Korean ethnic identity and also facilitates communication among family members; a few parents answered that teaching Korean also enhances job opportunities. The parents' rationale for not teaching Korean included "focusing on English education," "learning two languages is confusing," and "inability to teach Korean." Korean-Canadian children were mostly in agreement with their parents' rationale for Korean-language education: the mean score was 3.82 (SD=1.14) for a five-point Likert scale question (1 for *strongly disagree* and 5 for *strongly agree*) that asked how much Korean-Canadian children agree with their parents. To teach them Korean, 64 respondents reported that their parents spoke to them in Korean; 48 reported that their parents sent them to Korean-language school; 26 reported that their parents sent them to Korea; and 25 reported that their parents read to them in Korean. The low percentage of *reading in Korean* may have been due to a lack of Korean reading materials in immigrant homes. Studies on immigrant families in the United States have found that immigrant children's limited access to native-language reading materials is indeed common in various immigrant groups (McQuillan, 1998; Pucci, 1994).

An independent-samples t-test was conducted to compare the Korean proficiency for the groups of Korean youths whose parents taught and did not teach Korean. There was a significant difference in the Korean proficiency between these two groups; $t (49.20)=2.211$, $p=0.032$. The results suggest that Korean-language education in immigrant families affects Korean maintenance for 1.5- and second-generation Korean Canadians. The Korean proficiency of Korean immigrant youths whose parents teach them Korean is higher than that of Korean immigrant youths whose parents do not teach them Korean. However, the factors that are most important for Korean-language maintenance cannot be learned at this level of analysis.

Of the second-generation respondents, 54 per cent (27 out of 50) reported that they have attended Korean-language school. Additionally, 66.6 per cent (14 out of 21) 1.5-generation Korean Canadians who came to Canada before the age of eight also attended Korean-language school. The average period of attendance was three years and eight months, with an average of 1.7 days and 4.7 hours a week. Of the group, 37.5 per cent (24 out of 64) earned academic credits by taking Korean-language courses. A variety of Korean-language schools were available: 41 children attended Korean-language classes offered through the public schools, 13 through non-profit organizations, and 22 through religious organizations – twenty-one Christian churches and one Buddhist temple. A few respondents also attended Korean-language courses offered by more than one type of organization.

An independent-samples t-test was conducted to compare Korean proficiency between the groups of Korean youths who had and had not attended Korean- language schools. There was a significant difference in the Korean proficiency between the two groups: t (79.844)=2.542, p=0.013. These results suggest that Korean-language schools do have a positive impact on the Korean proficiency of 1.5- and second-generation Korean Canadians. The Korean proficiency of Korean immigrant youths who have attended Korean-language schools was higher than that of Korean immigrant youths who had not. These findings are in accordance with prior studies of the role of heritage schools in actual language maintenance. In her reviews of ethnic minority students in the United States, Tse (1998) found that heritage-language programs do have a positive impact on heritage-language maintenance through more exposure to and instruction in that language.

Attitudes and Language Proficiency

Using a five-point Likert scale with 1 representing *strongly disagree* and 5, *strongly agree*, the survey asked three categories of questions about language attitudes. There were thirteen questions for attitudes toward Korean, twelve questions for English, and two questions for bilingualism. The following table gives each question, the mean score, and the standard deviation of the responses to each question. As a whole, the results demonstrate positive attitudes toward both Korean and English. The mean score of English attitudes (4.27) was higher than that for Korean attitudes (3.78). For 1.5- and second-generation Korean Canadians, there was a strong desire to speak fluent Korean (4.53) and also English (4.50). The results – Korean (4.18) and English (4.11) – indicate that both languages are considered an important part of 1.5- and second-generation Korean-Canadian identity. They also regarded both Korean and English as beautiful languages – Korean (4.20) and English (4.01) and find pride in speaking Korean (4.16) and English (4.39). Korean Canadians do show strong support for Korean-language maintenance (the mean score for question 12 was 4.22). The results indicated the major differences between attitudes toward Korean and English in the following areas. The importance of Korean for academic success (3.28) and career (3.63) rated lower than the importance of English for academic success (4.77) and career (4.73).

Korean Canadians also rated the international status of Korean (2.95) significantly lower than that of English (4.73). The largest mean score difference was for the representativeness of each language in the Canadian media: Korean 2.50 versus English 4.76. Korean Canadians, however, do demonstrate positive attitudes toward bilingualism (questions 26 and 27).

According to the statistical analysis, the correlation between attitudes toward Korean language and Korean proficiency is strikingly stronger than the correlation between the attitudes toward English and English proficiency. Korean proficiency most strongly associates with how comfortable Korean Canadians feel when they speak Korean (Pearson correlation = .783, $p < 0.01$). This correlation is significantly higher than the correlation between English proficiency and the comfort in speaking that language (Pearson correlation = .395, $p<0.01$), still the strongest correlation between attitudes toward English and English proficiency. Viewing Korean as an important part of one's identity also strongly correlates to Korean proficiency (.555), followed by Korean pride (.510), and recognizing Korean as a beautiful language (.434).

In contrast, there is no significant correlation for Korean Canadians between English proficiency and the following measures of attitudes: regarding English as an important part of personal identity; pride in English; and regarding English as a beautiful language. Instrumental beliefs – the perceived usefulness of English for academic success and career – had a weak correlation with English proficiency. Between English-attitude measures and Korean proficiency, the comfort of speaking English appears to have a negative correlation to Korean proficiency (Pearson correlation = -.371, $p < 0.01$). English identity also appears to have a negative correlation with Korean proficiency (Pearson correlation = -.280, $p < 0.01$). In summary, these results indicate that positive attitudes toward the Korean language do affect the Korean-language proficiency of Korean Canadians. However, the correlation between English proficiency and attitudes toward English is not as significant as that for the Korean equivalents.

The correlation between language attitudes and family language use was notable. The mother's use of Korean with the first-born child positively correlated with that child's Korean- language attitudes (Pearson correlation = .402, $p < 0.01$); with the second-born (Pearson correlation = .396, $p < 0.01$); and with the third-born (Pearson correlation = .702, $p < 0.01$). The father's use of Korean with the first-born child also positively correlated with that child's Korean-language attitudes (Pearson

Table 9.3. Attitudes toward Korean, English, and Bilingualism, and the Correlation between Attitudes and Korean Proficiency

	Survey questions	M	SD	N	Corr.
Korean	1. Korean is important for academic success.	3.28	1.28	130	.321**
	2. If I speak Korean, I can get a better job.	3.63	1.19	130	.232*
	3. Korean is highly regarded internationally.	2.95	1.12	129	.221*
	4. In this country, Korean is well represented in the media (e.g., newspapers, TV, radio, etc).	2.50	1.26	130	.148
	5. Korean is a beautiful language.	4.20	1.07	130	.434**
	6. I feel comfortable when I speak Korean.	3.45	1.40	129	.783**
	7. I am proud to speak Korean.	4.16	1.16	128	.510**
	8. The Korean language is an important part of my identity.	4.18	1.16	130	.555**
	9. Children of Korean heritage should learn Korean.	3.98	1.17	130	.454**
	10. I want to speak Korean fluently.	4.53	0.89	129	.256**
	11. If I cannot speak Korean, it is shameful.	3.45	1.45	130	.236*
	12. For cultural reasons, Korean families should maintain the Korean language.	4.22	0.97	130	.355**
	13. I think that Korean will always be spoken in this country.	3.78	1.10	130	.324**
	Mean		*1.17*	*7.38*	
English	14. English is important for academic success.	4.77	0.67	132	.243**
	15. If I speak English, I can get a better job.	4.73	0.74	132	.290**
	16. English is highly regarded internationally.	4.74	0.72	132	.185*
	17. In this country, English is well represented in the media (e.g., newspapers, TV, radio, etc).	4.76	0.71	132	.147
	18. English is a beautiful language.	4.01	1.12	132	.087
	19. I feel comfortable when I speak English.	4.46	0.71	132	.395**
	20. I am proud to speak English.	4.39	0.92	132	.167
	21. The English language is an important part of my identity.	4.11	1.00	132	.135
	22. I want to speak English fluently.	4.50	0.93	130	.233*
	23. If I cannot speak English, it is shameful.	4.17	1.12	132	.027
	24. In this country, I should only speak English.	2.77	1.55	130	−.122
	25. To become Canadian, I need to speak English fluently.	3.91	1.23	131	−.049
	Mean		*0.95*	*5.41*	
Bilingualism	26. Becoming bilingual is beneficial for me.	4.55	0.84	132	.322**
	27. Learning two languages (e.g., Korean and English) confuses me.	2.70	1.45	132	−.070

Strongly disagree=1; strongly agree=5
** Correlation is significant at the 0.01 level (2-tailed).
* Correlation is significant at the 0.05 level (2-tailed).

correlation = .378, p < 0.01); with the second-born (Pearson correlation = .386, p < 0.01); and with the third-born (Pearson correlation = .564, p < 0.01). The mother's Korean-language use with children affected those children's Korean-language attitudes more than did the father's language use with the children. This difference in correlations may be due to the fact that mothers tend to spend more time with children than fathers do. Parents' Korean-language use with the third-born child was most strongly linked to the child's Korean proficiency. Further, Korean-language use among siblings has a stronger correlation with language attitudes than Korean-language use between parents and children. The first-born child's use of Korean with the second-born was highly correlated with positive Korean-language attitudes (Pearson correlation = .645, p< 0.01); and the first-born child's use of Korean with the third-born was also highly correlated with positive Korean-language attitudes (Pearson correlation = .693, p< 0.01). However, the findings do suggest that parents' Korean-language use with their spouses and with their own parents is not associated with their children's language attitudes toward Korean.

Conclusions

Applying the ecology of language approach, this study examines how societal, contact, and attitudinal factors link to the heritage-language maintenance of Korean Canadians by exploring the relationship between these factors and the language proficiency for Korean as well as English. The findings demonstrate that although Koreans are one of the most recent immigrant groups to arrive in Canada, a pattern of language shift is evident in Koreans in their language-use patterns, exposure to media, and literacy practices. The use of Korean appears to quickly diminish across generations. Even within the same generation, later-born Korean Canadians use less Korean than do earlier-born children. In other words, the intergenerational transmission of Korean across generations is failing. The domains of Korean-language use are also limited to family and relatives. Outside these domains, second-generation Korean Canadians mostly use English except in the domain of the church, where the use of English is less exclusive. Both 1.5- and second-generation Korean-Canadian exposures to media and literacy practices also indicates the dominance of English. As Korean-Canadian children progress through schooling, their exposure to Korean through the media quickly diminishes. The exposure to English in school-related literacy practices, such as textbooks and written homework, becomes the most predominant genre. In summary, "contact" factors, such as Korean-language use within family and in different domains, and exposure to Korean media and literacy practices, clearly point to a language shift from Korean to English.

These findings are disappointing, since the pattern of language shift among Koreans in Canada appears to be very similar to that of their counterparts in the United States (see Shin, 2005; Jeon, 2007, 2008), despite Canadian pro-active policies and initiatives to continue and support heritage-language instruction and maintenance. This study, however, has demonstrated an overwhelmingly strong correlation between Korean-language proficiency and Korean-language use in the family and in certain different domains, exposure to Korean media and literacy practices in Korean, and attendance at Korean-language schools. Positive attitudes toward Korean highly associate with Korean proficiency. In general, 1.5- and second-generation Korean Canadians have positive attitudes toward both English and Korean, although their positive attitudes toward English is slightly higher than toward Korean. The relationship between their attitudes toward English and English proficiency is weak, while the relationship between the attitudes toward Korean and Korean proficiency is particularly strong and convincing. This finding suggests that language attitudes do play a more significant role in the development and maintenance of heritage languages than do language attitudes in the development and maintenance of dominant languages. It also highlights the importance of attitudes toward a heritage language among its speakers when maintaining the heritage language. Korean-language use between immigrant parents and children is highly linked to positive attitudes toward that language, which clearly demonstrates the intersection between the contact and the attitudinal factors.

In order to foster heritage-language development and maintenance, immigrant parents need to speak their own heritage language with their children at home and encourage them to use that heritage language at home. It is also important to encourage and provide an environment where immigrant children can be exposed to media and literacy practices in their heritage language by acquiring reading materials in the heritage language and utilizing the Internet for access to heritage-language media. Further, promoting positive attitudes toward the heritage language and the heritage culture will foster children's heritage-language development. Of course, these efforts in immigrant homes and communities to maintain a heritage language cannot be successful without "considerable and repeated societal reinforcement" (Fishman, 1991, p. 371). However, it is impossible to maintain a heritage language if that language is not passed on to the next generation in the home.

REFERENCES

Allard, R. and Landry, R. (1994). Subjective ethnolinguistic vitality: A comparison of two measures. *International Journal of the Sociology of Language*, 108(1), 117–44.

Baergen, H. (2008). *Language losing and language keeping in Spanish-speaking families in Ontario: The mothers' perspective.* (Master's thesis). Available from ProQuest Digital Dissertations. (UMI #: AAT MR36290)

Burnaby, B. (2008). Language policy and education in Canada. In S. May & N.H. Hornberger (Eds.), *Encyclopedia of language and education (2nd ed.): Vol. 1. Language policy and political issues in education* (pp. 331–41). New York: Springer.

Canagarajah, A.S. (2008). Language shift and the family: Questions from the Sri Lankan Tamil diaspora. *Journal of Sociolinguistics*, 12(2), 1–34.

Cummins, J. (1992). Heritage language teaching in Canadian schools. *Journal of Curriculum Studies, 24*, 287–96.

———. (1996). *Negotiating identities: Education for empowerment in a diverse society.* Ontario, CA: California Association for Bilingual Education.

Duff, P. (2008). Heritage language education in Canada. In D. Brinton, O. Kagan, and S. Bauckus (Eds.), *Heritage language education: A new field emerging* (pp. 71–90). New York: Routledge.

Duff, P.A., and Li, D. (2009). Indigenous, minority, and heritage language education in Canada: Policies, contexts, and issues, *The Canadian Modern Language Review, 66*(1), 1–8.

Fishman, J.A. (1989). *Language and ethnicity in minority sociolinguistic perspective.* Clevedon, UK: Multilingual Matters.

———. (1991). *Reversing language shift.* Clevedon, UK: Multilingual Matters.

———. (Ed.). (2001). *Can threatened language be saved?: Reversing language shift, revisited: a 21st century perspective.* Clevedon, UK: Multilingual Matters.

Gibbons, J., & Ramirez, E. (2004). *Maintaining a minority language: A case study of Hispanic teenagers.* Clevedon, UK: Multilingual Matters.

Hakuta, K., and D'Andrea, D. (1992). Some properties of bilingual maintenance and loss in Mexican background high-school students. *Applied Linguistics, 13,* 72–99.

Hamers, J.F., and Blanc, M.H.A. (2000). *Bilinguality and bilingualism* (2nd ed.). Cambridge: Cambridge University Press.

Haugen, E. (1972). *The ecology of language.* Stanford: Stanford University Press.

Hong, Y.H. (2008). *Engendering migration in the transnational world: Highly skilled Korean immigrant women in the Canadian labour market.* (Doctoral dissertation). Available from ProQuest Digital Dissertations. (UMI #: AAT NR39920)

Hornberger, N. (2002). Multilingual language policies and the continua of biliteracy: An ecological approach. *Language Policy, 1,* 27–51.

Jeon, M. (2007). Language ideologies and bilingual education: A Korean-American perspective. *Language Awareness, 16*(2), 114–30.

———. (2008). Korean heritage language maintenance and language ideology. *Heritage Language Journal, 6,* 54–71.

Kim, Y. (1992). *The role of attitudes and motivation in learning a heritage language: A study of Korean language maintenance in Toronto.* (Doctoral dissertation). Available from ProQuest Digital Dissertations. (UMI #: AAT NN78824).

Krashen, S.D., Tse, L., and McQuillan, J. (Eds.). (1998). *Heritage language development.* Culver City, CA: Language Education Associates.

Kwak, M.J. (2004). *An exploration of the Korean-Canadian community in Vancouver.* Burnaby, BC: Vancouver Centre for Excellence.

Li, G. (2006). Biliteracy and trilingual practices in the home context: Case studies of Chinese-Canadian children. *Journal of Early Childhood Literacy, 6,* 355–81.

Mackey, W.F. (2001). The ecology of language shift. In A. Fill & P. Muhlhausler (Eds.), *The ecolinguistics reader: Language, ecology and environment London* (pp. 67–74). London, UK: Continuum.

McQuillan, J. (1998). The use of self-selected and free voluntary reading in heritage language programs: A review of research. In S.D. Krashen, L. Tse, and J. McQuillan (Eds.), *Heritage language development* (pp. 73–87). Culver City, CA: Language Education Association.

Mühlhäusler, P. (1996). *Linguistic ecology: Language change and linguistic imperialism in the Pacific region.* London: Routledge.

Noh, M.S. (2009*). Contextualizing ethnic/racial identity: Nationalized and gendered experiences of segmented assimilation among second-generation Korean immigrants in Canada and the United States.* (Doctoral dissertation). Available from ProQuest Digital Dissertations. (UMI #: AAT 3338459).

———. (2012). Gendered experiences of ethnic identity among second-generation Korean immigrants in Canada and the United States, chapter 11, this volume.

Park, S.M., and Sarkar, M. (2007). Parents' attitudes toward heritage language maintenance for their children and their efforts to help their children maintain the heritage language: A case study of Korean-Canadian immigrants. *Language, Culture and Curriculum, 20*(3), 223–35.

Pucci, S. (1994). Supporting Spanish language literacy: Latino children and free reading resources in the schools. *Bilingual Research Journal, 18*, 67–82.

Richard, B., and Yamada-Yamamoto, A. (1998). The linguistic experience of Japanese preschool children and their families in the U.K. *Journal of Multilingual and Multicultural Development, 19*, 142–57.

Shin, J.S. (2005). *Developing in two Languages: Korean children in America*. Clevedon, UK: Multilingual Matters.

Statistics Canada (2006). 2006 Census Canada. *Visible minority population and group reference guide* (Catalogue no. 97-562-GWE2006003). Retrieved 20 April 2010 from Statistics Canada: http://www12.statcan.gc.ca/census-recensement/2006/ref/rp-guides/visible_minority-minorites_visibles-eng.cfm20.

Subhan, S. (2007). *Heritage language maintenance among Bangladeshi immigrants in Toronto*. (Doctoral dissertation). Available from ProQuest Digital Dissertations. (UMI #: AAI3296090).

Tse, L. (1998). Affecting affect: The impact of heritage language programs on student attitudes. In S.D. Krashen, L. Tse, and J. McQuillan (Eds.), *Heritage language development* (pp. 51–72). Culver City, CA: Language Education Associates.

Tuominen, A. (1999). Who decides the home language?: A look at multilingual families. *International Journal of Sociology of Language, 140*, 59–76.

Wiley, T.G. (2001). On defining heritage languages and their speakers. In J.K. Peyton, D.A. Ranard, and S. McGinnis (Eds.), *Heritage language in America: Preserving a national resource* (pp. 29–36). McHenry, IL: Delta Systems and Center for Applied Linguistics.

Wong Fillmore, L. (1991). When learning a second language means losing the first. *Early Childhoods Research Quarterly, 6*, 323–46.

Young, R., and Tran, M. (1999). Language maintenance and shift among Vietnamese in America. *International Journal of the Sociology of Language, 140*, 77–8.

10 Ethnic Identity and Self-Concept among Korean-Canadian Youth

SAMUEL NOH, AYA KIMURA IDA, R. FRANK FALK,
NANCY B. MILLER, AND MIEA MOON

Introduction

What are the factors shaping the self-concept of minority youth? Self-concept involves cognitive and emotional images based on physical, social, and moral views of the self (Demo, 1992; Gecas, 1982; Owens, 2003). Adolescence and young adulthood represent developmental stages in which psychological distress and the incidence of most psychiatric disorders increases sharply (Gore & Aseltine, 2003; Steinberg, 1987); the psychological difficulties experienced during this period can affect health in later life (Lewinsohn et al., 2003). Developing a clear and positive view of oneself is critical for adolescents and young adults from minority groups, particularly when the group has low or underrepresented status in society (Sue et al., 1998). During adolescence and young adulthood, racial and ethnic minorities learn ethnic labels and meanings associated with the labels in wider social, cultural, and political contexts (Phinney, 1989). Through this process, they begin to define what it means to be a member of a particular ethnic group subjectively and objectively. The meanings they tie to their ethnic group membership can in turn help shape their overall self-concept (Tajfel, 1978).

The increasing arrival of new non-European immigrants and their high fertility trends are likely to maintain the rate of diversity growth in North American societies (Shields & Behrman, 2004). In 2001, about 73 per cent of immigrants to Canada were ethnic minorities, and the proportion has grown to 75 per cent in the successive five years (Statistics Canada, 2008). In 2006, there were 146,500 people of Korean origin living in Canada, constituting the seventh-largest non-European ethnic group in Canada (J. Park, chapter 2, this volume). Further, ethnic minorities represented 16 per cent of the entire Canadian population in 2006, and the proportion is expected to reach 20 per cent by 2017. Similarly, about half of the United States population will be ethnic minorities by 2050 (see Brown et al., 1999). Clearly, the future of North American society will largely depend on the economic productivity and political participation of these diversified young cohorts (Hernandez & Charney, 1998; Portes, 1996; Rumbaut, 1996; Shields & Behrman, 2004; Zhou, 1997). The increasing significance of non-European immigrants and their children to North American societies highlights the need to better understand the psychological processes of minority youth (Hernandez & Charney, 1998; Rumbaut, 1996; Zhou, 1997).

The purpose of this chapter is to investigate the roles of ethnic identity and identity as a member of the host society (i.e., Canadian identity) as potentially important resources in maintaining a positive self-concept among Korean, other ethnic minority, and white European adolescents and young adults.

Asian Adolescents and Young Adults in North American Society

Asian ethnic groups represent one of the fastest-growing segments of the North American population owing to the increasing rate of immigration from Asian countries in recent years (e.g., Schmidley, 2001). For example, the total number of Canadians of Korean origin has increased by 44 per cent since 2001 and has more than doubled since 1996 (J. Park, chapter 2, this volume). Furthermore, Asians represent over 65 per cent of all ethnic minorities in Canada (Statistics Canada, 2008) and about 17 per cent of all ethnic minorities in the United States (U.S. Census Bureau, 2000). Despite the significance of these figures, members of Asian ethnic groups are underrepresented in empirical research (Brown et al., 1999; Phinney, 1990; Porter & Washington, 1993; Williams, 2000).

Research including Asians suggests that there should be concern for their conceptions of self. Compared with blacks and Hispanics, a significantly higher number of Asian Americans exhibit negative self-images and report desires to belong to another, especially white, racial group (Phinney, 1989; Saucier et al., 2002). Asian Americans have also reported a desire to minimize their own ethnic characteristics and adapt to the dominant culture in society (Phinney, 1989). Frederick and colleagues (2007) showed that Asian-American men and women in college reported lower levels of satisfaction with their body image in contrast to their white counterparts (also see Forbes & Frederick, 2008). Other findings suggest that Korean and Japanese Americans tend to have a poorer body image compared with blacks and whites (see Porter & Washington, 1993).

Recent research, however, suggests that the formation of ethnic identity may serve to protect self-concept among Asians living in North America. In a qualitative study of Korean university students living in the United States and Canada, M.S. Noh (chapter 11, this volume) found that the formation or acceptance of Korean ethnic identity served as an effective coping mechanism against negative race-based gender stereotypes of Asian men and women.

Self-Concept

Self-concept is a product of how individuals subjectively and objectively define themselves (Callero, 2003; Falk & Miller, 1997; Gecas, 1982; Gecas & Burke, 1995; Owens, 2003). Self-concept develops in a reflective process by which individuals form cognitive and emotional images of themselves based on physical, social, and moral views of the self. Self-concept contains two dimensions: self-conceptions and self-evaluations (Demo, 1992; Gecas, 1982; Owens, 2003). Self-conceptions refer to identities or descriptive meanings that refer to the self as an object. These identities are descriptions of individuals' social positions and social roles (Gecas, 1982). Self-evaluations represent positive or negative views of the global or whole self. These two dimensions are closely tied. Evaluations of the whole self are based on descriptive self-conceptions, and these conceptions carry evaluative or emotional meanings that contribute to a positive or negative concept of the whole self.

Self-concept is perceived as a relatively stable construct across situations but can be modified over the life course based on biological, social, and psychological changes (Demo, 1992; Falk & Miller, 1997; Gecas, 1982). During adolescence and young adulthood, individuals continuously redefine their descriptions and evaluation of themselves in response to various changes, including new social roles, physical transformations, and increases in cognitive abilities (Demo, 1992). For this reason, self-concept, especially the evaluative dimension, is believed to highly influence psychological well-being during these periods (Harter, 1993; Phinney et al., 1997).

Self-conceptions or identities are often based on observable aspects of the self, while self-evaluations are a relatively hidden and subjective aspect of the self (e.g., Gecas & Burke, 1995). In other words, others may be able to speculate who one thinks one is in terms of social roles or social status, but they may not be aware of how one feels or evaluates oneself as a person. The main interest in this study is to understand how an observable aspect of self, namely, identity as a member of an ethnic group, affects the evaluative dimension of self-concept. Specifically, this study examines the relationship between two group identities: ethnic identity (self-conception as a member of an ethnic group) and Canadian identity (self-conception as a member of Canadian society), and two types of evaluative self-concept: physical and psychological evaluations of the self. In this study, psychological self-concept can be defined as one's evaluation of the overall self as a psychological being or as self-evaluations of one's psychological orientation. Similarly, physical self-concept is defined as one's evaluation of the overall self as a physical being or as self-evaluations of one's physical appearance.

Ethnic Identity and Self-Concept

Ethnic identity can be conceptualized as a description of the self as a member of an ethnic group. Callero (2003) asserts that the complete understanding of self-concept requires consideration of the historical and cultural contexts that surround the individual. A consideration of the roles of ethnic identity and host-society identity would help explicate the interdependence between social structure and self-concept.

Ethnic identity refers to a subjective sense of closeness to or acceptance of characteristics shared within a certain ethnic group (Phinney, 1989, 1990, 2003; Phinney et al., 2001a, 2001b). Empirical findings indicate that ethnic-language proficiency and ethnic peer interaction are positively related to ethnic identity (Phinney et al., 2001b). Further, ethnic identity can change and develop over time and across contexts (Phinney, 2003), and seems to be more salient for ethnic minorities compared with whites (Phinney, 1989). Porter and Washington (1993) have shown that positive attitudes and feelings toward one's ethnic group increase as one progresses through the stages of adolescence and young adulthood.

There are two dominant theories of ethnic identity and its relation to self-concept: *social identity theory* and the *ethnic identity development model* (Phinney, 2003). Social identity theory states that an individual holds multiple identities based on his or her membership in various social groups, such as those based on ethnicity, gender, race, and nationality (Hogg et al., 1995; Tajfel, 1978). People develop their ethnic identity by identifying with in-group members who share similar characteristics, and by contrasting with out-group members who are perceived to hold different characteristics (Shinnar, 2008; Stets & Burke, 2000; Stroink & Lalonde, 2009). Social identity theory suggests that a particular ethnic identity involves emotions, evaluations, and other psychological factors related to the ethnic group (Turner, 1991). Turner and colleagues (1987) explain that individuals have a tendency to evaluate their in-group characteristics more positively than their out-group characteristics. Thus, social identity is believed to have a self-enhancement function; by favouring in-group characteristics, individuals gain self-esteem or a positive self-concept based on membership in the "better group" (Porter & Washington, 1993; Stets & Burke, 2000). Moreover, individuals need a firm sense of belonging to or strong identification with the in-group to maintain a positive self-concept (Tajfel, 1978).

The *ethnic identity development model* (Phinney, 1990, 1989) is based on Erikson's (1968) theory of identity development. In the ethnic identity development model, ethnic identity develops in three stages (Phinney, 1989). First, at the unexamined ethnic identity stage, individuals do not have a particular notion of ethnicity or a sense of membership in an ethnic group. Individuals may not have had any experiences that have caused them to think about the meanings attached to their ethnicity in society. Second, at the ethnic identity exploration stage, individuals begin to think about what it means to be a member of a particular ethnic group. Individuals in this stage gain interest in their ethnicity and actively search for associated meanings. Finally, at the achieved or committed ethnic identity stage, individuals fully understand and accept the meaning of their ethnic group membership. Phinney (1990, 1989) emphasizes the importance of exploration prior to commitment to a certain ethnicity. The achievement of ethnic identity, following the accumulated exploration of the ethnic group, is believed to provide individuals with the basis of confidence in the self.

Ethnic identity measures often consist of a group-membership component based on social identity theory and a developmental component based on the ethnic identity development model (Phinney, 1990, 1992, 1999, 2003; Phinney et al., 2001b; Roberts et al., 1999). The group-membership component assesses *attachment*, or sense of belonging to an ethnic group, and *pride*, or positive attitude toward the ethnic group. The developmental component assesses *exploration*, or desire to seek more information about the ethnic group (Phinney, 1999).

Host-Society Identity and Self-Concept

The current study conceptualizes *host-society identity* as a changeable and subjectively defined sense of closeness to, or acceptance of, characteristics of the larger culture in a host society or nation (e.g., Canada). Immigrant or minority youth who grow up in a heterogeneous society may have both an ethnic identity and a national identity (Berry, 1990; Phinney, 2003; Phinney et al., 1997). In 2006, about 32 per cent of the Canadian population described their ethnicity, or part of their ethnicity, as "Canadian," with about half (43 per cent) also identifying other ethnic origins (Statistics Canada, 2008).

Ethnic and host-society identities are two separate but co-existing constructs that are particularly salient for members of ethnic minority groups (Phinney et al., 1997). Individuals may develop a host-society identity and the cultural characteristics of the dominant societal group while maintaining their ethnic identity and ethnic cultural characteristics (Berry, 1990; Phinney, 2003; Phinney & Devich-Navarro, 1997; Phinney et al., 2001a). In the process of acculturation, individuals may develop combinations of ethnic identity and host-society identity, each with varying levels of strength (LaFromboise et al., 1993; Phinney, 2003). Although host-society identity is important for psychological development and functioning, considerably less research has been conducted on host-society identity compared with ethnic identity (e.g., Mossakowski, 2003; Phinney et al., 2001a). Like ethnic identity, host-society identity possibly involves feelings of attachment, pride in host-society membership, and host-society cultural exploration.

Growing up bicultural can be challenging in North American society where assimilative adaptation is still emphasized for immigrants and ethnic minorities to attain socio-economic success (Portes, 1996). Despite the challenges associated with maintaining biculturalism, however, researchers show that bicultural identity, or the combination of strong ethnic and host-society identity, is the most advantageous status for a variety of outcomes, including greater self-esteem (Phinney et al., 1997), educational attainment (Feliciano, 2001), and a broader social network (LaFromboise et al., 1993). Bicultural individuals may feel that they are more grounded in the Canadian and ethnic community by having well-established social networks in both communities.

Hypotheses

This study has two main objectives. First, the roles of ethnic identity and Canadian identity in maintaining individuals' positive self-concept will be examined. Generally, researchers who consider ethnic identity or host-society identity as independent variables tend to disregard the specific functions of each dimension of identity on the outcome variables. In contrast, this study examines pride, attachment, and exploration as distinct dimensions of ethnic identity and Canadian identity in the analysis of their roles in global (overall), psychological, and physical self-concept. The study's hypotheses are as follows:

> **Hypothesis 1**: *Ethnic identity* is positively related to self-concept.
> **Hypothesis 1a**: *Ethnic pride* is positively related to self-concept.
> **Hypothesis 1b**: *Ethnic identity exploration* is positively related to self-concept.
> **Hypothesis 1c**: *Ethnic attachment* is positively related to self-concept.
> **Hypothesis 2**: *Canadian identity* is positively related to self-concept.
> **Hypothesis 2a**: *Canadian pride/attachment* is positively related to self-concept.
> **Hypothesis 2b**: *Canadian identity exploration* is positively related to self-concept.

The second objective of this study is to explore whether ethnic identity and Canadian identity function in the same way in maintaining overall self-concept across ethnic groups. The effect of the selected identity variables on self-concept will be compared.

> **Hypothesis 3a**: The role of ethnic identity varies for Korean Canadians, other ethnic minorities, and white Europeans.
> **Hypothesis 3b**: The role of Canadian identity varies for Koreans, other ethnic minorities, and white Europeans.

Sample and Data

The present study is a secondary analysis of data from the Growing Up

Canadian Project, a follow-up of a subsample of families in the Korean Mental Health Study (KMHS) (Noh et al., 1992; Noh & Kasper, 2003; see Noh & Avison, 1996, for details about KMHS). Out of 860 families who participated in KMHS, researchers selected 480 families, of whom 345 were traced. Another 234 families had one or more children between the ages of ten and twenty-five attending either elementary school, middle school, high school, college, or graduate/professional school full-time. A sample of 318 children from the 234 Korean immigrant families residing in Toronto were identified for the Growing Up Canadian Project. The data collection for the Growing Up Canadian Project was conducted in 1997 and 1998. Trained interviewers conducted a two-hour home interview with the children of the selected Korean immigrant families. After the interview, children were asked to nominate three non-Korean peers of the same gender and age in the same neighborhood regardless of their ethnic or immigrant status. One from each group of three nominees was contacted. A total of 267 non-Korean subjects, composed of 116 ethnic minorities and 151 white Europeans, completed the same interview. The total sample of 585 respondents includes 125 foreign-born and 460 native-born individuals (see table 10.1 for descriptive statistics).

Measurement

Self-Concept

Two aspects of overall self-concept were measured by the Student's Opinion on Self (SOS) questionnaire (Beiser, 1988). *Psychological self-concept* was measured by asking respondents to indicate how often they experienced the following feelings over the past six months: *I am pretty pleased with myself*; *I like the way I am leading my life*; *I am happy with myself*; *I am happy being the way I am*; and *I like the kind of person I am*. Responses to the five items were coded on a four-point Likert scale ranging from 1, *never*, to 4, *most of the time*. Responses were summed and standardized to compute a total score ranging from 0 to 100, with higher scores indicating more positve evaluations of the psychological self. This scale had a Cronbach's alpha of .89.

The *physical self-concept* scale consisted of five items that included two positive and three negative evaluations of the physical self. After the negative items were reverse coded, responses were summed to compute the total physical self-concept score, with higher scores indi-

Table 10.1. Descriptive Statistics of Study Variables (N=585)

Variable	Mean	SD	Coding and Distribution
Age	16.85	3.74	Age in years
Gender:			
Female gender	0.48	0.5	1 = Female (N=278; 47.5%)
			0 = Male (N=307; 52.5%)
Current School:			
Elementary School	0.18	0.38	1 = Elementary School (N=105; 17.9%)
High School	0.47	0.5	1 = High School (N=277; 47.4%)
(Reference group)			0 = College/University (N=203; 34.7%)
Ethnicity:			
Korean	0.54	0.5	1 = Korean (N=318; 54.4%)
Other Ethnic Minority	0.2	0.4	1 = Non-Korean Minority (N=116; 19.8 %)
(Reference group)			0 = European or white (N=151; 25.8%)
Nativity:			
Foreign-born (immigrant)	0.21	0.41	1 = Foreign-born (N=125; 21.4%)
(Reference group)			0 = Canadian-born (N=460; 78.6%)
Household Income	62.51	24.66	Actual dollars in $1,000 (missing = 7%)
Parental Education Level	3.21	1.2	1 = Less than high school (6.7%)
			2 = High school (26.2%)
			3 = Technical school (15.7%)
			4 = Bachelor's degree (32.0%)
			5 = Graduate degree or higher (13.7%)
			(Missing = 5.8%)
Psychological Self-Concept	60.23	17.01	5-item scale standardized to 0-100; α=.89
Physical Self-Concept	54.34	12.8	5-item scale standardized to 0-100; α=.82
Ethnic Identity	63.94	17.34	11-item scale standardized to 0-100; α=.88
Ethnic Pride	77.37	16.79	4-item scale standardized to 0-100; α=.80
Ethnic Attachment	58.27	21.39	3-item scale standardized to 0-100; α=.80
Ethnic Exploration	53.12	25.78	4-item scale standardized to 0-100; α=.81
Canadian Identity	69.5	15.39	9-item scale standardized to 0-100; α=.87
Canadian Pride/Attachment	74.89	16.06	7-item scale standardized to 0-100; α=.87
Canadian Exploration	50.6	21.87	2-item scale standardized to 0-100; α=.75

cating more positive evaluations of the physical self. The scale had a Cronbach's alpha of .82.

Ethnic Identity

Global ethnic identity was measured by fourteen items that were based on Phinney's conceptualization of ethnic identity (Phinney, 1992). Respondents were given a definition of *ethnic group* and were then asked to indicate how they felt about their own ethnic group. Responses were coded on a 4-point Likert scale from 1, *strongly agree*, to 4, *strongly disagree*. Scores were reverse coded to have higher scores represent stronger ethnic identity. Three items were dropped to achieve better internal consistency. The final global ethnic-identity scale consisted of eleven items and had a Cronbach's alpha of .88 (see table 10.1 for descriptive statistics).

Three dimensions of ethnic identity emerged in the exploratory factor analysis. The *ethnic pride* dimension was composed of four items measuring pride as a member of an ethnic group and had a Cronbach's alpha of .80. The *ethnic attachment* dimension consisted of three items measuring closeness and commitment to co-ethnic individuals, and had a Cronbach's alpha of .81. The *ethnic exploration* dimension consisted of four items measuring the behavioural and subjective desire to know more about one's ethnicity and had a Cronbach's alpha of .80. For each dimension, responses were summed and standardized to compute a total score ranging from 0 to 100.

Canadian Identity

The same items used to measure global ethnic identity were used to measure global Canadian identity, but were revised to measure how the respondent feels about being Canadian. Responses were coded on a four-point Likert scale ranging from 1, *strongly agree*, to 4, *strongly disagree*. Scores were reverse coded, summed, and standardized to compute a total score. This scale had a Cronbach's alpha of .87 (see table 10.1). An exploratory factor analysis showed two dimensions of Canadian identity: Canadian pride/attachment and Canadian identity exploration.

Canadian pride/attachment comprised seven items assessing closeness to and pride as a member of Canadian society, and had a reliability coefficient of .87. *Canadian identity exploration* consisted of two items assessing the behavioural and subjective desire to know more about Canadian society, and had a reliability coefficient of .75. All scores were summed and standardized to compute a total score ranging from 0 to 100.

Demographic Variables

Ethnic minority status was measured using dummy variables: Korean Ethnicity (Yes=1), Non-Korean Ethnic Minorities (Yes=1), and Whites/ Europeans (reference category). The effects of gender, developmental stage, age, nativity status, household income, and parental education were controlled in all regression models (see table 10.1 for the detailed coding).

Findings

Hypotheses 1 and 2: Ethnic Identity and Self-Concept

Multivariate regressions were conducted for psychological self-concept and physical self-concept. In each model, four ethnic identity variables (*global ethnic identity, ethnic pride, ethnic attachment,* and *ethnic exploration*) and three Canadian identity variables (*global Canadian identity, Canadian pride/attachment,* and *Canadian identity exploration*) were included. Each model also included demographic variables to estimate the effects of ethnic and Canadian identities when controlling for the effects of demographic characteristics. Results are presented in table 10.2.

In Model I (table 10.2), global ethnic identity and global Canadian identity were entered as independent variables in addition to the demographic variables. Results showed that only global Canadian identity had a significant positive impact on psychological self-concept, suggesting that Canadian identity (β = .240, p <.001) is more important than ethnic identity (β = .073, ns) for psychological self-concept when only global measures are considered.

In order to examine the specific roles of the identity dimensions, Model II examines dimensions of ethnic identity (ethnic pride, ethnic attachment, ethnic exploration), and Canadian identity (pride/attachment, exploration). Both ethnic pride and Canadian pride/attachment were significantly and positively related to psychological self-concept. Model III contained only the two variables that were significant in the second model. The purpose of running the third model was to compare the relative impact of ethnic pride and Canadian pride/attachment. The results indicated that both ethnic pride and Canadian-society pride/attachment remained statistically significant and had positive effects, although the effect of Canadian pride/attachment (β = .256, p < .001) was relatively larger than that of ethnic pride (β = .147, p < .01). Household income was the only significant demographic variable in all the psychological self-concept models.

In the right panel of table 10.2, the same models were replicated for physical self-concept. Overall, the results of the physical self-concept models were almost identical to the results of the psychological self-concept models.

Table 10.2. Regression Models of Self-Concepts

	Psychological Self-Concept						Physical Self-Concept					
	Model I: Effect of Global Identity		Model II: Effect of Dimensions		Model III: Effect of Pride		Model IV: Effect of Global Identity		Model V: Effect of Dimensions		Model VI: Effect of Pride	
Independent Variables	b (SE)	Beta	b (SE)	Beta	b (SE)	Beta	b (SE)	Beta	b (SE)	Beta	b (SE)	Beta
Ethnic Identity												
Total Scale	.073 (-.045)	.073					.050 (-.034)	.066				
Pride			.200** (-.058)	.197	.147** (-.044)	.145			.195*** (-.044)	.253	.125*** (-.034)	.162
Attachment			-.013 (-.039)	-.020					-.057 (-.029)	-.112		
Exploration			-.072 (-.047)	-.090					-.038 (-.036)	-.061		
Canadian Identity												
Total Scale	.268*** (-.053)	.240						.233				
Pride/Attachment			.221*** (-.057)	.207	.256*** (-.050)	.240			.167*** (-.043)	.205	.191*** (-.038)	.235
Exploration			.058 (-.043)	.074					.029 (-.032)	.049		
Intercept	30.793		22.060		23.229		25.939		17.826		19.189	
R²	.086		.102		.104		.080		.112		.107	

Note: The effects of all demographic variables (age, sex, nativity, ethnic minority status, developmental phase, household income, and parental education) are controlled in all models shown above. * p < .05, ** p < .01, *** p < .001.

The first set of hypotheses predicted that global ethnic identity and each of its dimensions would be positively related to self-concept. Contrary to Hypothesis 1, the results did not show a significant association between global ethnic identity and psychological or physical self-concept, controlling for demographic variables and global Canadian identity. Consistent with Hypothesis 1a, the association between ethnic pride and both physical and psychological self-concept remained significant and positive throughout the analyses. However, contrary to Hypothesis 1b and 1c, ethnic attachment and ethnic exploration did not show a significant association with psychological or physical self-concept.

The second set of hypotheses predicted that global Canadian identity and each of its dimensions would increase psychological and physical self-concept. Consistent with Hypothesis 2, global Canadian identity had a significant positive effect on both psychological and physical self-concept. Similarly, and consistent with Hypothesis 2a, Canadian pride/attachment remained statistically significant and positive throughout the analyses of both physical and psychological self-concept. However, contrary to Hypothesis 2b, Canadian identity exploration did not show a statistically significant impact on either psychological or physical self-concept.

Hypotheses 3a and 3b: Ethnicity, Identity, and Self-Concept

Data shown in table 10.3 present the results of analyses in three samples – Korean, other (non-Korean) ethnic minorities, and whites. Results revealed that Canadian pride/attachment had a significant impact on psychological and physical self-concept for all samples. On the other hand, ethnic pride was significantly associated with psychological and physical self-concept among only Koreans and non-Korean ethnic minorities. Ethnic pride was not relevant for psychological and physical self-concept among white respondents. However, statistical tests of cross-sample differences of coefficients suggested no significant differences. Thus, our data did not seem to support hypotheses 3a and 3b.

Subsequent analyses revealed that ethnic status significantly moderated the effect of gender on psychological self-concept (Korean versus whites, $p < .05$). While being a Korean female was associated with slightly higher psychological self-concept compared with being a Korean male, being a white female was associated with lower psychological self-concept compared with being a white male. Additionally,

Table 10.3. Regression Models of Psychological and Physical Self-Concepts for Subsamples of Korean, Other Ethnic Minorities, and White Europeans

	Subsample					
	Korean b (SE)	Beta	Non-Korean Minority b (SE)	Beta	White European b (SE)	Beta
Predictors	Dependent Variable: Psychological Self-Concept					
Ethnic Pride	.183** (−.062)	.175	.213* (−.087)	.230	.043 (−.102)	.043
Canadian Pride/Attachment	.192** (−.067)	.174	.294** (−.101)	.281	.373** (−.128)	.311
Constant	15.743		19.044		27.471	
Adjusted R²	(.075)		(.114)		(.136)	
Predictors	Dependent Variable: Physical Self-Concept					
Ethnic Pride	.110* (−.051)	.130	.173** (−.065)	.246	.092 (−.062)	.145
Canadian Pride/Attachment	.150** (−.055)	.168	.195* (−.075)	.245	.275** (−.078)	.304
Constant	25.504		−.738		23.870	
Adjusted R²	(.047)		(.160)		(.199)	

Note: The effects of all demographic variables (age, sex, nativity, ethnic minority status, developmental phase, household income, and parental education) are controlled in all models shown above. Also, * p < .05, ** p < .01, *** p < .001.

the results indicated that ethnic status moderates the effect of nativity (or immigration) status on psychological self-concept among Korean vs non-Korean ethnic minorities (p < .01). While being a foreign-born Korean was associated with lower psychological self-concept compared with being a Canadian-born Korean, among other ethnic minorities, being foreign-born was related to higher psychological self-concept compared with being Canadian-born.

Discussions and Conclusions

Results of this study highlight the salience of ethnic identity and Canadian identity for self-concept. Both ethnic identity and Canadian identity were positively related to psychological and physical self-concept. This finding is consistent with social identity theory and the ethnic identity development model, as well as the findings and suggestions of empirical and theoretical studies (Phinney et al., 1997; Porter & Washington, 1993).

Although global measures of Canadian identity showed the expected positive relationship with self-concept measures, this study demonstrated the importance of examining subdimensions of ethnic identity and Canadian identity. Results were clear in supporting the critical role of ethnic and Canadian pride in maintaining a positive self-concept, as both were positively and significantly associated with psychological and physical self-concept. This finding is inconsistent with a study that had found no relationship between ethnic pride and self-esteem (Valk, 2000). This inconsistency may be due to the use of different measures or different ethnic groups in each study, but further investigations into the pride aspect of identity are needed.

Contrary to the importance of pride, four other factors – ethnic attachment, ethnic exploration, and Canadian identity exploration – were not related to self-concept measures. This finding does not necessarily diminish the importance of measuring the attachment and exploration dimensions of ethnic and Canadian identity. It is possible that these dimensions are indirectly related to self-concept and other important psychological outcomes. An analysis of longitudinal data could explicate the assumptions in this study, which relied on cross-sectional data.

Based on the evidence that ethnic pride and Canadian pride/attachment were the most powerful factors of psychological and physical self-concept, these identity dimensions were used in the subsample analyses. Results from the subsample analyses did not support the hypotheses that there is a statistically significant difference in the effective role of group identities. However, the subsample analyses yielded interesting findings in regard to ethnic status.

Across ethnicity, results indicated significant effects of Canadian pride/attachment on both psychological and physical self-concept. However, ethnic pride had a significant effect for only visible minorities (Korean and non-Korean). It is possible that white Europeans may not have a strong sense of being ethnic persons in Canada, and being Canadian may be more salient to their identity. Thus, for white European Canadians, Canadian pride/attachment may have more important consequences for self-concept. Considering the finding that both ethnic pride and Canadian pride/attachment are significant factors of self-concept among ethnic minority adolescents and young adults, a bicultural identity may provide ethnic minorities with greater psychological and physical self-concept. However, biculturalism may not be as relevant to the self-concept among white adolescents and young adults.

Implications for Koreans in Canada

Ethnic pride and Canadian pride/attachment functioned differently for Koreans and non-Korean minorities. Among Koreans, ethnic pride was more important for the psychological self-concept, but Canadian pride/attachment was more influential in maintaining the physical self-concept. However, among non-Korean minorities, the opposite pattern was found; that is, Canadian pride/attachment was more important for the psychological self-concept, while ethnic pride was more influential for the physical self-concept. Future studies should consider investigating the potential differences in the functions of ethnic identity and Canadian or host-society identity across ethnic groups.

The amount of explained variance in both psychological and physical self-concept for Korean ethnicity was smaller compared with that of the other two groups considered in this study. Future studies could explore the ethnicity-specific factors that may explain Koreans' self-concept.

Although neither gender nor nativity (or immigration) status had direct relationships with self-concept, the subgroup analyses showed a significant interaction effect between ethnic groups and these two demographic variables on psychological self-concept. Because being a Korean female was associated with slightly higher psychological self-concept compared with being Korean male, and being a European/white female was associated with lower psychological self-concept compared with being a European/white male, Korean males and European females may be more likely to struggle in maintaining a positive perception of the self as a psychological being. Despite having minority status in both gender and ethnicity, Korean females were able to maintain a positive psychological self-concept. Furthermore, while being a foreign-born Korean was associated with lower psychological self-concept compared with being a Canadian-born Korean, being a foreign-born, non-Korean minority was related to higher self-concept compared with being a Canadian-born, non-Korean minority. This finding suggests that the impact of nativity status on psychological self-concept can vary by ethnicity. Future studies would benefit from careful examination of the various structural, contextual, and individual factors that may explain these differences across ethnicity, nativity status, and gender (for example, see Shields & Behrman, 2004).

It is important to interpret the results with caution. First, the direction of effect cannot be determined since this study employed cross-sectional data. Longitudinal data can help clarify how self-concept develops over time in relation to ethnic identity and Canadian or host-society identity. Second, the data were collected in the metropolitan area of Toronto, Canada, and therefore the generalizability of the findings is limited. Finally, the variance accounted for by the variables included in the analyses was small across all models, which may indicate that other important factors of self-concept were not included in the analyses. For example, Phinney and colleagues (1997) found that grade point average was an important factor related to self-esteem among adolescents. Despite these limitations, the findings of this study emphasize the importance of including measures of both ethnic identity and Canadian identity in the investigation of self-concept among Korean Canadians and other ethnic minorities living in Canada. Ethnic pride and Canadian pride/attachment were shown as consistently important resources in the maintenance of a positive self-concept, supporting Phinney's (1997) notion that it is not membership per se but rather the subjective sense of belonging and pride as a member of an ethnic group or host society that influence one's self-concept.

REFERENCES

Beiser, M. (1988). Influences of time, ethnicity, and attachment on depression in Southeast Asian refugees. *American Journal of Psychiatry, 145,* 46–51.

Berry, J. (1990). Psychology of acculturation. In J. Berman (Ed.), *Nebraska symposium on motivation* (pp. 201–34). Lincoln: University of Nebraska Press.

Brown, T.N., Sellers, S.L., Brown, K.T., and Jackson, J.S. (1999). Race, ethnicity, and culture in the sociology of mental health. In C.S. Aneshensel and J.C. Phelan (Eds.), *Handbook of the sociology of mental health* (pp. 167–82). New York: Kluwer Academic/Plenum Publishers.

Callero, P.L. (2003). The sociology of the self. *Annual Review of Sociology, 29,* 115–33.

Demo, D.H. (1992). The self-concept over time: Research issues and directions. *Annual Review of Sociology, 18,* 303–26.

Erikson, E.H. (1968). *Identity: Youth and crisis.* New York: Norton.

Falk, R.F., and Miller, N.B. (1997). The reflexive self: A sociological perspective. *Roeper Review, 20*(3), 150–3.

Feliciano, C. (2001). The benefits of biculturalism: Exposure to immigrant culture and dropping out of school among Asian and Latino youths. *Social Science Quarterly, 82,* 865–79.

Forbes, G.B., and Frederick, D.A. (2008). The UCLA body project II: Breast and body dissatisfaction among African, Asian, European, and Hispanic American college women. *Sex Roles, 58*(7–8), 449–57.

Frederick, D.A., Forbes, G.B., Grigorian, K.E., and Jarcho, J.M. (2007). The UCLA body project I: Gender and ethnic differences in self-objectification and body satisfaction among 2,206 undergraduates. *Sex Roles, 57*(5–6), 317–27.

Gecas, V. (1982). The self-concept. *Annual Review of Sociology, 8*, 1–33.

Gecas, V., & Burke, P.J. (1995). Self and identity. In K.S. Cook, G.A. Fine, and J.S. House (Eds.), *Sociological perspectives on social psychology* (pp. 41–67). Boston: Allyn and Bacon.

Gore, S., and Aseltine, R.H. (2003). Race and ethnic differences in depressive mood following the transition from high school. *Journal of Health and Social Behavior, 44*, 370–89.

Harter, S. (1993). Causes and consequences of low self-esteem in children and adolescents. In R. Baumeister (Ed.), *Self-esteem: The puzzle of low self-regard* (pp. 87–116). New York: Plenum Press.

Hernandez, D.J., and Charney, E. (1998). *From generation to generation: The health and well-being of children in immigrant families.* Washington, DC: National Academy Press.

Hogg, M.A., Terry, D.J., and White, K.M. (1995). A tale of two theories: A critical comparison of identity theory with social identity theory. *Social Psychology Quarterly, 58*, 195–211.

LaFromboise, T., Coleman, H.L.K., and Gerton, J. (1993). Psychological impact of biculturalism: Evidence and theory. *Psychological Bulletin, 114*, 395–412.

Lewinsohn, P.M., Rohde, P., and Seeley, J.R. (2003). Psychosocial functioning of young adults who have experienced and recovered from major depressive disorder during adolescence. *Journal of Abnormal Psychology, 3*, 353–63.

Mossakowski, K. (2003). Coping with perceived discrimination: Does ethnic identity protect mental health? *Journal of Health and Social Behavior, 44*, 318–31.

Noh, M.S. (2012). Gendered experiences of ethnic identity among early-adult second-generation Korean-Canadian and Korean-American immigrants, chapter 11, this volume.

Noh, S., and Avison, W.R. (1996). Asian immigrants and the stress process: A study of Koreans in Canada. *Journal of Health and Social Behavior, 37*, 192–206.

Noh, S., Avison, W.R., and Kasper, V. (1992). Depressive symptoms among Korean immigrants: Assessment of a translation of the center for epidemiologic studies depression scale. *Cross Cultural Research, 2*, 335–51.

Noh, S., and Kasper, V. (2003). Perceived discrimination and depression: Moderating effects of coping, acculturation, and ethnic support. *American Journal of Public Health, 93*, 232–8.

Owens, T.J. (2003). Self and identity. In J. Delamater (Ed.), *Handbook of social psychology* (pp. 205–32). New York: Kluwer Academic/Plenum Publishers.

Park, J. (2012) Demographic profile of Koreans in Canada, chapter 2, this volume.

Phinney, J.S. (1989). Stages of ethnic identity development in minority group adolescents. *Journal of Early Adolescents, 9,* 34–49.

———. (1990). Ethnic identity in adolescents and adults: Review of research. *Psychological Bulletin, 108,* 499–514.

———. (1992). The multigroup ethnic identity measure: A new scale for use with diverse groups. *Journal of Adolescence Research, 7,* 156–76.

———. (1999). The structure of ethnic identity of young adolescents from diverse ethnocultural groups. *Journal of Early Adolescence, 19,* 301–22.

———. (2003). Ethnic identity and acculturation. In K.M. Chun, P.B. Organista, and G. Martin (Eds.), *Acculturation: Advances in theory, measurement, and applied research* (pp. 63–81). Washington, DC: American Psychological Association.

Phinney, J.S., Cantu, C.L., and Kurtz, D.A. (1997). Ethnic and American identity as predictor of self-esteem among African American, Latino, and white adolescents. *Journal of Youth and Adolescents, 26*(2), 165–85.

Phinney, J.S., and Devich-Navarro, M. (1997). Variations in bicultural identification among African American and Mexican American adolescents. *Journal of Research on Adolescence, 7,* 3–32.

Phinney, J.S., Horencyzyk, G., Liebkind, K., and Vedder, P. (2001a). Ethnic identity, immigration, and well-being: An interactional perspective. *Journal of Social Issues, 57,* 493–510.

Phinney, J.S, Romero, I., Nava, M., and Huang, D. (2001b). The role of language, parents, and peers in ethnic identity among adolescents in immigrant families. *Journal of Youth and Adolescents, 30,* 135–53.

Porter, J.R., and Washington, R.E. (1993). Minority identity and self-esteem. *Annual Review of Sociology, 19,* 139–61.

Portes, A. (Ed.). (1996). *The new second generation.* New York: Russell Sage Foundation.

Roberts, R.E., Phinney, J.S., Masse, L.C., Chen, Y.R., Roberts, C.R., and Romero, A. (1999). The structure of ethnic identity of youth adolescents from diverse ethnocultural groups. *Journal of Early Adolescence, 19,* 301–22.

Rumbaut, R.G. (1996). The crucible within: Ethnic identity, self-esteem, and segmented assimilation among children of immigrants. In A. Portes (Ed.), *The new second generation* (pp. 119–70). New York: The Russell Sage Foundation.

Saucier, J.F., Sylvestre, R., Doucet, H., Lambert, J., Frappier, J.Y., Charbonneau, L., and Malus, M. (2002). Cultural identity and adaptation to adolescence in Montreal. In F. Azima and J. Cramer (Eds.), *Immigrant and refugee children and their families: Clinical research and training issues* (pp. 133–534). Madison, CN: International Universities Press.

Schmidley, A.D. (2001). Profile of the foreign-born population in the U.S.: 2000. *The U.S. Census Bureau Current Population Report* (pp. 23–206). Washington, DC: U.S. Government Printing Office.

Shields, M.K., and Behrman, R.E. (2004). Children of immigrant families: Analysis and recommendations. *The Future of Children, 14*(2), 4–15.

Shinnar, R.S. (2008). Coping with negative social identity: The case of Mexican immigrants. *The Journal of Social Psychology, 148*(5), 553–75.

Statistics Canada. (2008). *Canada's ethnocultural mosaic, 2006 census.* Ottawa: Ministry of Industry.

Steinberg, L. (1987). Impact of puberty on family relations: Effects of pubertal status and pubertal timing. *Developmental Psychology, 23,* 451–60.

Stets, J.E., and Burke, P. (2000). Identity theory and social identity theory. *Social Psychology Quarterly, 63*(3), 224–37.

Stroink, M.L., and Lalonde, R.N. (2009). Bicultural identity conflict in second-generation Asian Canadians. *The Journal of Social Psychology, 149*(1), 44–65.

Sue, D., Mak, W.S., and Sue, D.W. (1998). Ethnic identity. In L.C. Lee and N.W.S. Zane (Eds.), *Handbook of Asian American psychology* (pp. 289–324). Thousand Oaks, CA: Sage.

Tajfel, H. (1978). *The social psychology of minorities.* New York: Minority Rights Group.

Turner, J.C. (1991). *Social influence.* Pacific Grove, CA: Brooks/Cole Publishing.

Turner, J.C., Hogg, M.A., Oakes, P.J., Reicher, S.D., and Wetherall, M.S. (1987). *Rediscovering the social group: A self-categorization theory.* Oxford: Basil Blackwell.

U.S. Census Bureau. (2000). *Statistical abstract of the United States.* Washington, DC: U.S. Government Printing Office.

Valk, A. (2000). Ethnic identity, ethnic attitudes, self-esteem, and esteem toward others among Estonian and Russian adolescents. *Journal of Adolescent Research, 15,* 637–51.

Williams, D.R. (2000). Race, stress, and mental health. In C.J.R. Hogue, M.A. Hargraves, and K.S. Collins (Eds.), *Minority health in America* (pp. 209–43). Baltimore: The Johns Hopkins University Press.

Zhou, M. (1997). Growing up American: The challenge confronting immigrant children and children of immigrants. *Annual Review of Sociology, 23,* 63–95.

11 Gendered Experiences of Ethnic Identity among Second-Generation Korean Immigrants in Canada and the United States

MARIANNE S. NOH

Introduction

During the 1970s, social psychologists and micro-sociologists dominated identity research and generally defined identity as group membership, sameness, and an individual's identification with a social status, classification, or category (Marshall, 1994). Mead and Cooley theorized identity as static, stable, and as a core, objective sense of self (Cerulo, 1997). Indeed, such perceptions of identity swept and dominated social scientific investigations concerning the nature of self, self-identity, and individual subjectivity. Furthermore, the positivist notion of empirically measuring the intricate complexities of identity with simplistic instruments such as ethnic identity scales were developed, widely used, and quickly credited as comprehensive assessments of individual ethnic identity (see Phinney, 1992, for a leading ethnic identity measurement scale). The use of the term *identity* in this way, however, is currently considered problematic: *identity* is applied loosely, with the assumption that there is a universal understanding of what it is without specific or precise definition, and it has been widely criticized as essentialist (Cerulo, 1997).

Alternatively, contemporary understandings of identity constructs focus on the subjectivity, complexity, fluidity, and the situational aspects of forming identity. Individuals at different times and in a variety of settings report different degrees of ethnic attachment, practices, and pride (Bulmer & Solomos, 1998; Hall, 1999; Solomos & Back, 1995; Thorne et al., 2003). The social constructionist perspective frames ethnic identity as in a constant state of change, never quite reaching a stable or concluding state of identification (Cerulo, 1997). These changing states consist of varying degrees of feeling "ethnic" or "mainstream" in various situations. For visible minority immigrants, the inability to fully integrate into the American or Canadian mainstream, despite having been exposed to the dominant culture throughout their development (e.g., in school), creates inconsistent and dissonant senses of belonging and self-concept. Although born Korean, the respondents in this study were not born and raised solely according to Korean cultural practices in a Korean society. As such, second-generation Koreans, as is the case for second-generation immigrants in general, must personally resolve conflicting cultural norms and values, as well as demeaning stereotypes in both dominant and subordinate cultural settings.

As there is a large and growing Korean population in both the United States and Canada, it is important to examine the integration outcomes for the later generations of immigrants. The number of Korean immigrants in both the United States and Canada is steadily growing. Currently, Korean immigrants are one of the largest Asian groups in both countries. There were about 100,000 Korean Canadians and just over one million Korean Americans in 2000 (Statistics Canada, 2005; Reeves & Bennett, 2004). Furthermore, approximately one-third of all Asian-American immigrants were second generation in 2004. Koreans represent the fourth-largest Asian-American group, after the Chinese, Filipino, and Vietnamese, and represent the third-largest Asian-Canadian group, after the Chinese and Filipino.

The American and Canadian governments share a history of discrimination against Asians by exclusion through immigration rights (Bloemraad, 2006; Omi & Winant, 1994). Particular examples are the Asian exclusion acts, Japanese internment, and immigration systems that favour white Europeans. However, stereotypes of Asians, such as those portraying them as model minorities, hide this form of discrimination by implying successful integration into mainstream society. It is important to investigate how constructed notions of Asians living in North America affect second-generation Koreans who experience discrimination and exclusion based on their race and ethnicity on a daily basis (Korean Canadian Women's Anthology, 2007; Nam, 2001).

Extending previous studies of Korean Americans by investigating both Korean-American and Korean-Canadian experiences would be valuable. It is uncertain what role diaspora plays in the process of identity formation for American and Canadian immigrants (Reitz & Breton, 1994; Bloemraad, 2006). While Korean immigrants in the United States and Canada share characteristics in their home countries (White et al., 2003), their host societies currently hold different immigration policies and policies of tolerance and assimilation. Since pre-immigration characteristics are comparable, the differences in identity formation among second-generation American and Canadian immigrants may be attributable to the recent structure of their host societies. This study questions whether Eurocentric notions of Asians, ranging from the exotic to the "honorary" white and to the sexual deviant, will be interpreted the same way by second gens.[1]

The interaction of gender with ethnic identity is also important to examine. Men and women are found to experience ethnic identity formation differently owing to interacting gender and racial/ethnic norms and roles. A person's interpretation of his or her own ethnic or cultural experiences is highly influenced by his or her perceptions of gender norms, roles, and stereotypes. For ethnic and racial minorities, the formation of identity significantly involves the act of resolving degrading racialized gender stereotypes (Cho, 1997; Toro-Morn & Alicea, 2003). For example, dominant views of Asians as quiet and obedient are transferred to gender stereotypes of Asian men and women. Asian men are stereotyped as emasculate, weak, and physically less endowed compared with the "average" male. Furthermore, Asian women are depicted as hyperfeminine – anti-feminist, and sexually and domestically subservient to men. Furthermore, Asian men and women in North America, such as second gens, are frequently confronted with the challenge to resolve clashes between their family experiences and the degrading perceptions of their ethnic and gender statuses.

Background

The current literature on the social construction of ethnic identity finds that a "gendering of ethnicity" is also being produced (Espiritu, 1997, p. 88). For Asian-American men and women, there are stereotypes that both feminize and masculinize their Asian ethnicity. Asian-American men and women, contrary to the feminizing racialized gender stere-

---

1 During interviews and discussions with the respondents of this study, it was discovered that second-generation Korean immigrants referred to themselves as "second gen," both in Canada and the United States. I have adapted this term to refer to the respondents of this study and second-generation Korean immigrants in general.

otypes, are also portrayed as the Yellow Peril, threatening the occupations and civilizations of white male society. These opposing sexualized stereotypes are said to be used to maintain white male domination and subjugate Asians living in North America (Espiritu, 1997).

In-depth analyses of immigrant life have allowed for the examination of gendered experiences. For example, among Dominicans, West Indians, and Haitians in the United States, demeaning racialized gender stereotypes have been found to play a role in the functioning of their employment, albeit differently for men and women (Lopez, 2003). Caribbean men perceived a barrier in attaining employment while women were finding jobs but perceived little mobility in their positions. In other studies, Asian-American immigrant parents have been found to give their daughters more responsibility to maintain and practice ethnic traditions and values (Barajas & Pierce, 2001; Kurien, 2003). Unlike sons, daughters were taught that their responsibility to the family was to uphold and pass on the traditions of family practices.

Structurally, images of Asians further belittlement with stereotypes of physical or biological deficiencies. Kaw's (1993) analysis of medical documents, research articles, and interviews with physicians revealed how Asian physical features were *medicalized*, or constructed as features deviating from normative physical appearance and functioning.[2] In this way, the physical features of Asians were used to construct a racial "Other," justified and rationalized by a scientific and institutionalized discourse of fact and logic. Although the effects of medicalizing physical Asian features on identity formation have not yet been documented, there is evidence that Asian Americans struggle with body image ideals of "whiteness" (Kaw, 1993; Mckee, 2001). Furthermore, Cho's (1997) critical analysis of racialized sexual harassment emphasizes the "surgency" of race and gender subjugating Asian women in school and workplaces. Racialized gender stereotypes were used to harass Asian-American women in their everyday lives. Cho's article also indicated that there were negative material outcomes for receivers of racialized gender stereotypes.

A number of studies examine Asian-American women's experi-

---

2 See also Schur (1984) for discussions on the normalization and stigmatization of physical appearance. In Kaw's 1993 study, stereotyped Asian eyes, in the medical field, were documented as preventing Asians from socially and economically integrating into U.S. society.

ences and accounts of gendered ethnicity (Cho, 1997; Espiritu, 2003; Gibson, 1988; Lee, 2007; Williams, Alverez, & Andrade Hauck 2002; Zhou & Bankston, 1996). Pyke (2004) spoke with Korean-American and Vietnamese-American women about their views on Asian and white masculinities. It appeared that Asian women internalized racialized gender stereotypes of masculinity, which characterized Asian men (especially Korean men) as sexist, angry, and overbearing. White men, in turn, were idealized as "angelic liberators" with egalitarian, caring, and sensitive characteristics. In groups, Pyke's respondents repeatedly presented Asian men and white men as opposites. Although there are Asian men who embody liberating qualities and white men who are sexist, angry, and overbearing, such reality is obliterated by the use of racialized gender stereotypes. Although this and other studies that include interviews with Asian women provide useful insights into the internalization of racialized gender stereotypes and identity formation, how Asian men internalize and resolve demeaning stereotypical messages is examined to a lesser degree.

Some studies examine Asian males' experiences and accounts of gendered ethnicity (Barajas & Pierce, 2001; Kurien, 1999; Lopez, 2003; Maira, 2002). In Qin and colleagues' (2008) study, Chinese-American school-age males face the challenge of having to resolve conflicting notions of masculinity. A Chinese idiom "strong limbs, simple minds" is issued to contradict Western views of masculinity, which values athleticism and physical strength. The Chinese-American youths needed to create balance between their ethnic cultural values and the values upheld and practiced in their school culture. These conflicting masculinities served as sources of distress for young Chinese-American males, as their stereotyped smaller stature and physical weakness constantly attracted bullying victimization.

The purpose of this study is to develop a social-constructionist understanding of identity using the example of second-generation Korean immigrants in Canada and the United States. There are numerous factors involved in identity formation; however, this study pays particular attention to the fluidity and complexity of ethnic identity in national and gendered contexts. Ethnicity, gender, and nationality are significant status elements in constructing one's identity largely because they are experienced as ascribed statuses. These are the statuses that individuals feel they are born with and that are in their blood oftentimes (Kibria, 2002).

Methods

In February 2008, I interviewed thirty-one second-generation Korean-American and Korean-Canadian undergraduates from two large universities, one in southern Ontario, Canada, and one in the midwestern United States. Both campuses are located in university towns. The schools are also similar in national prestige, with rankings in the top 10 per cent for overall public undergraduate programs.[3] I recruited participants through Korean ethnic student organizations, with mostly second-generation immigrant members. Each participant engaged in an in-depth, face-to-face semi-structured interview, which lasted for an average of one and a half hours. The participants were asked to talk about their lived experiences in childhood, adolescence, and young adulthood while focusing on family, peer, school, and work settings. The interview questions primarily inquired into personal views and experiences of the meaning of race, ethnicity, gender, and nationality.

The Sample

All except three of the American respondents were originally from outside the university town. Most grew up in cities with high concentrations of Korean Americans, such as New York City and Chicago. The Canadian respondents were also likely to have come in from other cities and provinces. Most of the Canadian participants grew up in central or southwestern Ontario. More American respondents, compared with the Canadians, had parents in professional occupations with graduate degrees. Small-business ownership, however, was clearly the dominant occupation of the participants' parents.

Table 11.1 provides a summary of the respondents, which includes their pseudonyms, places of birth, ages, and study majors. Most of the informants were second generation – Canadian-born children of immigrant parents. Only one American was foreign-born and five Canadians were born outside Canada. Of the thirty-one participants, fifteen were American, with a mean age of twenty years, ranging from eighteen to twenty-six years; the mean age for the sixteen Canadian respondents was also twenty years, ranging from eighteen to twenty-three years.

---

3 The U.S. school holds a higher ranking nationally and internationally, according to *Times Higher Education* (2007).

Table 11.1. Respondent Information

American Males

Respondent	Foreign-Born	Age	Major
Benjamin	No	21	Political Science
Dennis	No	19	Engineering
Doug	South Korea	26	Business
Edwin	No		Business
Jacob	No	21	Education
Joel	No	20	Business
Scott	No	20	Psychology
Sean	No	21	Business

American Females

Respondent	Foreign-Born	Age	Major
Carrie	No	19	Psychology
Jane	No	21	Architecture
Jessica	No	18	Undecided (Sociology, Biopsychology)
Pobae	No	20	Arts
Suzy	No	20	Math, Economics
Taesuk	No	19	Undecided (Sociology, Psychology)
Yoona	No	20	International Language, Foreign Languages

Canadian Males

Respondent	Foreign-Born	Age	Major
Albert	No	22	Engineering
Bruce	No	20	Business and Management
Edan	United States	19	Business
Ethan	No	19	Science
Eugene	No	23	Biology, Physiology, Anthropology
Jack	South Korea	19	Business
Jeffrey	South Korea	18	Business
John	No	21	Economics
Josh	South Korea	18	Business
Peter	No	22	Business

Canadian Females

Respondent	Foreign-Born	Age	Major
Alison	No	21	Pre-Med
Caroline	No		Business and Management
Helen	No	20	Social Work
Hena	No	20	Physiology, Psychology
Lena	South Korea	21	International Relations
Lucy	No	20	Science

The most frequent major among the sample was business (or busi-ness and management). Both universities have highly ranked business schools, which may explain the frequency of business majors. Ten of the eighteen male respondents were majoring in business, whereas only one of the thirteen female respondents was majoring in business and management. The female informants were most commonly majoring in the social sciences, followed by basic sciences. The researcher sought referrals for non-business, engineering, and science majors through the interview process. Overall, there was a wide range of majors rep-resented in the sample, from the arts to social work to basic sciences.

Results

The Development of Racialized Gender Using Religious Narratives

In order to assess the respondents' perceptions of femininity and mas-culinity, they were asked to define what it meant to be a man or woman. Similar to Puerto Rican (Toro-Morn & Alicea, 2003), Caribbean (Waters, 1996), and other Asian ethnic second generations (Espiritu, 2003; Kur-ien, 1999), the second-generation Koreans in this sample associated masculinity and femininity with concepts that they believed originated in their ethnic communities. These concepts countered the negative and demeaning stereotypes persistent in the dominant white North Ameri-can society. They regarded their Korean ethnic values as superior to those of the mainstream and more responsible than egalitarianism.

Many respondents were Christian and viewed positively the tradi-tional notions of gender that their parents and Korean churches had "ingrained" in them, describing gender in biblical terms. This presenta-tion appeared to be a way of constructing their views as superior to the gender practices of white Americans (see also Espiritu, 2003). Alison, a Korean Canadian, suggested that traditional femininity aligned with Christian morals and was preferable and "God given." For example, women who behaved aggressively were seen as going against nature:

> I think that men and women have different characteristics that God pos-sesses and together we complement each other and are able to show the world ... are able to represent God, sort of thing. So, for women I think that women are God's way of showing his tender, more warm, kind of caring side. And something that I've always – my views on feminism and women's rights and stuff – I think it's good that women should have rights

and stuff and equal opportunities as men, but for me I don't think there's anything wrong with women staying at home with their kids. And you know there's so many people who sacrifice their education, their careers and stuff because they feel like they're called, or more comfortable, or they need to be at home for the kids to provide that support. So I don't know – I think that's like a God-given ability for women to be the caregivers, like the more nurturing aspect of humans. Even though guys – even though women can be aggressive and like that kind of thing I think their overall nature is to be, like, that warm kind of role. (twenty-one-year-old female Korean Canadian)

Scott, a Korean American, explained that a woman's role is to support her man, a position reflecting Christian tenets. He also implied that aggressiveness in women is not a desirable trait: "… man is the head but women are the neck. Not to demean men or anything, but I think behind a great man there's a great woman. You know … someone who really is able to see things that guys can't … that men can't. Who can really provide, like, a different perspective and to be gentle about it too. I think a woman really knows to work around man's pride" (twenty-year-old male Korean American).

The male respondents commonly preferred patriarchal rules and ideology over egalitarianism, especially in the home. For all the male respondents, gender norms and roles in the home were "responsible," and fitted well with the way they saw Christian doctrine regarding the place of men and women. Traditional male and female roles (i.e., male breadwinner and female homemaker) did not seem to be practiced in mainstream settings, according to these second-gen men.

"Somewhere in Between": The Development of Gendered Ethnicity through Family Experiences

Across the entire sample, Korean households were distinguished from mainstream households by the former's apparent embrace of conservative patriarchal values and gender inequality. Eugene, for example, a Korean Canadian, felt that men should be the providers and protectors, and he regarded as irresponsible women who aspire to successful careers instead of devoting themselves exclusively to their families' well-being. Not sympathetic to the egalitarianism of the broader Canadian society, Eugene saw traditional Korean gender relationships as a closer reflection of "natural" male-female differences.

The] Canadian side ... I think this side is a lot more equal, egalitarian. I think it's sometimes very irresponsible – the lack of difference between men and women ... There's a distinct difference between men and women and then you just treat them the same it just ... Like, the tall tale male-female difference, like, men being assertive and women being reserved, I think that's a universal trait. I don't know if it's genetic or if it's culture or whatever it is. Like, it hasn't even been answered in anthropology, but it's just there is a difference between the way men and women act and psychology and everything... Women are just born more emotional or more irrational. I'm not going to say irrational because that's not true but in a more, like, intuitive metaphysical sense, men are just, like, straight, direct, right? What you see is what's there. What you don't see isn't necessarily there. I guess in that way I recognize that difference that Koreans, Canadians, anyone, like, this whole world recognizes the difference ... I think a median between both choosing between Korean and the way Koreans and Canadians treat men is – they're both sort of extremes to me and I sort of choose the middle ground of that. (twenty-three-year-old male Korean Canadian)

All the respondents shared Eugene's perceptions of the ethnic differences in gender norms: masculinity was equated with taking responsibility for the family; Korean men were described as family-oriented, stoic, and reliable decision makers. Western men, on the other hand, were seen as "lazy," "selfish," and less family-oriented. The male respondents felt "somewhere in between Korean and American/Canadian" views on gender, and most of the men felt closer to the "Korean" end on the subject of affinity for patriarchy.

As well, the men seemed to experience and benefit from a privileged status in the home due to their gender. With their relatively more conservative notions of gender rooted in family roles, the male respondents saw themselves as "more Korean." Although American or Canadian social environments are not fully egalitarian, the male (and female) respondents overwhelmingly thought that members of American/Canadian families were entirely equal, even "too equal," as one respondent stated.

The second-generation men described first-generation Korean men their own age as wimpy, spoiled, uptight, and bad tempered; however, the second gens would often use their image of their fathers (older first-generation immigrants) to typify masculinity. In their families, the male respondents were given head-of-household benefits not available to their mothers and sisters. In relation to "Asian male disadvantage"

(Noh, 2008), the men felt they had more access to power, status, and privilege in Korean society and in ethnic Korean settings. Describing what it means to be a man, Benjamin, a Korean American, reflected on his father's leadership: "… in my head where, like, when they say 'man of the household' it's just truly man of household. When a man enters the room, when a husband or a father enters a room, he sets the tone. I would always remember growing up, if my dad didn't have a good day at work and he entered the house, the mood would go down, you know? It's just really important to have that leadership to make sure that your family is like in a good environment and your children and your wife are responding positively to the mood that you set" (twenty-one-year-old male Korean American).

The female respondents also maintained that patriarchal values served the family's well-being. It was often stated by the entire sample that American and Canadian women are louder and more aggressive than Korean women, who were seen positively as quiet and submissive. The male respondents felt that American/Canadian women are as capable, driven, and motivated as men to succeed in the paid labour force. Such ambition, however, was described as selfish; their mothers' sacrifice of individual interest for the family was far more highly esteemed and regarded as the respectable feminine norm.

While second-generation Korean men received privileged status and treatment in the home, second-generation Korean women experienced strict treatment by their "very traditional" parents. It appeared to me that the Korean-American women focused on the differences between mainstream and Korean notions of gender when they thought about their mothers' attitudes and behaviours. The Korean-Canadian women, however, focused more on the restrictive treatment they received from their parents due to gender inequality.

All the female respondents portrayed "Korean Korean" and older first-generation women as ultra-conservative, a major distinction from their own and North American values and attitudes. In this sense, nearly all the Korean-American women identified themselves as more American because they viewed a woman's role as extending beyond that of homemaker. However, they distinguished themselves from "American American" women, who were described as overly aggressive (a perceived masculine trait) and lacking in family values. As was the common pattern for all respondents, the Korean-American female respondents identified themselves somewhere in between North American and Korean in terms of gender conservatism and progressiveness.

Their ideal woman was one who assumed financial responsibility with an emphasis on caring for her family. In the words of Taesuk, a Korean-American woman,

> When I think of a Korean woman, the image that pops into my mind is really like a housewife. Someone who really, really attends only to family needs. And then when I think of an American woman I think of, you know, corporate America. Like a woman in a suit, taking over Wall Street …
>
> A woman can set goals for herself just as well as men. They have the freedom to be ambitious, but then I feel like they also have an obligation to really hold the family together. Whether it be the mother or even the head of the household. I feel that they have to be that strong, or the big responsibility of keeping family together and connected all the time. (nineteen-year-old female Korean American)

Unlike the Korean-American respondents, the Korean-Canadian women commonly described their parental discipline as sexist. Daughters lacked freedom and missed out on the opportunities that mainstream Canadian girls were given by their parents. For the Korean-Canadian women, growing up in a restrictive household impeded their ability to form a balance between occupational success and caring for the family, a balance that was the central concern for the Korean-American women.

Lucy, a second-generation Korean Canadian, expressed a desire for independence from men and for the freedom to experience life outside the home. The Korean-Canadian women seemed to appreciate diversity in women's roles, a departure from the traditional "Korean way." Lucy describes some variations between her attitudes and her parents': "What it means to be a woman? I guess nowadays being strong and confident about yourself is important. I guess back then, I guess in the Korean society … I don't know if it's still like this or not, even in my household, just cause my parents are traditional still and like it's almost as if females are … it's a stereotypical thing – having to stay home, cook and clean, take care of the kids or whatever. But I think nowadays it's more important to get out there and experience things for yourself and not be so dependent on a guy, I guess. So I guess being a woman is being independent, being able to do things for yourself now and not always having to rely on someone else" (twenty-year-old female Korean Canadian). At the same time, she found that she maintained some of the traditional practices of gender, which, for her, added to the difficulty of internally resolving culturally different notions of gender.

As the model of multiculturalism in Canada connotes heterogeneity in the meaning of *Canadian*, so also does the model manifest the difficulty in identifying normative gender roles. Alison is a second-generation Korean Canadian who discovered that growing up in a Korean household strongly affected her perception of the way gender and ethnicity intersect. She found partial resolution of the way gender is expressed in her dominant and minority settings through understanding Korean gender conservatism as it relates to the Asian wish to avoid shame and save face. Alison concluded that her parents' strictness upheld her honour: "I know for me growing up being the oldest [and] being a girl in a Korean household I was not given opportunities. My parents would stop me from doing things I would see my friends doing. Even sleepovers and stuff like that – they wouldn't want me to do that. I really didn't understand that when I was younger. but I feel that Korean women/girls are more sheltered or protected or something. Restricted? I think it's more like a negative kind of thing, like, we aren't given, allowed to be as free as my white friends" (twenty-one-year-old female Korean Canadian).

Although Alison's feelings about her upbringing were not fully resolved, she was beginning to see value and benefit in the "Korean parenting style," which aims to prevent daughters from becoming overly aggressive and devoid of family values. Nevertheless, the Korean-Canadian females emphasized that they did not agree with the way they had been raised and believed they were able to become responsible women without the strict parenting.

The Korean-American and Korean-Canadian female respondents held clearly opposing views on the matter of parenting daughters, as the former did not recall or mention sexist treatment by their parents. There can be multiple reasons for this difference, resulting from the two models of assimilation and identity formation: the multicultural Canadian model may be more accepting of variations in custom in comparison with the American ethnic model (Kibria, 2002), which may help to explain Korean-American parenting styles. Perhaps because the term *Canadian* is meant to be inclusive of immigrants and their cultural practices, diverse parenting styles are more tolerated than in the United States. Korean-American immigrants may also feel greater pressure to accommodate white American styles, which, compared with Korean parenting styles, do not favour corporal punishment, are less controlling, and encourage closer parent-child relationships. For example, many of the Korean-American respondents indicated that their parents eschewed the typical Korean parents' insistence on high academic achievement for their children.

For the Korean-American females, having ultra-conservative parents in a dominant society that values and encourages progressive gender norms and roles led to their own questioning of the Korean way. It appeared that the Korean-American women's parents were also more Americanized in their messages of gender than the Korean Canadians' parents. However, all the female respondents indicated that their attitude to being female was not entirely contemporary and that their more westernized ideas of gender did not impinge on their identification as Korean. Most of the women felt comfortable interacting in Korean ethnic settings, even preferring them to mainstream social settings. This finding is dissimilar to one found in Pyke and Johnson's (2003) investigation into the lives of Korean-American women.

Conclusions

The relationship between assimilation and ethnic identity formation cannot be fully understood without consideration of gender constructs in dominant and minority settings. For second gens in Canada and the United States, formations of the self reflected racialized gender stereotypes such as Asians being extremely patriarchal and white Americans and Canadians being truly egalitarian. It did not appear that concepts of the melting pot or the cultural mosaic were predominant influences on ethnic identity formation.

The conditions of gendered ethnicity employ the social constructionist model, in which one's gendered and ethnicized self-concept is fluid and circumstantial. Ethnic identity formation for men and women is experienced differently because gendered norms and roles interact with perceptions of ethnicity. Lived experiences and interpretations of others' experiences of ethnicity are influenced by perceptions of gender norms, roles, and stereotypes. For example, though the respondents' views of ethnicity are not essentially driven by their gender, their impressions are highly coloured by gendered stereotypes of Korean Americans/Canadians, Americans/Canadians, and Korean Koreans.

Study Limitations and Contributions

A limitation to using qualitative methods is the inability to generalize the findings to any larger population. The results of this study are not generalizable to the larger second-generation Korean North American population because of the small sample size and the non-random sampling methods utilized. Also owing to the small sample size, the analysis and interpretation from this study cannot provide predictive power to substantiate that the comparisons in analysis are actually due to group factor differences. However, the analysis of data for this study achieves validation through the systematic application of theoretical perspectives and themes that emerged from previous empirical investigations (Maxwell, 1996). In addition, qualitative studies can have validity to the extent that quoted interview material corresponds with the concepts discussed. The reader can make this determination to a greater extent than with quantitative research.

Given the small sample size used in this study, these findings may not represent the relationships between assimilation, gendered ethnicity, and identity formation for second-generation Koreans who are not attending high-ranking universities or pursuing a university degree. This sample also largely represents members of Korean ethnic student organizations, which could present patterns of ethnic identification dissimilar to second-generation Koreans who are non-members. Further investigation is needed to provide some answers about whether and to what extent university students differ from non-students, and members differ from non-members, as well as the larger question of representation.

Whether racial or ethnic identity formations have any significant consequential effects on the well-being of second gens cannot be identified in the scope of this study. Future investigations into this matter would provide information on the direction of identity politics for Asians in the United States and Canada. Kibria (2000), for example, suggests that Asian Americans should move toward developing a pan-Asian identity rather than adhering to disconnected Asian ethnic identities. A singular and collaborative pan-Asian identity and agenda, hypothesized by Kibria, would enhance and strengthen resources, political influence, and minority self-esteem. Because the results from this study indicate that more second-generation Korean Canadians than Korean Americans are experiencing different identity formations, cross-border comparisons may provide more empirical background for the development and direction of such race-relations agendas.

However, based on the findings in this study, it is likely that different Canadian and American standards and variables are required to enhance the acceptance and inclusion of diversity for citizens. As a consequence, a comparison between these two countries is complicated by factors such as government-level reception of immigrants and diversity. Recent variation in the countries' histories of race relations also complicates the matter in predicting and suggesting ethnic and race politics. Although their implications need further investigation, this study provides an illustration of some comparisons between American and Canadian second-generation Koreans.

This study has illustrated the importance of analysis of contextualized ethnic identity formation. Through this investigation, it has been found that the barriers to assimilation relate to the challenges in forming a complete sense of belonging for second-generation Korean Americans and Korean Canadians. More studies are needed to validate and contribute to the models of acculturation and identity formation presented in this study. The results also suggest that further investigations into the validity, impact, and consequence of internalizing stereotypes and formation of dissonant ethnic identity are needed. The findings here, however, provide substantial evidence of dissonant identity formation due to experiences of conflicting and challenging racialized gender stereotypes.

Contextualizing Ethnic Identity

For racial minorities, identity formation is heavily affected by degrading racialized gender stereotypes held by individuals of both dominant and minority groups (Cho, 1997; Espiritu, 1997; Pyke, 2004; Toro-Morn & Alicea, 2003). Dominant mainstream views of Asians as quiet and obedient are transferred to gender stereotypes of Asian men and women. Korean men in this study are stereotyped as wimpy and spoiled. Racialized gender stereotypes depict Korean women as untouched by feminism, and sexually and domestically subservient to men. Second-generation Korean men and women in the United States and Canada are constantly confronted with the challenge to resolve the clash between their family experiences and the degrading perceptions of their ethnic/racial and gender status. It may be that a "somewhere in between" Korean and American/Canadian ethnic identity is being formed.

The resulting gendered ethnicity for the second-gen men and women in this study illustrates the complexity and interacting relationship between gender and ethnicity in identity formation. Gender norms and practices are complex, and range widely from strict patriarchy to gender progressiveness in Canadian, American, and Korean families; however, stereotypes appear to be used to provide justification for the reality of ethnic, racial and gender inequalities in Canada and the United States. The reality is that racialized gender stereotypes are so well established in North American mainstream society that although they clash with lived experiences, visible minorities who have grown up in Canada or the United States cannot help but use these stereotypes in the formation of their ethnic identity.

REFERENCES

Barajas, H.L., and Pierce, J.L. (2001). The significance of race and gender in school success among Latinas and Latinos in college. *Gender & Society, 15,* 859–78.

Bloemraad, I. (2006). *Becoming a citizen: Incorporating immigrants and refugees in the United States and Canada.* Los Angeles: University of California Press.

Bulmer, M., and Solomos, J. (1998). Introduction: Re-thinking ethnic and racial studies. *Ethnic and Racial Studies, 21,* 819–37.

Cerulo, K.A. (1997). Identity construction: New issues, new directions. *Annual Review of Sociology, 23,* 385–409.

Cho, S.K. (1997). Converging stereotypes in racialized sexual harassment: Where the model minority meets Suzie Wong. In R. Delgado and J. Stefancic (Eds.), *Critical race theory: The cutting edge* (pp. 532–42). Philadelphia: Temple University Press.

Espiritu, Y.L. (1997). *Asian American women and men: Labor, laws, and love.* Thousand Oaks, CA: Sage.

———. (2003). Gender and labor in Asian immigrant families. In P. Hondagneu-Sotelo (Ed.), *Gender and U. S. immigration: Contemporary trends* (pp. 81–100). Los Angeles: University of California Press.

Gibson, M.A. (1988). *Accommodation without assimilation: Sikh immigrants in an American high school.* Ithaca, NY: Cornell University Press.

Hall, S. (1999). Old and new identities, old and new ethnicities. In S. Hall, L. Back, and J. Solomos (Eds.), *Theories in race and racism* (pp. 144–53). New York: Routledge.

Hankut: Critical art and writing by Korean Canadian Women. (2007). Toronto: Inanna Publications and Education.

Kaw, E. (1993). Medicalization of racial features: Asian American women and cosmetic surgery. *Medical Anthropology Quarterly, 7,* 74–89.

Kibria, N. (2000). Not Asian, black, or white? Reflections on South Asian American racial identity. In J.Y.S. Wu & M. Song (Eds.), *Asian American studies: A reader* (pp. 247–54). New Brunswick, NJ: Rutgers University Press.

———. (2002). *Becoming Asian American: Second-generation Chinese and Korean American identities*. Baltimore: The Johns Hopkins University Press.

Kurien, P. (1999). Gendered ethnicity: Creating a Hindu Indian identity in the United States. *American Behavioral Scientist, 42*, 648–70.

———. 2003. Gendered ethnicity: Creating a Hindu Indian identity in the United States. In P. Hondagneu-Sotelo (Ed.), *Gender and U.S. immigration: Contemporary trends* (pp. 648–70). Los Angeles: University of California Press.

Lee, S.J. (2007). The "good" news and the "bad" news: The "Americanization" of Hmong girls. In B.J. Ross Ledbeater and N. Way (Eds.), *Urban girls revisited: Building strengths* (pp. 202–217). New York: New York University Press.

Lopez, N. (2003). Disentangling race-gender work experiences: Second-generation Caribbean young adults in New York City. In P. Hondagneu-Sotelo (Ed.), *Gender and U.S. immigration: Contemporary trends* (pp. 174–93). Los Angeles: University of California Press.

Maira, S.M. (2002). *Desis in the house: Indian American youth culture in New York City*. Philadelphia: Temple University Press.

Marshall, G. (1994). *Concise dictionary of sociology*. New York: Oxford University Press.

Maxwell, J.A. (1996). *Qualitative research design: An interactive approach*. Thousand Oaks, CA: Sage.

Mckee, K. (2001). The other sister. In V. Nam (Ed.), *Yell-oh girls! Emerging voices explore culture, identity, and growing up Asian American* (pp. 142–3). New York: Harper Collins.

Nam, V. (Ed.). (2001). *Yell-oh girls! Emerging voices explore culture, identity, and growing up Asian American*. New York: HarperCollins.

Noh, M.S. (2008). *Contextualizing ethnic/racial identity: Nationalized and gendered experiences of segmented assimilation among second generation Korean immigrants in Canada and the United States*. (Doctoral dissertation). Available from ProQuest Digital Dissertations (UMI #: AAT 3338459).

Omi, M. and Winant, H. (1994). *Racial formation in the United States: From the 1960s to the 1990s* (2nd ed.). New York: Routledge.

Phinney, J.S. (1992). The multigroup ethnic identity measure: A new scale for use with diverse groups. *Journal of Adolescent Research, 7*, 156–76.

Pyke, K.D. (2004). *Asian American women's accounts of Asian and White masculinities: An example of internalized gendered racism*. Department of Sociology University of California Riverside CA 92521-0419. (Unpublished manuscript.)

Pyke, K.D., and Johnson, D.L. (2003). Asian American women and racialized femininities "doing" gender across cultural worlds. *Gender & Society, 17*, 33–53.

Qin, D.B., Way, N., and Mukherjee, P. (2008). The other side of the model minority story. *Youth and Society, 34*, 480–506.

Reeves, T., and Bennett, C. (2004). We the People: Asians in the United States. *Census 2000 Special Reports.* Washington, DC: U.S. Census Bureau.

Reitz, J., and Breton, R. (1994). *The illusion of difference: Realities of ethnicity in Canada and the United States.* Toronto: C.D. Howe Institute.

Schur, E. 1984. *Labeling Women Deviant: Gender, Stigma, and Social Control.* New York: Random House.

Solomos, J., and Back, L. (1995). *Race, politics, and social change.* London: Routledge.

Statistics Canada. (2005). Canadian statistics: Visible minority population, by provinces and territories (2001 Census). Retrieved from http://www40.statcan.ca/101/cst01/demo52a.htm.

Thorne, B., Orellana, M.F., Lam, W.S.E., and Chee, A. (2003). Raising children, and growing up, across national borders: Comparative perspectives on age, gender, and migration. In P. Hondagneu-Sotelo (Ed.), *Gender and U.S. immigration: Contemporary trends* (pp. 241–62). Los Angeles: University of California Press.

Times Higher Education. (2007). *The top 200 world universities.* Retrieved from http://www.timeshighereducation.co.uk/hybrid.asp?typeCode=243&pubCode=1& navcode=137.

Toro-Morn, M.I., and Alicea, M. (2003). Gendered geographies of home: Mapping second- and third-generation Puerto-Ricans' sense of home. In P. Hondagneu-Sotelo (Ed.), *Gender and U.S. immigration: Contemporary trends* (pp. 194–214). Los Angeles: University of California Press.

Waters, M.C. (1996). The intersection of gender, race, and ethnicity in identity development of Caribbean American teens. In B.J. Ross Ledbeater and N. Way (Eds.), *Urban girls: Resisting stereotypes, creating identities* (pp. 65–84). New York: New York University Press.

White, M.J., Fong, E., and Cai, Q. (2003). The segregation of Asian-origin groups in the United States and Canada. *Social Science Research, 32*, 148–67.

Williams, L.S., Alvarez, S.D., and Andrade Hauck, K.S. (2002). My name is not Maria: Young Latinas seeking home in the heartland. *Social Problems, 49*, 563–84.

Zhou, M., and Bankston, C.L. (1996). Social capital and the adaptation of the second-generation: The case of Vietnamese youth in New Orleans. In A. Portes (Ed.), *The new second generation* (pp. 197–220). New York: The Russell Sage Foundation.

PART III

Social Roles and Relationships in Korean Families

12 Social Support and Elderly Korean Canadians: A Case Study in Calgary

GUILSUNG KWAK AND DANIEL W.L. LAI

Introduction

Late-life immigration presents complex adjustment and resettlement challenges. Many elderly immigrants lack the cultural skills and resources to manage these challenges. In such stressful circumstances, they are more likely to rely on personal networks for physical, emotional, and psychological support (Giles et al., 2004; Kim & Nesslerade, 2003; Wu & Hart, 2002) rather than formal social support services (Statistics Canada, 2004). Therefore, it is important for newer immigrants to develop new social networks within their ethno-cultural communities and in the host society (Cheang, 2002; Cnaan et al., 2005). The increase in the number of elderly immigrants also highlights the importance of ethnic social support as an alternative to inadequate standard local social and health services, which lack specific cultural and linguistic competence (Kabir et al., 2002; Kaniasty & Norris, 2000; Keyes, 2002; Litwin, 2001).

Social Support as an Asset

Two perspectives about social support continue to prevail. The stress-buffering model establishes that social support protects individuals from the potential harmful influences of stressful events (Cohen & Willis, 1985). In contrast, the main (direct) effect model proposes that a perception of a high degree of social support contributes directly to well-being (Robinson & Garber, 1995).

Social support refers to the exchange of "resources between at least two individuals perceived by the provider or the recipient to be intended to enhance the well-being of the recipient" (Shumaker & Brownell, 1984, p. 13). Dunst and colleagues (1988) considered that social support includes five major components: (1) relational support, (2) structural support, (3) constitutional support, (4) functional support, and (5) support satisfaction. This definition of social support takes into consideration the specific structures (e.g., family, friends), functions (e.g., informational, instrumental), and positive and negative interactions or exchanges. However, the different concepts of social support are interrelated. In a broad sense, social support can be referred to as any process that might promote well-being, health, and relationships through a degree of interaction (Cohen et al., 2000).

During the settlement period of immigrants who often encounter harsh challenges in the new land, social support produces beneficial outcomes (Litwin, 1997; Newsome et al., 2003). Specifically, social support provides information about access to available services, facilitates cognitive functioning, and strengthens the role identity of older immigrants (Everard et al., 2000; Kim, 2002; Wu & Hart, 2002). Research demonstrates that social support helps elderly immigrants use social services better (Aroian et al., 2001), provides direct assistance in daily living tasks (Giles et al., 2004), and maximizes information and resources that facilitate independent living (Kim & Lauderdale, 2002).

Cultural Diversity and Social Support

The acculturative process leads to changes in customs, habits, language usage, lifestyle, social supports, and value-oriented behaviours/attitudes, which present a critical challenge to elderly immigrants who have limited resources to help them adjust to a new life in their old age (Kim, 2002; Kwak & Berry, 2001; Lee et al., 2004; Lee et al., 2000). Cultural differences, limited English competence, and transportation problems are closely associated with negative perceptions toward health care and a lower level of service utilization (Jang et al., 2005). A variety of studies have identified a lower level of health service use by elderly immigrants despite their higher levels of need for health services (Aroian et al., 2001; Lai, 2004; Liu, 2003).

Different cultural values and unfamiliar social conditions are either directly or indirectly connected to elderly immigrants' adjustment challenges such as acculturation, accessing health and social services, maintaining their well-being, living and care-giving arrangements, and coping with changing family relationships (Choi & Gonzalez, 2005; Lee et al., 2004; Nandan, 2005; Oh et al., 2002; Taylor et al., 2004). Several studies show that elderly immigrants tend to rely on informal support from family, friends, and ethnic churches or organizations in the new society (Koh & Bell, 1987; Moon & Pearl, 1991). The effective utilization of social support is essential to dealing with adjustment challenges (Carbonell & Polivka, 2003; Litwin, 2004; Lubben & Lee, 2001).

However, identifying available support resources or preferred resources is not easy because support resources are unequally distributed in society across members and groups of different socio-cultural status (Ho et al., 2000). Therefore, it is important to understand how social support is manifested, what it looks like, what it does, and the socio-cultural context in which it works. The role and nature of social support differ according to the needs and socio-cultural factors associated with social support in the new country (Ho et al., 2000). The distinct culture of each ethnic group affects the nature of social support as immigrants combine cultural values from the homeland with challenges encountered in the new country.

Despite the importance of social support among elderly immigrants, there is little examination of the concept and construction of social support among minority elderly immigrants. Existing research on elderly immigrants has focused on large ethnic groups such as South Asians and Chinese immigrants (Durst, 2005; Lai, 2004; Luhtanen, 2005). Researchers have paid less attention to addressing issues of social support in small groups, including Korean immigrants. This chapter identifies the meaning and nature of social support, and acquires valuable information on how social support operates in a group of Korean elderly immigrants living in Calgary, Alberta. There is a well-recognized positive relationship between the availability of social support resources and positive resettlement. It is important to identify the factors promoting social support in the specific socio-cultural context of elderly Korean immigrants.

Research Objective and Questions

Researching social support in ethnic and cultural minority groups requires the careful consideration of both cultural values and language barriers. Cultural and language barriers not only hinder the use of social and health services but also determine the ways in which immigrants from ethnic minority groups conceive of social support and develop personal social networks. This chapter describes the nature and roles of social support in the socio-cultural context of Korean elderly immigrants, using a sample of Korean elderly immigrants living in Calgary, Alberta, as a case study.

In this ethnic group, the nature of social support is based on the way that Korean elderly immigrants experience interpersonal relations. The availability of social support and its receipt by the intended beneficiaries can enhance their ability to cope with the adverse effects of life stressors. Using a qualitative method, the study aims to provide a comprehensive illustration of how elderly Korean immigrants conceive of social support, how they construct and reorganize their social relations, and how they characterize the functions and effects of social support. More specifically, this chapter describes an ethnographic study of the process of reorganization and re-characterization of social support within the context of late-life immigration as a social phenomenon.

Methods

Research Setting

The setting for the study is Calgary, Alberta, the fourth-largest city in Canada. In 2009, there were 1,065,455 residents in the city (City of Calgary, 2009). According to the national 2006 Census, 6,835 Korean immigrants lived in Calgary (Statistics Canada, 2006). This number represents a substantial increase from 3,985 in the 2001 Census (Statistics Canada, 2006). The City of Calgary reported that 481 new Korean immigrants settled in Calgary in 2003 (City of Calgary, 2003). However, Korean community leaders had assumed that over 10,000 Korean immigrants would live in Calgary by 2008. It was also assumed that approximately 1,000 Korean seniors would live in Calgary in 2004 (Luhtanen, 2005), although there are no official data on the population available at the present. Despite the numbers of Korean immigrants, there does not appear to be a distinct Korean enclave in the city (Luhtanen, 2005).

There are several key organizations within the Calgary Korean community. The Calgary Korean Association that emerged in the early 1970s continues to provide Korean newcomers with settlement information, but it has only a minor influence in the community. The Korean Senior Association was established in 1977 to provide camaraderie and support to seniors speaking the Korean language (Luhtanen, 2005). In 2008, there were approximately 100 seniors who were registered members of this association. Ethnic churches exert the most influence within the Korean community. At present, there are eighteen Protestant churches and one Roman Catholic church. A Buddhist service is held every Sunday.

Korean immigrants have limited access to social and health services in Calgary. For example, despite the importance of bilingual medical services, there are no Korean-speaking family and specialist doctors, nurses, or pharmacists. In addition, other than the Korean Association and the Korean Senior Association, no ethnic social service agency has been established to date. Furthermore, no mainstream social service agencies, including agencies for new immigrants, have Korean-speaking counsellors or full-time staff. Therefore, for Korean immigrants, culturally and linguistically competent services are not available in Calgary.

Study Participants and Data

Participants for this study, twelve Korean elderly immigrants, were recruited by using purposive sampling to enlarge the scope or range of data as well as with the likelihood that multi-dimensioned realities of elderly immigrants' life would be unveiled (Lincoln & Guba, 1985). To ensure maximizing theoretical saturation in the small sample size, data from each participant in the study were diversified to make sense of individual cases. Participants with different backgrounds were intentionally selected based on the selection criteria of the study (Sandelowski, 1995). The inclusion criteria were organized into eight categories: (1) gender, (2) types of immigration, (3) duration of immigration, (4) types of living arrangements, (5) living alone/with spouse, (6) distance from support networks, (7) religious involvement, and (8) driving ability.

There were twelve participants, three men and nine women, ranging in age from sixty-six to eighty-five. Participants were divided into two categories of residence in Canada: short-term and long-term settlers. The average length of residence for the long-term settlers was 18.5 years. For the short-term settlers, the average was 5.3 years. None of the participants lived in a nursing facility: eight were living at a seniors' apartment, and two lived in other rental accommodations. One of these two rented a subsidized apartment. Two seniors were living with their sons. All participants resided with their children before moving to their current accommodation. Most of the participants were either unable to speak English or spoke limited English. About two-thirds of the participants reported specific illnesses or physical conditions, but all participants rated themselves as being in overall good health. Table 12.1 provides the demographic characteristics of the study.

Table 12.1. Demographic Characteristics, Social Support for Elderly Korean Canadians Study

Characteristics	# of Participants (N=12)	% of total	Characteristic	# of Participants (N=12)	% of total
Gender			Religion		
Male	3	25%	Protestant	7	58.30%
Female	9	75%	Catholic	3	25%
Age			None	2	16.70%
65–70	2	16.70%	Marital Status		
71–75	5	41.70%	Married	3	25%
76–80	4	33.30%	Widowed	9	75%
81–85	0	0%	Spouse died in Korea	6 (N=9)	66.70%
86 and over	1	8.30%	Spouse died in Canada	3 (N=9)	33.30%
Immigration type			Work History		
Family immigration	2	16.70%	Employed	3	25%
Child sponsorship	9	75%	None	9	75%
Other	1	8.30%	Education Level		
Years in Canada			None	1	8.30%
1–5 years	3	25%	Elementary school	2	16.70%
6–10 years	5	41.70%	Middle school	2	16.70%
11–15 years	1	8.30%	High school	3	25%
16–20 years	1	8.30%	University	4	33.30%
21 or more	2	16.70%	ESL Level		
Dwelling			Very poor	5	41.70%
Senior Apt.	8	66.70%	Poor	3	25%
Rented Apt.	1	8.30%	Middle	4	33.30%
Subsidized Apt.	1	8.30%			
Child's house	2	16.70%			

In-depth interviews were conducted to collect detailed personal information on characteristics, culture, behaviours, beliefs, and practice of the Korean elderly immigrants in forming and utilizing social support in the community. The interviews, which lasted 90 to 120 minutes, took place at the participants' homes.

For data analysis, the completed interviews were transcribed in Korean and translated into English. Each line of the transcripts was reviewed and marked according to main themes such as social support and its types, challenges, cultural characteristics, the seniors' understanding of social support, their help-seeking behaviours, and so forth. After initially screening the data manually, the researcher used the computer software Atlas.ti for further coding work. Data interpretation and analysis involved making sense of what people said, looking for patterns, and integrating what different people had said (Patton, 2002, p. 347). The data analysis method used in the study was based on the tool suggested by LeCompte, Schensul, Nastasi, and Borgatti (1999). In this study, three levels of data analysis were undertaken as a systematic cognitive process: the item level of analysis, the pattern level of analysis, and the constitutive or structural level of analysis (LeCompte & Schensul, 1999).

Member checking was mainly used for ensuring the accuracy of the results and interpretation of the research through scrutiny of the participants. After the data were analysed, the summary of the research findings was provided to three research participants to obtain their viewpoints on the findings. They confirmed that the findings were consistent with their own experiences and perceptions.

Findings

The research findings showed that elderly Koreans defined social support in relation to their social and cultural contexts. Social support was provided within personal boundaries defined by family, friends, and ethnic and religious communities. The findings also indicated how changes in cultural expectations affected the participants' adjustment to the new society. After settling down in a new country, the Korean elderly reconstructed their lives by making use of major resources of social support. The findings also revealed some of the distinctive characteristics of ethnic Korean elderly immigrants in situations of adjustment and settlement during their later lives. The overall results indicated how changes in cultural expectations affected their adjustment to the new society, and how the elderly immigrants later reconstructed the shape and nature of the social support they accessed, based on their socio-cultural values.

"Treating Others": A Cultural Conception of Social Support

Social support of Korean elderly immigrants is deeply rooted in Korean culture. In the study, the raw units of social support were family and friends from Korean communities. The definition and nature of social support were culturally formed and maintained. Traditional Koreans carry a cultural mindset of treating others without expecting anything in return. The Korean cultural concept of "treating others," that is, caring for others, emerged as a concept central to social support. It is based on and reinforces a high degree of reciprocity between the elderly immigrants and their family and friends. Social support and supportive relations that Korean elderly immigrants experience have a sociocultural dimension that embodies a system of shared meanings. These meanings emerged as social interactions and the expectations that the participants have of their relationships with others.

Knowing the cultural context in which social support is exchanged expands the understanding of how norms, attitudes, beliefs, and behaviours shape the interaction of the social support network within an ethnic group (Gellis, 2003). The elderly Korean participants in this study explained social support in the context of their world view emphasizing the social norm of "treating others," sharing *jung* (affection), and interconnectivity. Social support was conceived of and experienced as a circular process of "treating others," as expressed in the Korean (and English) proverb "One good turn deserves another." When one person helped another, he/she believed that the help provided would come back to him/her in the end. The notion of interconnectedness was understood in the context of interpersonal relationships as the level of engagement one had with others. It was associated with a sense of belonging and the enhanced feelings of well-being (Cornwell et al., 2008).

Sources and Nature of Social Support

Children were the most dominant resource from which the Korean elderly requested and sought help. Their central role in social support was seen in the context of the universal importance of family in Korean culture and values, although it became evident in the study that the notion of filial piety was weakening in Korean immigrant families. One of the participants simplified it by saying, "Children protect me unconditionally because we are their parents." One male participant gave a clear explanation of the importance of children from the typical traditional perspective of filial piety shared by most Korean elderly: "There are no ways without your kids. Of course, they are still kids but they are also our guardians. The kids become the guardians … I am always living with help from kids. They do everything for us. They protect me from difficulties. I consider kids like that. Kids are my shield."

The gender of children influenced the nature of the social support available. The traditional values of Korean culture were manifested in large gender differences in the nature of social support and roles between sons and daughters. In general, sons were expected to provide a sense of security to their aging parents, whereas daughters were supposed to have more intimate relationships with their parents. One female participant in the study commented, "Although my son makes me feel secure, he doesn't talk about the usual matters in his daily life. However, my daughter talks all about what to do and what happened at her work and home. I like my son because he gives me emotional security, but I also like my daughter because she is lovely. My daughter is like an old friend to me."

The traditional Korean cultural values limited the degree to which participants would depend on a daughter-in-law or son-in-law for social support compared with a family member. Some of the research participants described their relationships with their sons-in-law in a metaphor, referring to a son-in-law as "a guest for a hundred years." This meant that sons-in-law were always an awkward and uncomfortable presence in their lives. A daughter-in-law was depicted as an "uncomfortable" person that needed to be managed or controlled or, at best, handled with care. Nonetheless, wives make critical decisions about family matters in many immigrant families. In the study we found that daughters-in-law exert significant influence on the amount and nature of support their husbands may provide to their parents.

Friends gave a feeling of comfort to the seniors, similar to their experience of comfort from their children. Unlike the comfort they get from their children, however, the support from friends did not affect more than the daily events in a senior's life. A female participant, who was in an emergency situation late at night that made her realize the difference between children and friends, said, "The difference is big … I can ask my children anything I need, from petty little things to big requests … However, if I really don't have anyone else to lean on, in the end I would tell my difficulty to my children and ask them to resolve it … And the help I get from my friends is about every little thing that occurs in my daily life like 'Let's go shopping or drink tea after golf.'"

However, close friends are important. Koreans conceive of and experience close friendships in terms of "sisterhood" or "brotherhood." They believe that a close (or best) friend could and should ask for help without feeling burdensome, just as a sister and brother could and should.

Social Support and Challenges

Our participants reported multiple factors that could impede successful adjustment in Canada, including language, transportation, living arrangements, and financial conditions. Social support played a critical role in alleviating the adjustment difficulties. The participants in this study noted that social support mainly came from family members, i.e., children. As well, they obtained additional support from social networks based on friends, church, and ethnic organizations. Most of the participants were unable to solve the problems caused by the language barrier and had to depend on their children. The most critical challenge was to secure assistance when receiving medical or health-care services. Most of the participants did not ask for the help of their friends with such issues because their friends did not speak English fluently.

In addition to the language barrier, transportation problems were another hardship that the participants encountered. Difficulties with getting a ride and being picked up posed limitations on social involvement. Securing the means of transportation greatly changed the daily lives of the elderly. There were two ways for the elderly to meet their need for a ride: using public transportation and getting a ride from friends or children. The elderly generally used public transportation for personal needs such as shopping, banking, or meeting friends, but otherwise they usually relied on rides from their children or friends to go to regular destinations such as church, the doctor's office, and the hospital.

The availability of social support helped the participants to adjust to the new society. Most reported that support from family or friends was useful in solving their daily problems. However, many participants were ambivalent about the quality of their lives in Calgary. Although they had adapted to a new lifestyle as elderly immigrants, they described themselves as living like "a comfortable frog in the well" – in short, accepting the stress and curtailment consequent on the resettlement experience. Whether a participant was nervous about meeting an English-speaking senior depended on whether he or she had lived in Canada for a long or a short time, revealing that the participants had limited social interaction with mainstream networks. One female participant explained her situation: "I am afraid of meeting English-speaking residents. [Do you not have difficulty with English when you are out there?] No, it is not hard because I do something in my range where I can afford. I have never gone over my limitation. When I meet new people out there, they try to talk me by asking, where I am coming from, when did come. When they are going into deep conversations, I tend to avoid or stop by saying sorry."

Korean elderly immigrants have some difficulty in accessing health and social services by themselves, so they sometimes asked the help of family or friends. However, the problems and limitations that Korean elders encounter were often accepted as their destiny. Therefore, they could not address their challenges or problems without the help of others.

Adaptation meant overcoming the hardships that one faced and feeling a sense of peace. All the participants felt better about immigration as they began to learn more about the new environment. Gradually they settled into their new surroundings, and their anxiety disappeared as they went where they wanted to without needing anyone's help.

The Changing Life in the New Society

The fact that the daily lives of the elderly were becoming busier was a positive indicator of adaptation to their lives as immigrants. One male participant stated that his experience contrasted with "an old saying" that elderly immigrants needed to be protected by others, and that there was nothing they could do for themselves. He explained, "We are busy for sure since we all have our personal to-do lists. We have to go to the hospital … People who go to church attend services and volunteer; for me, I have to go work in the senior community, volunteer at the casino; I am really busy now that I think about it. It is good to be busy when you are old. It is better than sitting around and resting because while you live busily, your worries disappear and you sleep better too; I like being busy. However what seniors do is pretty much the same."

Busy seniors in the study tried to enjoy life by choosing to do what they wanted. They spent considerable time on hobbies, learning English, meeting friends, or studying the Bible. They alleviated their loneliness by discovering things to do and planning enjoyable events. Visiting a child's home or store frequently was one of the activities that seniors liked in order to strengthen their well-being and relationships with family members. Having a hobby gave seniors a chance to meet others and was a good way to spend leisure time. For example, playing golf, a sport enjoyed by many Korean elderly, enabled them to increase their participation in society while making new friends. More important, it was a pro-active way to avoid loneliness in a positive way.

Independent living involved an adjustment in family relations and a change in the nature of social support and its use. The seniors who chose independence encountered enormous improvements in their lives. They began to accept problems as daily aspects of their independent living and to seek the help of others to resolve their difficulties. As they lived independently from their children, they began to experience the freedom that would represent the biggest change in their lives: the seniors were actually awakened to the importance of receiving social support from their friends and family members.

Securing Social Support

Securing social support was one of the major daily activities of the elderly Koreans in the study. The social support that they intentionally or unintentionally gathered was a valuable asset for meeting their basic needs and helping to achieve successful resettlement. Positive factors related to social support were gaining information, increasing confidence, developing a positive attitude, maintaining confidentiality, and active social involvement. Negative factors preventing seniors from securing social support included financial insecurity, worries about being a burden to one's children, discomfort with seeking help, and uncertainty about the quality of social support.

Information was one of the types of social support that the participants sought from their social networks. One participant emphasized the importance of obtaining valuable information about a better quality of life. "There are plentiful things to enjoy in Canadian life. Unfortunately, we [Korean seniors] don't have enough information to enjoy our life fully, so that we have easily lost our benefits and rights. In the Korean Seniors Seminars, I learned many things that elderly people should know to enjoy their life and I received a lot of information on senior life in Canada. The City of Calgary offers some classes for us."

Positive attitudes fostered the opportunity for seniors to adjust to the new society. Such attitudes were seen as important in helping the seniors spend their later years happily and also helping them make wiser decisions when interacting with others. A participant explained that a positive attitude is essential for elderly people. "We are in our old age. We don't have enough time to live and there is a limited chance to do good things even though we try to understand everything we should do. We have a short time, so we must always do good things. When I am in a conflicting relationship with others, my soul feels tired and then I will be sick. I always try to think positively and to live happily so I ignore bad words that others say. Bad words make me sad or unhappy."

Staying home was one of the greatest barriers to seniors' adapting to the new environment. Actively participating in the society and not just staying home were very good ways for seniors to gain social support. Seniors' just staying home (in their children's home) could quickly lead to discord with their children. A participant explained that staying home increased dependence on their children and decreased their chances to acquire ways of coping with daily life. Going out and having fun was a way for them to overcome the boredom in their lives.

The settlement and adaptation of seniors were affected deeply by their degree of financial stability. Without that, they could make very few choices for themselves. Seniors who were not financially independent were forced to depend on their children, which often led to a lack of satisfaction with their lives. The importance of financial security was best illustrated by a statement from a participant: "It is also very important to be financially sustainable … Your happy senior life probably reaches the end if you are old and you have to lean on your children for financial support. Isn't that right? It will be definitely hard if you are not financially stable when you are old. There are many chances to earn money when you are young, but there are a lot of restrictions on seniors, and so they must contemplate their financial capability before they decide to immigrate. Definitely, that is very important."

The sense of being a burden associated with asking for help from children or friends seemed to play a role in lowering the quality of life of the elderly. For fear of inconveniencing their children, seniors in a difficult situation might avoid asking for help. A participant explained: "My son is too busy carrying out his own life to live for his parents; I have to ask my son for help if I want to do something, but that is limited to one or two favours … If I ask, my son will do what I ask, but I cannot continue to burden him when I know of his situation."

Reconstructing Social Support

The study revealed that the elderly immigrants had accepted changes in their lifestyle and culture. As they became more adjusted to the sociocultural contexts of the new society, they began to reconstruct the shape and nature of the social support they accessed. This reconstruction, or re-formation, is typically evident in relation to the living arrangements of those who are newly settled. The effect of seniors' living on their own has implications for several sub-themes identified in the study, such as traditional Korean family relations, modified intra-family relationships, and the rebuilding of social support and its use to fit existing circumstances. The seniors typically chose to live as close as possible to their children: proximity to family members was important to facilitate access to social support in the new culture. A participant, whose daughter lives just fifteen minutes from him and his wife, spoke about his reconstructed family relationships: "Her children visit us a lot once a week. The kids go, 'I want to see grandmother and grandfather,' and so they call a lot, phone me, come often; it's like that. We just spend time with our kids like that. I can go back and forth since my daughter's house is close. If there is something, I go; I go to see the kids; also if there is something to eat we both go back and forth to bring it to each other. Today, they came to stay while the car was being repaired."

The study revealed that the seniors expected adult children who lived separately from them to perform filial duties partly through frequent contact by phone or by visiting. Adult children could thereby stay up to date with their parents' financial, emotional, language, or transportation needs, which the younger ones could then respond to. Most seniors considered such supports and activities related to the changed culture to be essential aspects of filial responsibility, respect, and affection for the aged parents.

Some of the participants said that the government acts as the "second son" for the Korean elderly because it provides various benefits and services to seniors. This concept of "government as the second son" showed how almost all the participant seniors, influenced by traditional Korean child-parent relationships were moving toward the Western norm of independence for the elderly as the ideal. Most of the seniors could maintain their independent life owing to government pensions and other forms of official financial subsidy, which enabled them to avoid complete financial dependence on their children and allowed them some autonomy. As a result, they expressed gratitude to Canada for the benefits available. A female participant said,

Here is a perfect place for seniors, like heaven! I love living here in Canada. I have what I always appreciate in both Korea and Canada. In Korea, I must pay medical expense when I see a doctor. In addition, I had a serious concern on an increase of an apartment rental fee whenever I renewed the rental contract for either a one-year or two- year term. The rental fee was always increasing. Here, public housing is provided to me. The cost is not increasing. Furthermore, I am not asked to leave my apartment. How wonderful and good the Canadian society is! I appreciate it. I can get pre-scriptions free of charge. The medications work well. With the Blue Card, I can buy drugs cheaply. I don't pay when I see a doctor, there is no exami-nation fee. Almost everything is free. How wonderful! I really appreciate Canada where I live.

Despite the socio-cultural changes associated with immigration, the support of family and friends for the Korean elderly remained the dominant source of help to meet their needs. The focus on family and co-ethnic friends as the primary sources of social support needs to be re-evaluated in the context of changing socio-cultural circumstances, with particular reference to the question of where the elderly should live in late life. Although various social services are available, the services are not substitutes for the support of family and friends. The research suggests that support from government and social agencies alleviated some of the immediate pressures on the children, strengthening their capacity to support their aging parents for longer, thereby enabling the children to maintain their responsibilities toward their immigrant parents.

Discussion and Conclusions

The research findings on social support revealed that there were sig-nificant cultural characteristics associated with why and how elderly Koreans sought help when facing difficulties or solving problems in the context of immigration in later life. Social support was seen as a shield against their hardships in a different social environment. All family members are vital to aged immigrants; however, the findings indicated significant differences in the nature of the participants' preferences and in the quality of support available. The parents had expectations of the roles of son, daughter, and their children's spouses, based on their Korean culture and values. Traditionally, aged parents tend to strongly rely on a son rather than a daughter. The son, seen as a decision maker, provides financial support; the daughter mainly provides emotional support. Importantly, it should be noted that often the daughter-in-law is the actual service provider and decision maker in the Korean fam-ily, although her role and influence in family matters are not immediately evident. Due to the value placed on family harmony, Korean elderly immigrants do not want to let others know if, for example, they have a conflict with their daughter-in-law. Identifying the dynamics of the family is a crucial factor in building professional relationships and working with Korean elderly immigrants.

Language barriers and transportation problems were noted as barriers to accessing social and health services for the Korean elderly in Calgary (Trang, 2008). The study indicated that the participants did not have negative attitudes toward using social and health services, but they found it inconvenient to do so. The availability of Korean translation services in social service and medical settings is very limited in Calgary. When family members or friends are not on hand as translators, service areas should be equipped with teleconferencing devices. At the very least, professionals should be aware of language and cultural barriers when they work with Korean elderly immigrants.

Cultural and linguistic competence are closely related to meeting the challenges and dealing with problems that elderly immigrants encounter in making use of existing social and health services in Calgary. Elderly immigrants in stressful circumstances tended to rely on their own social-support resources that provided them with both tangible and intangible support. However, such social support was not enough to meet their social and health-service needs in Calgary, where there are no Korean-speaking family doctors or social-service professionals. Given the difficult conditions inherent in the immigrant experience, health and social-service providers should not only take a greater interest in the service needs and help-seeking patterns of elderly Korean immigrants but also try to "eliminate access barriers and challenges in the health professional setting" (Lai, 2004, p. 825). The research findings illustrate that the development of culturally and linguistically competent services depends on the possibility of providers' increasing their comprehensive knowledge of ethnic minority groups and applying it to the provision of services.

Our participants shared their experiences and understandings of how they developed and extended their social support networks. They also described social support as deeply important to the lives of elderly immigrants during the period of adjustment/resettlement. The characteristics and extent of the social support were strongly influenced by socio-cultural factors. Social interactions were mainly focused on their own families, friends, and their own ethnic community. The importance to adjustment of one's social network was illustrated by social interactions such as attending church, meeting with friends, and attending group events. These social contacts were all strongly associated with better adjustment in the new life. A key aspect of establishing an optimized relationship network was to maximize contact with old settlers who could direct the newcomers to specific resources. Newcomers benefited from the opportunities provided by older settlers within shared ethnic and cultural boundaries.

One of the important conclusions from the research results was that the family continues to be central to the lives of the participants and a major source of social support although the older generation may live separately. Most of the adult children still contributed considerable financial and emotional help to their aging parents, meeting the expectations of filial responsibility. Parents got support from their children even after their move to independent living in the community, so geographical distance from children did not mean that the children's helping relationship was discontinued. Instead, the parents' social support was reconstructed. Through the parents' independent living arrangements, child-parent relationships were transformed. The seniors were moving toward the Western ideal of independence for the elderly, even as they retained their traditions and cultural practices. Social services from governmental agencies reinforced the children's ability to meet their responsibilities to their parents by alleviating some pressures on them and supplementing their ability to support their aged parents for a longer period.

Most of the "old" settlers considered their way of life to be stable, seeing government as their "good second son." However, the phrase is also relevant to the level of social support provided by children. It implies that their children perhaps did not give money on a regular basis but the government did. The support of children was not always sufficient to help the elderly parents maintain their independent way of life. Increasing dependency in old age was seen as normal for the elderly. A combination of social support and social services was necessary for their successful adjustment to a new environment.

As the Korean elderly became acclimatized to their life in Calgary, they extended their support networks, continued to develop their own independent lifestyle, and reconstructed many aspects of their lives. The seniors' daily lives were becoming busier, and they tried to live in a way that met their own social and cultural needs. It was important for them to be fully occupied, to make various plans, and to participate in activities in order to live healthy and fulfilling lives. Their extended social networks and a high level of interaction with family members, relatives, and friends helped facilitate adjustment to the new society.

REFERENCES

Aroian, K.J., Khatutsky, G., Tran, T.V., and Balsam, A.L. (2001). Health and social service utilization among elderly immigrants from the former Soviet Union. *Journal of Nursing Scholarship, 33,* 265–71.

Carbonell, J., and Polivka, L. (2003). The aging networks and the future of long-term care. *Journal of Gerontological Social Work, 41,* 313–21.

Casado, B.L., and Leung, P. (2001). Migratory grief and depression among elderly Chinese American immigrants. *Journal of Gerontological Social Work, 36,* 5–26.

Cheang, M. (2002). Older adults' frequent visits to a fast-food restaurant: Non-obligatory social interaction and the significance of play in a "third place." *Journal of Aging Studies, 16,* 303–21.

Choi, N.G., and Gonzalez, J.M. (2005). Barriers and contributors to minority older adults' access to mental health treatment: Perceptions of geriatric mental health clinicians. *Journal of Gerontological Social Work, 44,* 115–35.

City of Calgary. (2003). *Fact sheet: Immigration.* Calgary: Community Strategies, Policy and Planning Division. Retrieved from http://www.calgary.ca/docgallery/bu/community_strategies/immigration_fact_sheet_June2003lh.pdf.

City of Calgary (2009). *2009 Civic Census.* Calgary, AB: Retrieved from http://www.calgary.ca/DocGallery/BU/cityclerks/city.pdf

Cnaan, R.A., Boddie, S.C., and Kang, J.J. (2005). Religious congregations as social services providers for older adults. *Journal of Gerontological Social Work, 45,* 105–30.

Cohen, S., Gottlieb, B.H., and Underwood, L.G. (2000). Social-relationships and health. In S. Cohen, L.G. Underwood, & B.H. Gottlieb (Eds.), *Social support measurement and intervention* (pp. 3–25). New York: Oxford University Press.

Cohen, S., and Willis, T.A. (1985). Stress, social support, and the buffering hypothesis. *Psychological Bulletin, 98,* 310–57.

Cornwell, B., Laumann, E.O., and Schumm, L.P. (2008). The social connectedness of older adults: A national profile. *American Sociological Review, 73,* 185–203.

Dunst, C.J., Trivette, C.M., and Deal, A.G. (1988). *Enabling and empowering families: Principles and guidelines for practice.* Cambridge, MA: Brookline.

Durst, D. (2005). Aging amongst immigrants in Canada: Population drift. *Canadian Studies in Population, 32*, 257–70.

Everard, K.M., Lach, H.W., Fisher, E.B., and Baum, M.C. (2000). Relationship of activity and social support to the functional health of older adults. *Journal of Gerontology: Social Sciences, 55B*, S208–12.

Gellis, Z.D. (2003). Kin and nonkin social supports in a community sample of Vietnamese immigrants. *Social Work, 48*(2), 248–58.

Giles, L.C., Metcalf, P.A., Glonek, G.F.V., Luszcz, M.A., and Andrews, G.R. (2004). The effects of social networks on disability in older Australians. *Journal of Aging and Health, 16*, 517–38.

Ho, E.S., Cheung, E., Bedford, C., and Leung, P. (2000). *Settlement assistance needs of recent migrants.* Wellington, New Zealand: New Zealand Immigration Service. Retrieved from http://www.immigration.govt.nz/NR/rdonlyres/C15CAC9B-1A98-4A19-90E9-5E8980E413CA/0/SettlementAssistanceNeedsofRecentMigrants.pdf.

Jang, Y., Kim, G., and Chiriboga, D.A. (2005). Health, healthcare utilization, and satisfaction with service: Barriers and facilitators for older Korean Americans. *Journal of American Geriatrics Society, 53*, 1613–17.

Kabir, Z.H., Sxebehely, M., and Tishelman, C. (2002). Support in old age in the changing society of Bangladesh. *Aging and Society, 22*, 615–36.

Kaniasty, K., and Norris, F.H. (2000). Help-seeking comfort and receiving social support: The role of ethnicity and context of need. *American Journal of Community Psychology, 28*, 545–81.

Keyes, C.L.M. (2002). The exchange of emotional support with age and its relationship with emotional well-being by age. *Journal of Gerontology: Psychological Science, 57B*, P518–25.

Kim, J.E., and Lauderdale, D.S. (2002). The role of community context in immigrant elderly living arrangements: Korean American elderly. *Research on Aging, 24*, 630–53.

Kim, J.E., and Nesselroade, J.R. (2003). Relationships among social support, self-concept, and wellbeing of older adults: A study of process using dynamic factor models. *International Journal of Behavioral Development, 27*, 49–65.

Kim, Y. (2002). The role of cognitive control in mediating the effect of stressful circumstanced among Korean immigrants. *Health and Social Work, 27*, 36–47.

Koh, J.Y., and Bell, W.G. (1987). Korean elders in the United States: Intergenerational relations and living arrangements. *The Gerontologist, 27*, 66–71.

Kwak, K., and Berry, J.W. (2001). Generational differences in acculturation among Asian families in Canada: A comparison of Vietnamese, Korean, and East-Indian groups. *International Journal of Psychology, 36*, 152–62.

Lai, D.W.L. (2004). Impact of culture on depressive symptoms of elderly Chinese immigrants. *Canadian Journal of Psychiatry, 49*, 820–7.

LeCompte, M.D., and Schensul, J.J. (1999). *Designing and conducting ethnographic research. Vol. 1: Ethnographer's toolkit.* Walnut Creek, CA: AltaMira Press.

LeCompte, M.D., Schensul, J.J., Nastasi, B.K., and Borgatti, S.P. (1999). *Enhanced ethnographic methods: Audiovisual techniques, focused group interviews, and elicitation techniques, Vol. 1: Ethnographer's toolkit.* Walnut Creek, CA: AltaMira Press.

Lee, H.Y., Moon, A., and Knight, B.G. (2004). Depression among elderly Korean immigrants: Exploring socio-cultural factors. *Journal of Ethnic & Cultural Diversity in Social Work, 13*(4), 1–26.

Lee, S.K, Sobal, J., and Frongillo, Jr., E.A. (2000). Acculturation and health in Korean Americans. *Social Science and Medicine, 51*, 159–73.

Lincoln, Y., and Guba, E.G. (1985). *Naturalistic inquiry.* Newbury Park, CA: Sage.

Litwin, H. (1997). The network shifts of elderly immigrants: The case of Soviet Jews in Israel. *Journal of Cross-Cultural Gerontology, 12*, 45–60.

———. (2001). Social network type and morale in old age. *The Gerontologist, 41*, 516–24.

———. (2004). Social networks, ethnicity and public home-care utilization. *Aging and Society, 24*, 921–39.

Liu, Y.L. (2003). Aging service need and use among Chinese American seniors: Intragroup variations. *Journal of Cross-Cultural Gerontology, 18*, 273–301.

Lubben, J.E., and Lee, A. (2001). Social support networks among elderly Chinese Americans in Los Angeles. In I. Chi, N.L. Chappell, and J.E. Lubben (Eds.), *Elderly Chinese in Pacific rim countries: Social support and integration* (pp. 53–65). Hong Kong: Hong Kong University Press.

Luhtanen, E. (2005). *Cultural cues: A resource guide for service providers working with Calgary's culturally diverse seniors.* Calgary: The City of Calgary, Seniors Services Division, Community and Neighbourhood Services.

Mickelson, K.D., and Kubzansky, L.D. (2003). Social distribution of social support: The mediating role of life events. *American Journal of Community Psychology, 32*, 265–81.

Moon, J., and Pearl, J.H. (1991). Alienation of elderly Korean American immigrants as related to place of residence, gender, age, years of education, time in the U.S., living with or without children, and living with or without a spouse. *International Journal of Aging and Human Development, 2*, 115–24.

Nandan, M. (2005). Adaptation to American culture: Voices of Asian Indian immigrants. *Journal of Gerontological Social Work, 44*, 175–203.

Newsom, J.T., Nishishiba, M., Morgan, D., and Rook, K.S. (2003). The relative importance of three domains of positive and negative social exchanges: A longitudinal model with comparable measures. *Psychology and Aging, 18,* 746–54.

Oh, Y., Koeske, G.F., and Sales, E. (2002). Acculturation, stress, and depressive symptoms among Korean immigrants in the United States. *The Journal of Social Psychology, 142,* 511–27.

Patton, M.Q. (2002). *Qualitative evaluation and research methods.* Newbury Park, CA: Sage.

Robinson, S.N., and Garber, J. (1995). Social support and psychopathology across the life span. In D. Cicchetti and D.J. Cohen (Eds.), *Developmental Psychopathology,* Vol. 2 (pp. 162–209). New York: John Wiley & Sons.

Sandelowski, M. (1995). Sample size in qualitative research. *Research in Nursing & Health, 18,* 179–83.

Shumaker, S.A., and Brownell, A. (1984). Toward a theory of social support: Closing conceptual gaps. *Journal of Social Issues, 40,* 11–36.

Statistics Canada (2004). *Highlights of the longitudinal survey of immigrants to Canada, wave 1, 2000–2001.* Ottawa: Statistics Canada.

———. (2006). 1996, 2001, 2006 Census. Retrieved November 14, 2009, from http://www40.statcan.ca/l01/cst01/demo50a-eng.htm.

Taylor, S.E., Sherman, D.K., Kim, H.S., Jarcho, J., Takagi, K., and Dunagan, M.S. (2004). Culture and social support: Who seeks it and why? *Journal of Personality and Social Psychology, 87,* 354–62.

Thoits, P.A. (1995). Stress, coping and social support processes: Where are we? What next? *Journal of Health and Social Behavior, 35,* 53–79.

Trang, A. (2008). What older people want: Lessons from Chinese, Korean, and Vietnamese immigrant communities. *Generations, 32,* 61–3.

Wu, Z., and Hart, R. (2002). Social and health factors associated with support among elderly immigrants in Canada. *Research on Aging, 24,* 391–412.

13 Korean Fathers on Canadian Shores[1]

YOUNG IN KWON AND SUSAN S. CHUANG

Introduction

Since the early 1970s, the role that fathers play in children's lives has gained significant attention. We now recognize that men's family roles are not limited to only being economic providers but also include other roles such as caregiving and nurturing of children (Lamb, 2004). The quality and quantity of paternal involvement have been important resources for children's development – their future communication skills (Beatty & Dobos, 1993), emotional maturation (Zimmerman et al., 1995), and social skills (Verschueren & Marcoen, 1999). Fathering roles have also been found to be closely related to men's well-being (Eggebeen & Knoester, 2001). More recently, researchers have reported that the roles and responsibilities of mothers and fathers have changed or transformed over the years. Normative parental roles are no longer viewed as a stark dichotomy (maternal caregiver and paternal bread-winner) but, rather, seen as shifting from traditional roles to more egalitarian relationships, with fathers engaging in childcare and household chores and mothers contributing to household income (e.g., Chuang & Moreno, 2008; Chuang & Su, 2008).

Most of our current understanding of fathering, however, has focused on families of European background. Given the tremendous changes of the ethnoprofiles of many countries, greater focus is needed

1 This work was supported by the Post-Doctoral Research Fellowships (PDRF) funded by the Government of Canada International Scholarship Programs, Canadian Bureau for International Education (CBIE). We also recognize research support from the University of Guelph. We thank the Korean-Canadian fathers and mothers who willingly participated in our interview.

to better understand families of varying ethnicities, and the implications of immigration on the dynamics and relationships of families. For Canada, the immigrant population is the second highest in the world. According to Statistics Canada 2006, the immigrant population rose from 17.9 per cent in 2001 to 19.8 per cent in 2006, the biggest increase in seventy-five years. This was four times the growth rate of native-born Canadians (Statistics Canada, 2006). In particular, the number of Korean immigrants in Canada has been remarkable. From 2001 to 2006, the number of Korean immigrants has grown from 100,600 to 141,890, which is more than a 40 per cent increase (J. Park, chapter 2, this volume). Korea is currently the fifth-largest source country for Canada, with Korean immigrant families even outnumbering those in the United States (Han & Ibbott, 2004). Despite the notable growth of the Korean immigrant population in Canada, there is no actual study that critically questions the conceptions and transitions of fatherhood for Korean-Canadian men across the lifespan.

To place this chapter into the context of fathering and Korean-Canadian families, we first begin with a historical account of fathering within the Korean culture and how the socio-cultural changes have shaped current fathering. Before delving into the research on Korean immigrant fathers, we must first provide a brief overview of the fathering literature, with the primary focus on father involvement. We then explore the development of fatherhood and the immigration processes for first-generation Korean-Canadian fathers. To consider the broader influences of society and culture, we examine the paternal roles and role transitions for two distinct age groups of first-generation fathers: older fathers who came to Canada before and younger fathers who came after the mid-1980s.

An Overview of Contemporary Father Involvement

With the advent of fathering research, researchers were primarily concerned with the notion of the "good dad"–"bad dad" dichotomy. A good dad was conceptualized as the economic provider who could financially support his family as opposed to the bad dad (or deadbeat dad) who had limited or no financial resources. Thus, the father's primary role was that of breadwinner (Pleck, 2004). Unfortunately, this narrow focus on fathers excluded the investigation of other paternal roles of fathers (i.e., caregiving).

It was not until the 1970s that researchers began to re-conceptualize the roles of fathers to reflect a more accurate portrayal of contemporary fathers. This re-conceptualization was greatly influenced by the era's second-wave feminist movement, along with society's view that fathers needed to be positive role models for their children (Lamb, 2004). These societal shifts steered researchers to explore what fathers should do (father involvement). Lamb, Pleck, Charnov, and LeVine's (1987) conceptualization of fathering was one of the first models that explicitly delineated a multidimensional framework that allowed researchers to explore the behavioural levels of father involvement and the effects on their children's lives. Their model was based on three dimensions: (1) paternal engagement, which included direct interaction with the child such as caretaking and play; (2) accessibility or availability to the child (within earshot of the child); and (3) responsibility for the child (e.g., making doctor's appointments, decision making regarding children's education) (Lamb, 2004). Fathering could be understood differently depending on the dimensions considered. Although paternal involvement has been investigated over the years, closer examination revealed that the increased involvement was primarily based on direct engagement or accessibility. Responsibility for a child's welfare and decision making on childcare issues, on the other hand, received considerably less attention (Kwon & Roy, 2007; Lamb, 2000).

To understand fatherhood, it is also critical to distinguish between changing socio-cultural expectations for fathering, and the actual shifts and transitions in men's behaviours as fathers (LaRossa, 1988, 1997). For instance, socio-cultural factors such as increased maternal employment and governmental policies that promote father involvement (e.g., paternity leave) may influence how fathers conceptualize fathering and their roles in the family. However, pragmatically, their economic situations may force many fathers to continue the traditional ways of fathering. Thus, there can be a perceived disconnect between how fathers view fathering and what they actually do. Such discrepancies between ideal expectations and actual behaviour may be related to diverse factors including their work and family environments, economic situations (Kwon, 2010). Moreover, how fathers and others view parenting roles may undergo various redefinitions as families encounter rapid and dynamic social and contextual shifts over their life course.

Historical Transitions of Socio-cultural Contexts

The unique socio-cultural and historical experiences of fathers requires receive full consideration. Fatherhood is an adaptive process that is constantly shaped and reshaped by the social world (Marsiglio et al., 2005; Roggman et al., 2002). With the dramatic influx of newcomers in North America, scholars have been increasingly intrigued by the ways immigrants have changed and adapted to their host countries. Immigrant fathers were found to create their paternal roles within different and often paradoxical contexts of both country of origin and destination throughout their lives (Chan, 1998; Jasso, 2003). Kwon and Roy's (2005) exploration of Korean-American fathers' roles and cultural identity development revealed that fathers created their roles and cultural identities by applying not only the contexts of their host country but also the changing socio-cultural environment of South Korea.

The Confucian Tradition in Korea

To place Korean fathers in their cultural contexts, one needs to better understand the influences of Confucian traditions on Korean families. South Korea is typical of East Asian countries that share Confucianism as the ideological basis of family and value systems. Confucianism originated in China as a conservative philosophy and religion that governed East Asian society for more than twenty-five centuries. Although Confucian tradition in South Korea has faded away or has mixed with Western values since the industrialization and modernization of the country (Lee, 1997), some researchers believe that Confucianism still influences people's everyday lives and provides the guidance and values of good fathering to families.

The two most important principles of Confucianism that shaped expectations on fatherhood were filial piety and gender segregation (Lee, 1997; Park & Cho, 1995). According to Confucianism, there is a clear hierarchy between parents and children, and between men and women. Thus, fathers had all the power and authority in the family. K. Lee (1997) explained traditional Korean fathers' three main rights and obligations as family heads: represent the family, supervise family members, and control family property. Although fathers were considered as primary providers for the family, economic contribution was not a prerequisite for the fathers' rights or obligations. In traditional Korea, financial support was not the criterion for defining a good father; rather, the focus was on the father's level of power and authority.

Father-child relationships were highly valued under Confucian tradition. However, Confucian ideology led to the longstanding popular

image of "strict father, kind mother," and assigned fathers responsibility for children's discipline and training (Shwalb et al., 2010). For
example, in Han's (1997) study on Korean fathers, middle-age men
remembered their fathers as "blunt," "not talking," or "punishing," but
they also interpreted those behaviours as positive fathering in those
days. Similarly, Ishii-Kuntz (1993) studied Japanese families and also
reported that traditional families were taught to fear "earthquakes,
thunders, fire, and fathers."

Owing to the strict gender segregation, the worlds of fathers and
mothers were explicitly distinct from each other as "outside the home"
and "inside the home." Caregiving and nurturance were only the
mothers' responsibility, and fathers were segregated from daily family
activities. Fathers' participation in childcare or child-rearing activities
was thought to be negative and not masculine by the cultural norms (K.
Lee, 1997; Park & Cho, 1995).

The Industrialization of Korea

Compared with other East Asian countries such as China and Japan,
industrialization and Westernization in Korean society started fairly
late. It was only after the Korean War (1950–3) when Confucian ideals
were challenged. Changes in traditional family ideals in South Korea
were exacerbated by the industrialization that started from the mid-
1960s. Under the motto of rehabilitation of the country, the government undertook a series of economic development plans (S. Lee, 1997).
Those plans mainly focused on expanding the size of the South Korean
economy rather than increasing families' well-being. It was during this
period that Korean fathers dedicated themselves to their work. Fathers'
authority and privilege were no longer top priority but became rewards
for (or equated with) being a good provider. As breadwinners, fathers
spent most of their time and energy at work, leaving minimal time for
their families. Fathers were, therefore, separated from their families'
lives, and good fathers in South Korea became redefined as hard workers rather than good caregivers (Han, 1997; Suh & Lee, 1999).

Another reason that accentuated the importance of fathers' provider
role during this period was the emphasis on providing the necessary
means and infrastructure (e.g., funds for tuition) for their children to
attain high levels of education. Education was seen as the best vehicle
for upward social mobility to ensure a comfortable life in the future.
Thus, giving such educational opportunities to their children was per-

ceived as one of the most important criteria for being a good father (S. Lee, 1997).

The Rapid Westernization of South Korea and Dual Expectations for Fathering

The rapid westernization of Korean society started in the mid-1980s, along with the 1988 Seoul Olympics and termination of the travel overseas restriction policy. Korean people had more opportunities to interact with people from other parts of the world. For instance, the number of Koreans departing the country for overseas travel, education, and migration in 2003 was fourfold compared with travel in 1987 (Statistics Korea, 2004).

As South Korean society became westernized, traditional images of fathers were challenged, and the generous image of fathers as paternal caregivers became the spotlight (Kim, 1997; Suh & Lee, 1999). In the mid-1990s, the South Korean government made great efforts to encourage fathers to be more involved in childcare as one way of balancing work and family life for dual-earner couples in Korea. The Ministry of Health and Welfare (founded in 1994), and the Ministry of Gender and Family (founded in 2005), guided family-friendly policies to target fathers: for instance, the "papa quota policy," a paternal-leave policy, promoted active family participation among fathers (Yun, 2005).

Although the Korean people adopted westernized notions of fathering, there continues to be a significant structural gap between fathers' emerging roles as caregivers and their image as hard workers (Kwon, 2010; Suh & Lee, 1999). Unfortunately, before fathers' emerging roles as caregivers were settled, South Korean society underwent another series of economic and social changes that produced dual messages for fathers. One major change was the Asian economic crisis (also known as the IMF crisis) in November 1997, which significantly decreased the value of the Korean currency. On November 30, 1997, the South Korean government decided to invite the International Monetary Fund, whose involvement became a key factor in the economic crisis in the country. All the symptoms of economic downturn emerged at once: the GNP per capita fell from $10,300 to $6,000 (Lee et al., 2000, many people lost their jobs, and the unemployment rate increased enormously (Statistics Korea, 1998, 2000).

With the country's financial downturn, many family problems that had been ignored since the industrialization era surfaced. For example, from 1997 to 1998, divorce rates increased 28 per cent (Statistics Korea, 1998, 2000), and the rates of domestic violence also escalated (Lee et al., 2000 Sung, 1998). However, when the first serious and sudden economic crisis occurred, the South Korean government was not fully prepared to protect the families from its negative impact on family life. The media and government started to emphasize traditional family values and relationships such as reconstituting fathers as the head of the family, and traditional gender roles were promoted (Sung, 1998). In this context, fathers received dual messages on fathering – be a generous caregiver as well as a successful provider.

Moreover, as the societal stresses of attaining higher levels of education constantly pressed parents to provide better educational opportunities for their children, fathers' burden of economic provision became heavier. For instance, to deal with the educational pressure, many middle-class fathers resorted to sending their wives and children to English-speaking countries for a better educational future for their children while they stayed behind (Lee, 2001). These strains on families led to the reconstruction of the roles of the father into one role, that of economic provider.

The ongoing economic and social transitions in South Korean society also created enormous social ambivalence around culture and the conduct of fathering, which, in turn, resulted in tension and conflict for Korean fathers. Kwon and Roy (2007) studied middle-class and working-class Korean fathers. They found that middle-class fathers accepted the new concepts and ideologies of fatherhood; however, their actual performance as fathers had not changed, mostly owing to their heavy workload. This difference made the fathers identify themselves as "inappropriate" fathers.

Immigration in Canada

The influx of Korean immigrants to Canada began in the mid-1960s with the reform of the Canadian immigration laws (Han & Ibbott, 2004). As mentioned from the beginning of this essay, many Korean immigrants have been migrating to Canada during the past forty-five years. However, our understanding of Korean families remains limited, with a dearth of information on fathering. The general focus has been on older first-generation Korean parents and their conflicts with their second-generation children (e.g., see Foner, 1997; Kim, 2008; Kim & Kim, 1995). According to those study findings, Korean immigrant men were viewed as still following the Confucian family values of being aloof and uninvolved. They did not take part in caregiving activities or in their families' daily lives (Kim, 2008).

In contrast, Chuang and Su (2008) examined Chinese and immigrant Chinese-Canadian fathers' conception of their parenting roles in the family. They reported that both Chinese and immigrant Chinese fathers viewed their roles as multidimensional, including breadwinner, caregiver, playmate, and educator. When assessing self-reports on parenting styles, some researchers challenged the Asian traditional roles of parenting. Chao and Kim (2000) examined parenting differences among immigrant Taiwanese-American mothers and fathers of elementary-school-age children. The findings revealed that mothers and fathers did not significantly differ from each other in relation to how they rated their parenting styles, as well as their views on how parents should train their children.

Current Study on Korean Immigrant Fathering in Canada

The various socio-cultural contexts that Korean fathers experience in their lifetimes have received minimal attention. Currently, we are one of the first to examine the attitudes and values of Korean-Canadian fathers. We designed a comprehensive interview to explore fathering among first-generation Korean immigrant fathers in two life stages (middle and late adulthood). Using the samples of fathers at two life stages, we were able to better understand the extent to which Confucianism and western culture have influenced paternal expectations as well as fathering behaviour.

The interviews were conducted with eighteen younger and fifteen older Korean immigrant fathers living in Ontario. Younger first-generation fathers came to Canada after the mid-1980s, when the westernization of Korean society had started. Their ages ranged from thirty to the mid-forties. These fathers had children who were pre-adolescent or younger. Five fathers had experiences of raising children in Korea, and the others had their first child after they came to Canada. The younger fathers were engaged in diverse occupations, including pastor, student, office worker, engineer, business owner, and househusband.

Older first-generation fathers, whose ages ranged from the early sixties to late seventies, had at least one grandchild. Different from those of the younger fathers, the occupations of the older participants were somewhat similar. Most of the older fathers (n=12) were retired at the time of the interview, and the occupations of ten of them were grocers or laundry owners. Five fathers were working or had been working as a professor, an engineer, a business owner, and a translator. During the interviews, lasting about forty minutes to two hours, we asked about their lives after immigration, memories about their own fathers, their notion of ideal paternal roles, and their actual participation in childcare.

To increase credibility of the interview data, we also asked the wives about paternal roles in the family. Wives provided the most intimate and meaningful context in their husbands' role development (Allen & Hawkins, 1999; Arendell, 1996), and interviewing wives enhanced our knowledge about Korean immigrant fathers' paternal involvement in childcare their family contexts. Not all wives, however, agreed to participate in the interview, resulting in seven younger wives and five older wives.

The Development of Paternal Expectations and Behaviours of Older Korean Immigrant Fathers

Older fathers in our sample were born in an era when Confucian tradition was still influential on their own fathers' ideologies of parenting (from 1934 to 1948). For example, they described their fathers as "traditional," "indifferent to family life," and "always busy." Although his father had not worked during his whole life, one man explained that his father had great authority over his family. "My father was very stern and strict about Confucian tradition. Even if he loved his kids, he never said that … He was so stern that I had never talked with him. I ran away when he came home" (sixty-six-year-old father).

Among fifteen older fathers, six had little memory of their absentee fathers, who had passed away before the respondents' childhood. Others, however, described themselves as fatherless. "My father wandered around the country before he died. It was not because of his work. He just wandered around. When he met me, he said I was cute. But other than that, we never talked. And since I went to middle school in the city, I seldom saw him" (sixty-seven-year-old father).

Only one mentioned that his own father was a "good man"; however, his perception also was not very distinct from others. "My father was a construction worker. He was a really good man … He did not talk much, but he loved his children, and he did not say anything even when we did something wrong" (seventy-year-old father).

As many older fathers in our sample were fatherless or afraid of their fathers, they tried to be sincere with their own family and children. The notion of being "sincere" is closely related to the social contexts of Korea they have experienced. The older participants became fathers during South Korea's industrialization period (mid-1960s to late 1970s), and they focused on providing economic resources for their families during their whole lives. For example, one reported that he was satisfied with his paternal role as breadwinner: "I am not ashamed to my kids, because I had to work and I had to feed them. I did not take any vacation for the first eight years. Now my kids say I was foolish" (seventy-year-old father). These results are consistent with Kim and Hong's (2007) findings that first-generation Korean immigrant fathers were described as "not expressing affection or emotion." It was instead through successful provision of housing, food, and education that children viewed their fathers as expressing their love for them (Kim & Cain, 2008).

The older Korean immigrant fathers' notion of ideal fathering also provided a strong motivation for their migration to Canada. Two-thirds of our older participants (n=9) stressed that the "better economic condition" was the most important reason for moving to Canada, especially in the 1960s to '70s, which confirms a finding from past studies. One man recalled his rationale for migration, stating, "At that time, Korea was too poor. I was working at SuWon city hall in Korea. But we just could not live on a public employee's salary" (seventy-year-old father).

Although the older fathers worked more hours after migration than they did in Korea, it is hard to conclude that their excessive focus on economic provision for their families forced their migration to Canada. For example, three older fathers also mentioned that their provider role in Canada was not as critical as in Korea. One felt less burdened by breadwinning when he came to Canada because his wife also worked. "I was 100 per cent responsible for economic providing in Korea. I felt a huge responsibility because our standard of living could be changed depending on how I worked. But since I came here, my wife also worked. Well, here I wasn't really thinking about making money so much" (sixty-three-year-old father).

In many immigrant families, wives contributed to the household finances (Kibria, 1993; Min 1995, 2000). The older fathers in our sample were no exception. Most of the older fathers (n=11) were sole economic providers in Korea; however, all their wives shared the economic responsibilities when they moved to Canada. As was previously found, Asian immigrant wives often suffered from being overworked and overstressed as their employment did not mean an increase their husbands' participation in household labour (Hurh & Kim, 1984; Min 1995, 2000).

Many older Korean-Canadian fathers in our sample were rarely involved in child-rearing responsibilities. For example, although his wife worked full-time, a man with two children reported that he relied on her to make most of the family- and work-related decisions. "My wife always makes right decisions, much better than me. So, I follow 99 per cent to what she wants to do. If we have different opinions, I just follow her decision. Her decision is better for our family, business, and kids. It is a hundred times better than my decision" (sixty-seven-year-old father).

Similarly, when asked about child-rearing decisions, another man also stated that he just accepted his wife's. "That [making child-rearing decisions] was my wife's job. When Korean women meet their friends, they chit-chat and they make all decisions there. We [husbands] are drivers. We just follow our wives to shopping, to here and there" (seventy-year-old father).

Five fathers, however, had attempted to share childcare duties with their working wives. One who defined his paternal role as the "driver" took care of his children while his wife was working the night shift. "I changed diapers, fed milk ... pretty much all. I also washed them. I heard that now fathers in Korea are doing those things as well. Anyway, I had no choice since we both worked. I had to do all. I also cleaned the house. We worked different times. When I came from work, my wife went to work" (seventy-year-old father).

For more than fifteen years, a seventy-year-old father of three had worked during the night while his wife worked during the daytime. Although he mentioned that he did not participate much in childcare, his wife reported, "When I was at work, he did all. He feed the kids, cook food like spaghetti. He did his best."

The equal division of work and family responsibility was the norm for two older fathers. According to the wife of a sixty-four-year-old man, equal sharing of childcare duty with her husband was not unusual. "Without demanding on one person, we shared everything together. Whoever was available did the work. [Changing diapers and everything?] Yes, everything. Well, some families were different. But when I see my close college friends, they all live like us."

One father admitted that he had no idea how to take care of infants. Nevertheless, he participated in many childcare activities, since his wife was also a graduate student. "I did not know what to do. But there were only two of us. When changing diapers, I often pricked the child with a little pin by mistake. I was like that first. I also feed the kids. Especially for our older daughter, because she was a little restless before sleeping I sang all kinds of lullabies. I don't sing well, but back then I held the child and sang to make her sleep. And I played a lot with the kids. I mean, a lot! I let them try whatever they could" (seventy-five-year-old father).

Different from the rest of the older fathers, these two were co-parents and played a significant role in their children's everyday activities. Closer examination of the commonalities between the two fathers revealed that both came to Canada to pursue higher educational degrees, along with their wives who were graduate students. This link between education and the concept of egalitarian parenting supports Kwon and Roy's (2005) earlier study on first-generation immigrant Korean-American fathers. The authors found that Korean immigrant fathers with professional occupations, or those who migrated to the United States for their graduate education or for professional reasons, tended to participate more equally in childcare duties and responsibilities than fathers with non-professional occupations who migrated for economic reasons or for their children's education.

Among ten fathers who had limited experiences of early childcare, four insisted that they were engaged in their children's lives through sports. For example, a man with two sons recalled that he concentrated his efforts on teaching sports to his boys. "They needed to practice ice hockey, and rinks are available only in the early morning, like 3:00 or 4:00 a.m. So, high school students are practicing early. My responsibility was to send the kids to the rink, and I could not sleep enough" (sixty-seven-year-old father).

A father of three mentioned that he always checked his children's math homework, since he was good at math himself. For these fathers, paternal involvement started when their children entered school. These examples stress the importance of exploring paternal involvement throughout the lives of children rather than at particular points during early childhood.

New Fathering Expectations and Behaviours for Younger Korean Immigrant Fathers

Younger fathers who participated in this study were born during the industrialization and westernization era, from 1962 to 1975. Their experiences with their own fathers, who were in the same cohort as the older fathers in our sample, were also based on the economic-provider concept of fathering. One man emphasized the importance of his father as breadwinner during his life. "The first thing I can think of about my father is ... he was very sincere. He wasn't drinking or smoking at all. He never stayed out for whole night. Every day he went to work early in the morning when all other family members were sleeping. He was the first one to wake up. And because of his work, he went back home late, not to drink or spend time with his friends. He showed us how to be sincere" (thirty-eight-year-old father).

Many younger fathers viewed their fathers' focus on work as natural and appropriate: "Well, I don't think I wanted more from my father. When I was little ... I don't think it is just me. All Korean fathers are busy. I feel sorry that I could not have more time with my father. But Korean society did not let fathers have much time with their children" (forty-one-year-old father).

However, the characteristics of ideal fatherhood for Korean men have now changed. According to Kim (1997), younger Korean fathers live in an era when fathers' caregiving is no longer optional but required for being a good father. This new notion of fathering may have shaped younger first-generation immigrant fathers' expectations of paternal roles since they grew up during these societal changes before migrating to Canada. In contrast to what first-generation Korean immigrant fathers experienced as children, the younger fathers' personal ideal fathering roles centred on "taking good care of their children," "becoming a good friend to their children," "spending time with children," and "having as much communication as possible with the kids."

In the words of one, "I think spending time with children is important. Well, quality time might be important, but I don't think quality could not come without quantity. Quality and quantity of time with children should be balanced. Spending quality time is impossible if you just spend one or two hours with children. It is important to have much time with children. And in terms of emotions, I want my son to be proud of his daddy and wish to follow whatever Daddy is doing" (forty-year-old father).

One man moved to Canada when his sons were five and seven to pursue his postgraduate education. He had placed great emphasis on caring for his children even before coming to Canada, owing his flexible work schedule in Korea: "I washed the kids, took care of them when they were crying. I was with kids all the time after work. I did not have a busy job in Korea" (thirty-nine-year-old father).

The principle of fathers' becoming more actively involved in their children's lives has been supported by Kwon's (2010) cross-cultural study of Korean fathers living in South Korea and in the United States. Her findings reveal that the cultural setting (South Korea versus the United States) had no significant impact on paternal involvement in childcare. Rather, fathers had already accepted a more egalitarian approach to fathering and expected to be involved in their children's lives. This "new" conceptualization of Korean fatherhood was in line with the way other fathers around the world were redefining fatherhood (see Chuang & Moreno, 2008).

Younger immigrant fathers who came to Canada after the mid-1980s experienced two often contradictory messages of fathering in South Korea. Specifically, they had to deal with the new ideal of the caregiving father while balancing their heavy workload. Because of Korean society's expectation of hard work for men, a serious challenge for younger fathers to act upon their new fathering role was created. Most of the younger immigrant fathers came to Canada due to their educational or professional careers without thinking about migration. However, many of them preferred to live in Canada because the local lifestyle affords them more time to spend with their families. As an immigrant father reflected, "I like my life here, because in Korea I had a very busy schedule and life. But ever since I came here, I am just concentrating on my studying and that is all. I have more time with my children" (thirty-five-year-old father).

In contrast with the older fathers who came to Canada to become better breadwinners, most of the younger fathers in our sample (n=16) considered the Canadian context a more supportive culture where better caregivers were regarded as better fathers. One father commented, "Here, people think about family. Everything can be excused if there is a family business. In Korea, work is more important than family. When I talked with my friends in Korea, there is a big difference in the time they spend with family and kids. Here, there is nowhere to go after work. But in Korea, if I do not participate in social meetings [outside the family], I will be singled out. Wives also accept this situation. Thus, in Canada, I can be more sincere to my family" (forty-year-old father).

Min (2002) defined immigrant people as "active social actors" who explicitly attempt to negotiate identities and behaviours by presenting positive and advantageous identities in particular situations. The younger participants in our sample also emphasized their family lives as following what they believed to be valued by Canadian society. According to one father, "My role is similar to [that of] other Canadian fathers. Even if I am at work, everything could be excused when I have to pick up my kids. I am behaving more in that way unintentionally. If I have to go to my kids' school, I do not schedule any other stuff. Nothing is more of priority to family. That's the Canadian way of thinking, and I think I am somewhat changed compared with when I first came here" (thirty-seven-year-old father).

Moreover, fathers not only reconstructed their roles based on the socio-cultural values of the host country but also seemed very satisfied with such family values. When asked to compare their fathering behaviours with those of their counterparts in South Korea, many fathers emphasized that younger fathers in South Korea shared similar beliefs. However, as one father pointed out, "Even if they [fathers in South Korea] want to be with their children, they just can't because the tight working environment in Korea does not allow them to act on their ideology" (forty-two-year-old father). Another father stated, "Although I really want to be involved in childcare, I think I might not be able to do so in Korea" (forty-year-old father). He preferred living in Canada because his personality and role as an involved father were better suited to the Canadian context. Thus, paternal expectations that men develop within their socio-cultural and historical contexts do not necessarily correspond with their actual behaviours as fathers (LaRossa, 1988, 1997).

As evidenced in our study of younger first-generation Korean immigrant fathers in Canada in their thirties and forties, most of the fathers had conceptualized fathering as multi-dimensional (economic provider, caregiver, educator) even before migrating to Canada. Specifically, they wished to live in a country where family life was valued and balanced with the workplace. Thus, fathers were able to engage in a variety of caregiving activities, including changing diapers, bathing and feeding, putting children to bed, playing with them, and helping them with their homework. A father with a four-year-old son explained that he might have participated more in childcare than his wife. "Feeding him, washing him, and most importantly playing with him. I do all those things. I thought I had to do those activities because my wife was caring for him all day alone. But I figured out that when our son goes to the daycare at 8:00 a.m., he comes back at 1:00 p.m. And he is taking a nap for an hour or two. Then my wife actually takes care of him for only two or three hours before I come back! But by the time I realized it, we already had a routine. So he refused to take a bath with his mom [in charge]" (forty-year-old father).

One father whose wife was older than he was said that his active involvement in childcare was because his wife was physically weak. "Because she gave birth when she was over forty, I needed to help her a lot every day. I cleaned diapers, pretty much all … and did all the laundry. Those need to be hand washed. But it was hard for me to wash the baby. So, a lady from our church helped us a lot. Other than that, I did all."

The younger mothers who participated in the interview also welcomed their husbands' active engagement in childcare. A mother of two children, for instance, explained that her husband was worth "120 points as a father."

Six fathers of school-age children paid particular attention to their children's education. Many fathers perceived that they were more responsible for checking their children's homework because their English ability was better than their wives'. A forty-one-year-old father said that he spent one or two hours with the children's homework. Similarly, a man with two daughters strongly believed the importance of paternal involvement in a child's education: "If reading the same book, I think reading with Daddy is more effective than reading with Mommy at their age. Math and other subjects as well … learning could be more effective with dads than with moms. I don't know whether that's in general or just for my kids. I think a father should take care of education and, as I explained, that is easier in terms of language" (forty-two-year-old father).

Supporting earlier discussion of the paternal role in child development (Lamb, 2004; Chuang & Moreno, 2008) was our finding that the immigrant fathers' feeling of overall responsibility for the family did not change as much as their direct engagement in everyday duties did. Whereas all the fathers took part in caregiving, six fathers did not actively participate in decision-making processes (responsibility). For example, a father of two preschoolers was dependent on his wife to make the decisions: "Until now, I don't think my wife is making any strange decision. I trust my wife's choice. Because I spend long hours working, I don't have much time to focus on those things. If my wife needs my help, I help her. But she is making decisions and she has made positive decisions" (thirty-eight-year-old father).

Nevertheless, compared with the older participants, the majority of the younger fathers (n=12) were involved in making various kinds of decisions for the family. For instance, a father with one daughter would make the choices related to her education. "Where you live is important in the child's education because of the school location. In fact, we now live in an inexpensive neighbourhood. I searched school websites, and the school grades were near the bottom. I think we have to move and ... of course I discuss with my wife, but that's my decision" (thirty-five-year-old father).

The wife of another thirty-five-year-old father explained that his was the last word. "Making the final decision is his responsibility while I suggest many things. Most of my suggestions are denied, but I don't want to do what he doesn't want ... I thought this and that is good for the kids ... I should teach kids many things. But when I think back, my husband was right in many things. So, I am trying to follow my husband's decision."

Other fathers, in contrast, reported that they had equal weight in decision making through discussions and negotiations with their wives on all child-rearing issues. This collaboration between Korean immigrant parents is similar to the practices of Chinese immigrant parents and Chinese parents of young children (Chuang & Su, 2009).

An important finding that emerged from the interview data with younger fathers is the relationship between their work and their paternal involvement. Although younger fathers in our sample placed priority on their family life, their actual engagement in child rearing was more likely shaped by their work situation. As described in the previous section, flexible and less demanding work motivated younger fathers to immigrate to Canada. Of the five fathers who first raised their children in South Korea, three reported that their paternal involvement had increased when they settled in Canada, partly due to their reduced working hours. A man with two children had his first son in South Korea and said that he "rarely took part in childcare because [he] went out for work early and came back late in Korea" (forty-nine-year-old father).

Different from most immigrant fathers, two in our sample worked more hours and were less involved in childcare activities in Canada than they had been in South Korea. A father of two sons came to Canada for his postgraduate education. He also served as a youth pastor. "I spent more hours with my family and kids when I was in Korea. There, I had enough time because I worked just nine to five, and we lived near my wife's family. So we all got together on weekends. Even now, the kids say that they miss those days. I had good time with the boys" (forty-five-year-old father).

Among the fathers who had their first child in Canada, two mentioned that their childcare participation level had changed relative to their working hours. Similar to the older fathers, they had limited interaction with their children due to the focus required for their new businesses. Their active involvement started when they changed occupation, affording them more time with their families. A father of two was a full-time graduate student. When he first came to Canada, he owned his own business, which left him little opportunity to take care of his first son. "No, I didn't do anything. Not at all, because I owned a business in Toronto. I was an owner of a small store and I could not do any of those [childcare]. Mom did all. At that time, I went work at 3:00 a.m. and came home at 10:00 a.m." (thirty-five-year-old father). When he became a student, he could devote the same amount of time as his wife to childcare chores.

The occupations of the younger fathers in our sample did not influence their fathering, but the time required for their work could have an impact on childcare, as similarly illustrated in previous study findings (e.g., Almeida & McDonald, 2005; Berry & Rao, 1997; Elliot, 1986). Korean immigrant fathers may not adhere to traditional paternal practices but instead actively participate in childcare as their work situation permits. Thus, a Korean immigrant man's work context rather than his cultural background may be regarded as the greater indicator of his individual paternal involvement in childcare (Kwon, 2010).

Discussions

Although the history of Korean immigration to Canada dates back fifty years, little academic attention has been paid to the evolving experience of fatherhood in Korean-Canadian families. In this chapter, we have attempted to explore the way fathering has been re-conceptualized and transformed over the developmental (i.e., various fathering stages from infancy to adolescence of offspring) and socio-cultural contexts (e.g., migration, dual cultures, work) of their lives. To support our premise that the subject needs examination, we have provided evidence from our comparative study of two different cohorts of first-generation Korean-Canadian fathers (in their sixties and seventies, and in their thirties and forties).

Recently, researchers such as ourselves (e.g., Chuang & Su, 2008, 2009;

Kwon, 2010; Kwon & Roy, 2005) and others (e.g., Akira & Chao, 2008) have challenged the relevance of Confucianism to contemporary Asian families. Our present study further supports the contention that Confucianism may not be as influential on Korean families as once thought, particularly for younger fathers. Our results suggest the possibility that Korean immigrant fathers are not traditional or distinct from other fathers of various ethnic backgrounds (see Chuang & Moreno, 2008; Chuang & Tamis-LeMonda, 2009). Rather, Korean immigrant fathers have a multi-dimensional view of the roles of fathers. We also found that Korean immigrant fathers were active participants in society who not only adjusted their fathering conceptions to their new socio-cultural environments in Canada but also chose the cultural setting where they could be better fathers based on their notions of ideal fathering. Moreover, we raised the importance of exploring socio-cultural and historical contexts that fathers had known before coming to Canada.

The older Korean immigrant fathers who came to Canada before the early1980s had developed their notions of ideal fathering during South Korea's economic-boom period after the Korean War. Although their fathering experiences of their own fathers were mostly related to Confucianism (father as the authority figure), the ideal fathering concept that they developed within their socio-cultural context was to be successful economic providers in order to offer educational opportunities for their children.

Although older Korean immigrant fathers could not spend significant amounts of time in caregiving, they were not necessarily following the traditional paternal role as defined by Confucian principle. Different from previous studies that showed mothers' overwork and fathers' unchanged gender-role attitude after migration (see Hurh & Kim, 1984; Kibria, 1993; Min 1995, 2000), ours indicated that older fathers' lack of involvement in childcare duties after coming to Canada was the result of time constraints imposed by their work duties. Levels of paternal involvement, in general, increased in Canada as fathers shared childcare with their wives. However, responsibility for childcare (e.g., childcare-related decisions, making doctor's appointments) remained limited for older Korean immigrant fathers. This result supported previous findings about the various levels of paternal involvement (direct engagement versus responsibility in the abstract) (McBride & Mills, 1993).

Consistent with the few studies on first-generation Asian immigrant couples with young children in North America (e.g., Chao & Kim, 2000;

Chuang & Su, 2008), the Confucian traditions and norms of paternal involvement were rarely examined in roles of younger Korean immigrant fathers in our study. Different from the older fathers, younger Korean-Canadian fathers were actively involved not only in direct caregiving activities (engagement and accessibility) but also in the childcare decision-making processes (responsibility).

As a Korean immigrant father explained, South Korean society has undergone rapid changes, and younger first-generation Korean-Canadian fathers were experiencing the effect of westernized values on family roles even before they came to Canada (Kwon, 2010). "They [fathers in Korea] love their kids as much as I love my kids. When I talked with my friends in Korea, they felt really confused with and sorry about their roles. If they could finish their work on time, and could spend their evening with the kids ... wow, their family life would blossom!" (thirty-seven-year-old father).

Thus, their parental role expectations of an engaged father were realized as they encountered the family-focused values of Canadian society. This cultural emphasis on appreciating family time and relationships was also expressed as a motivating factor for some Korean families to migrate to Canada.

As LaRossa (1997) pointed out, it is important for researchers to explicitly explore the distinction between paternal expectations and actual behaviours. For example, although Korean men's paternal involvement was limited, this limitation was not reflective of Confucian norms and traditions. Rather, the social and economic contexts around fathers prevented them from following their wish to be fully engaged with their children. Within various contexts and situations, the work contexts for younger fathers and dual earning status in Canada for older fathers emerged to be important indicators of fathers' actual involvement in childcare. Many theories and studies about contextual influences on individual behaviours (e.g., Bubolz & Sontag, 1993; Kwon, 2010) also stressed how diverse contexts indirectly shaped individual behaviours. Our findings also support this contention.

There were some limitations of the present study that need to be taken into consideration. First, our qualitative study featured a small sample, limiting the generalizability of our results. Second, we had a homogeneous sample, with most fathers being well educated and in successful marriages. Although we tried to recruit families from varying socio-economic backgrounds, recruiting strategies were less fruitful than anticipated. As Lamb (2008) asserts, immigrant life for fathers could be understood differently by taking into account factors such as their reasons for immigration and their socio-economic status. Thus, to understand the diversity and dynamics of Korean-Canadian fathering and family relationships, it would be important to include participants from different backgrounds, family experiences, and immigration statuses. In addition, there were some fathers who lived in South Korea while their spouses and children resided in Canada (so-called wild-goose [*kirogi*] fathers). This type of family arrangement and the consequent lack of physical interaction critically shapes the level of fathering in their children's lives.

In sum, this study provides insight into a number of issues uncovered in research on Korean (and other Asian) immigrant fathers in North American countries. By comparing two cohorts of fathers, we have brought into focus the need to consider their personal relocation experiences relative to the societal and cultural dynamics in both their country of origin and their new home. Moreover, we have emphasized the active agency of Korean immigrant fathers in their own paternal role development as they adapt to socio-cultural changes. Building on our examination of the lives of Korean immigrant fathers in Canada, further exploration of the construction of fatherhood in various ethnic and socio-economic groups would advance scholarship on ethnic minority families and fathering in transition from one culture to another.

REFERENCES

Akira, K., and Chao, R.K. (2008). Asian immigrant fathers as primary caregivers of adolescents. In S.S. Chuang and R.P. Moreno (Eds.), *On new shores: Understanding immigrant fathers in North America*, (pp. 151–74). Lanham, MD: Lexington Books.

Allen, S., and Hawkins, A. (1999). Maternal gatekeeping: Mother's beliefs and behaviors that inhibit greater father involvement in family work. *Journal of Marriage and the Family, 61,* 199–212.

Almeida, D.M., and McDonald, D.A. (2005). The national story: How Americans spend their time on work, family and community. In J. Heymann and C. Beem (Eds.), *Unfinished work: Building equality and democracy in an era of working families* (pp.180–203). New York: New Press.

Arendell, T. (1996). *Co-parenting: A review of the literature.* Philadelphia: National Center on Fathers and Families.

Beatty, M.J., and Dobos, J.A. (1993). Adult males' perceptions of confirmation and relational partner communication apprehension: Indirect effects of fathers on sons' partners. *Communication Quarterly, 41*, 66–76.

Berry, J.O., and Rao, J.M. (1997). Balancing employment and fatherhood: A systems perspective. *Journal of Family Issues, 18*, 386–402.

Bubolz, M.M., and Sontag, M.S. (1993). Human ecology theory. In P.G. Boss, W.J. Doherty, R. LaRossa, W.R. Schumm, and S.K. Steinmetz (Eds.), *Sourcebook of family theories and methods: A contextual approach* (pp. 419–48). New York: Plenum Press.

Chan, S. (1998). Families with Asian Roots. In E.W. Lynch and M.J. Hanson (Eds.), *Developing cross-cultural competence* (pp. 251–344). Baltimore: Maple Press.

Chao, R., and Kim, K. (2000). Parenting differences among immigrant Chinese fathers and mothers in the United States. *Journal of psychology in Chinese societies, 1*, 71–91.

Chuang, S.S., and Moreno, R.P. (Eds.) (2008). *On new shores: Understanding immigrant fathers in North America*. Lanham, MD: Lexington Books.

Chuang, S.S., and Su, Y. (2008). Transcending Confucian teaching on fathering: A sign of the times or acculturation? In S.S. Chuang and R.P. Moreno (Eds.), *On new shores: Understanding immigrant fathers in North America* (pp. 129–50). Lanham, MD: Lexington Books.

———. (2009). Says who?: Decision-making and conflicts among Chinese-Canadian and mainland Chinese parents of young children. *Sex Roles, 60*, 527–36.

Chuang, S.S., and Tamis-LeMonda, C. (2009). Gender roles in immigrant families: Parenting views, practices, and child development, *Sex Roles, 60*, 451–5.

Eggebeen, D.J., and Knoester, C. (2001). Does fatherhood matter for men? *Journal of Marriage and Family, 63*, 381–93.

Elliot, F.R. (1986). *The family: Change or continuity?* London: Macmillan Education.

Foner, N. (1997). The immigrant family: Cultural legacies and cultural changes. *International Migration Review, 31*, 961–74

Han, K. (1997). Change of fatherhood in Korea. Korean woman research institute (Ed.), *Men in the Korean society* (pp. 33–52). Seoul: Socio-Cultural Research Institute.

Han, J.D., and Ibbott, P. (2004). *Korean migration to North America: Some prices that matter*. Retrieved from http://www.unb.ca/fredericton/arts/departments/ economics/acea/ pdfs/ 2004_4.pdf.

Hurh, W., and Kim, K. (1984). *Korean Immigrants in America: A structural analysis of ethnic confinement and adhesive adaptation*. Madison, NJ: Fairleigh Dickinson University Press.

Ishii-Kuntz, M. (1993). Japanese fathers: Work demands and family roles. In J.C. Hood (Ed.), *Men, work and family* (pp. 45–67). Newbury Park, CA: Sage
———. (2000). Diversity within Asian American families. In D. Demo, K. Allen, and M. Fine (Eds.), *Handbook of family diversity* (pp. 252–73). New York: Oxford University Press.

Jasso, G. (2003). Migration, human development, and the life course. In J.T. Morimer and M.J. Shanahan (Eds.), *Handbook of life course* (pp. 331–64). New York: Kluwer Academic/Plenum Publishers.

Kibria, N. (1993). *Family tightrope: The changing lives of Vietnamese Americans.* Princeton: Princeton University Press.

Kim, C. (1997). Problems and movements of young generation. In H. Ahn, S. Kim, C. Kim, and H. Kim (Eds.), *Young generation of Korea: Conflicts and responses of 30s* (pp. 95–145). Seoul: Korean Research Institute of Young Generation.

Kim, E. (2008). Korean immigrant fathering: Dealing with two cultures. In S.S. Chuang and R.P. Moreno (Eds.), *On new shores: Understanding immigrant fathers in North America* (pp. 175–95). Lanham, MD: Lexington Books.

Kim, E., and Cain, K. (2008). Korean American adolescent depression and parenting. *Journal of Child and Adolescent Psychiatric Nursing, 21*, 105–15.

Kim, E., and Hong, S. (2007). First-generation Korean American parents' perceptions on discipline. *Journal of Professional Nursing, 23*, 60–68.

Kim, K.C., and Kim, S. (1995). Family and work roles of Korean immigrants in the United States. In E.T.H. McCubbin, A. Thompson, and J. Fromer (Eds.), *Resiliency in ethnic minority families. Vol. 1: Native and immigrant American families* (pp. 225–43). Madison: University of Wisconsin.

Kwon, Y. (2010). Paternal involvement within contexts: Ecological examination of Korean fathers in Korea and in the U.S. *International Journal of Human Ecology, 11*, 35–47.

Kwon, Y., and Roy, K.M. (2005, November). *Cultural negotiation and fatherhood for first and   second generation Korean immigrant fathers.* Paper presentation at the annual meeting of the National Council on Family Relations, Phoenix.
———. (2007). Changing social expectations and work and family experiences for middle-class and working-class fathers in Korea. *Journal of Comparative Family Studies, 38*, 285–304.

Lamb, M. (2000). A history of research on father involvement: An overview. *Marriage and Family Review, 29*, 23–42.

Lamb, M.E. (Ed.). (2004). *The role of the father in child development* (4th ed.). New York: Wiley.

Lamb, M., Pleck, J., Charnov, E., and Levine, J. (1987). A biosocial perspective on paternal behavior and involvement. In J. Lancaster, J. Altmann, A. Rossi, and L. Sherrod (Eds.), *Parenting across lifespan: Biosocial dimensions* (pp. 111–42). Hawthorne, NY: Aldine de Gruyter.

LaRossa, R. (1988). Fatherhood and social change. *Family Relations, 37,* 451–7.

———. (1997). *The modernization of fatherhood.* Chicago: University of Chicago.

Lee, K. (1997). *Korean family and kinship.* Seoul: Jipmoondang.

Lee, S. (1997). Fathers' professional work and family conflict. Korean Woman Research Institute (Ed.), *Men in the Korean society* (pp. 53–80). Seoul: Socio-cultural Research Institute.

Lee, M. (April 2001). *Reality of Korean education and diverse aspects of children's studying abroad.* Paper presented at the Korean Educational Development Institute Conference, Seoul, Korea.

Lee, M., Kho, S., and Kwon, H. (2000). Economic stress, marital conflict, and the quality of life under economic crisis. *Korean Journal of Home Economics, 138,* 117–32.

McBride, B.A., and Mills, G. (1993). A comparison of mother and father involvement with their preschool age children. *Early Childhood Research Quarterly, 8,* 457–77.

Marsiglio, W., Roy, K., and Fox, G.L. (2005). *Situated fathering: A focus on physical and social spaces.* Boulder: Rowman and Littlefield.

Min, P. (1995). The relationship between Korean immigrant parents and children. *The Academic Review of Korean Studies, 18,* 119–36.

———. (2000). Korean American families. In R. Taylor (Ed.), *Minority families in the United States: A multicultural perspective* (3rd ed.), (pp. 193–211). Upper Saddle River, NJ: Prentice Hall.

———. (2002). Introduction. In P. Min (Ed.), *Second generation: Ethnic identity among Asian Americans* (pp. 1–17). Lanham, MD: AltaMira Press.

Park, J. (2012). Demographic profile of Koreans in Canada, chapter 2, this volume.

Part, I., and Cho, L. (1995). Confucianism and the Korean family. *Journal of Comparative Family Studies, 26,* 117–34.

Pleck, E.H. (2004). Two dimensions of fatherhood: A history of the good dad – bad dad complex. In M.E. Lamb (Ed.), *The role of the father in child development* (4th ed.), (pp. 32–57). New York: Wiley.

Pleck, J.H., and Masciadrelli, B.P. (2004). Paternal involvement by U.S. residential fathers: Levels, sources, and consequences. In M.E. Lamb (Ed.), *The role of the father in child development* (4th ed.), (pp. 222–70). New York: Wiley.

Roggman, L.A., Fitzgerald, H.E., Bradley, R.H., and Raikes, H. (2002). Methodological, measurement, and design issues in studying fathers: An interdisciplinary perspective. In C.S. Tamis-LeMonda and N. Cabrera (Eds.), *Handbook of father involvement* (pp. 1–30). Mahwah, NJ: Erlbaum.

Shwalb, D.W., Nakazawa, J., Yamamoto, T., and Hyun, J. (2010). Fathering in Japan, China, and Korea. In M.E. Lamb (Ed.), *The role of the father in child development* (5th ed.), (pp. 341–87). New York: Wiley.

Statistics Canada. (2006). *The daily: 2006 Census: Immigration, citizenship, language, mobility and migration.* Retrieved from http://www.Statcan.ca/Daily/English/071204/d071204a.htm.

Statistics Korea (1998). *1997 Annual report of Korean society.* Seoul: Statistics Korea.

———. (2000). *1999 Annual report of Korean society.* Seoul: Statistics Korea.

———. (2004). *2003 Annual report of Korean society.* Seoul: Statistics Korea.

Suh, H., and Lee, S. (1999). The relations of work-father role conflict with parent satisfaction and parenting sense of competence. *Korean Journal of family relations, 4,* 257–80.

Sung, S. (1998). Familism in the IMF period and gender identity crisis. *Journal of Korean Feminism, 18,* 75–91.

Verschueren, K., and Marcoen, A. (1999). Representation of self and socioemotional competence in kindergartners: Differential and combined effects of attachment to mother and to father. *Child Development, 70,* 183–201.

Yun, H.S. (2005). Restructuring the family policy from the gender-integrating perspective: Reconciling work and family life. *Korean Social Welfare, 57,* 291–319.

Zimmerman, M.A., Salem, D.A., and Maton, K.I. (1995). Family structure and psychological correlates among urban African-American adolescent males. *Child Development, 66,* 1598–1613.

14 *Kirogi* Families as Virtual "Families": Perspectives and Experiences of *Kirogi* Mothers[1]

JUNMIN JEONG AND DANIÈLE BÉLANGER

Introduction

The *kirogi*, or wild goose, has long been considered a "good" animal by Koreans. Because they are believed to keep the same partner for life and diligently take care of their young, wild geese have symbolized the virtues married couples should follow in Korea (Portal, 2000). A pair of carved wooden geese can always be seen at traditional Korean weddings to symbolize the hope that the new couple will stay together forever.

However, such togetherness is not what defines families referred to as *kirogi gajok*, or "wild-geese families" in Korea. This term, coined by the Korean media in the mid-1990s, refers to "split-household transnational families" (Yeoh et al., 2005), in which the familial arrangement generally involves the overseas migration of mothers and their children to English-speaking countries, mainly the United States, Canada, or Australia. Fathers remain in South Korea as breadwinners, working and sending money to their families overseas, and occasionally travelling to visit their families.

The main objective of *kirogi* migration is to enable children to be educated in the English language, a desire shared by many families since

1 A previous version of this paper was presented at the forty-fifth Annual Meeting and Conference of the Canadian Sociological Association, Montreal, Quebec, in June 2010. We express our gratitude to all study participants who generously shared their stories with us. We thank Guida Man, Tania Das Gupta, Rina Cohen, Ann Kim, and Alan Simmons for their insightful comments and suggestions. We also thank Byunghoon Jeong, Sungyee Kim, and Kyungshin Park for their help, particularly in searching the Korean literature. We extend our recognition to Gale Cassidy for editing.

the recent "English Boom" in South Korea, a trend that began in the 1990s. Two key events – the South Korean government's active implementation of *sekyehwa woondong* (globalization campaign), and South Korea's admission to the Organization for Economic Cooperation and Development (OECD) in 1996 – have glamourized the importance of Koreans' becoming global citizens. As a result, being fluent in English began to be perceived as an important advantage in both the South Korean educational system and the job market (Lee & Koo, 2006). In addition, South Korea's large diaspora produced a second generation of bilingual South Koreans. Because some elect to work in South Korea, they are seen as competing with young, educated, Korean graduates who have not mastered English to the same extent. In response, many Korean parents who are able have chosen to send their children overseas with the hope that they can reach near-native fluency. In Chew's (2009, p. 34) words, these parents are in "pursuit of linguistic gold" because they now live in a society where "linguistic capital" – English – is a much-desired commodity.

Based on thirty interviews with Korean women migrants who are members of *kirogi* families living in a Canadian mid-size city, this chapter examines how the *kirogi* family arrangement affects family relationships. Our analysis focuses on women's perspectives on their family dynamics since migration. We examine how being a family while living apart repositions family members toward each other in new ways. We document some of both positive and negative experiences of *kirogi* family members.

Our main argument is that while distance may be a challenge in keeping the family together, it is also a catalyst for redefining the boundaries of previously established roles and relationships. Our data underscore how gender and intergenerational relations change after migration. The chapter analyzes shifts in relationships between husbands and wives, mothers and children, and fathers and children. Through communication technology, family members in Canada and South Korea can maintain daily conversations, exchanges, and sharing. Results show how a post-migration "virtual intimacy" creates a new relational space in which family dynamics are transformed. Interestingly, most family members physically separated since migration spend more time communicating with one another after migration than before; study participants generally feel that this time together was quality time, and that in-depth sharing and mutual understanding are enhanced. The chapter proposes a typology of families and the changes that they experienced by linking family relations prior to and following migration. The findings are situated within the literature on transnational families, virtual intimacy, and the impact of migration on gender and intergenerational relations.

First, this chapter is informed by the literature on transnational families. Past research indicates that transnationalism for Asian families often results from "strategic intents." Among these intents, children's education has been documented as being a "strong impetus for [Asian] families to go transnational" (Yeoh et al., 2005, p. 307). Transnational families are also studied for how they negotiate intimacies and power relations across space (Pratt & Yeoh, 2003). An examination of how transnationalism may, or may not, lead to the reconfiguration of power and gender relations in families is needed. Some scholars note that some forms of transnationalism may "fail to transcend, or trouble, the ideological gender bases upon which social identities are built" (Yeoh et al., 2005, p. 311).

Second, the chapter is situated within research about transnational communication. Among the various forms of transnational activities performed by migrants, communication with family members abroad stands as the most frequent and common one (Vertovec, 2009). Scholars of transnationalism argue that communication between family members today differs in nature from what migrants used to do, suggesting that information and communication technology (ICT) has allowed for a steadiness, intensity, and frequency of communication that was impossible to imagine a few decades ago (Vertovec, 2009). With webcams, individuals can spend virtual time with each other – talking, partaking in meals, and sharing daily activities while seeing the other. The Internet and cell phones also allow for news to be shared immediately. The concept of being together takes on new meaning when migrants create transnational family spaces for expression and sharing. Other researchers, however, disagree that ICT has transformed transnational family life and see ICT as an extension of earlier means of communication, such as letters or phone calls (Wilding, 2006). The degree to which ICT shapes transnational family relations varies according to countries of origin and destination, cultural ideals of family relations, and preferences for mode of communication based on age and gender.

Kirogi Families

Migration patterns similar to the one of *kirogi* families have been observed previously in other Asian countries, such as Hong Kong, Taiwan, China, and Japan (e.g., "parachute kids," "astronaut families"; see Pe Pua et al., 1996; Waters, 2002). The uniqueness of *kirogi* families is that they are initiated by Korean parents, who, for the sake of their children's education, are willing to maintain a fractured family for many years, even at the cost of a possible family dissolution (Cho, 2007; Lee & Koo, 2006).

The exact number of *kirogi* families is unknown, but one can infer their increase by the dramatic rise in the number of Korean students studying abroad since the new millennium. Korean students attending schools abroad from kindergarten through Grade 12 numbered 27,349 in 2008, compared with only 7,944 in 2001. During the same period, the increase in the number of elementary school students studying abroad has outpaced that of middle and high school students – from 2,107 students to 12,531 students (Korean Educational Development Institute, 2009). Meanwhile, the most popular destination for *kirogi* families has been the United States. In 2008, 13,156 Korean students left for the United States (32.1 per cent), followed by 7,983 for Southeast Asia (19.5 per cent), 5,415 for China (13.2 per cent), 5,172 for Canada (12.6 per cent), 2,046 for Australia (5.0 percent), and 1,636 for New Zealand (4.0 per cent) (Korean Educational Development Institute, 2009).

In recent years, research has responded to the increases in the number of *kirogi* families, and a number of studies have documented the various experiences and difficulties encountered by its members. Earlier literature has mainly focused on three areas.

First, a variety of studies have looked into the reasons behind the growing number of *kirogi* families in South Korea (e.g., Cho, 2007; Kim & Yoon, 2005; Lee & Larson, 2000; Sohn, 2005). Much of the emphasis has been on the overly competitive nature of the Korean education system. Many authors discuss how the education system forces South Korean parents to seek alternative measures for their children's education overseas. For example, Kim and Yoon (2005) point out two main problems in South Korea's current education system: (1) the inadequate quality of public school education, and (2) the "exam hell" that South Korean students must endure to gain admission to college, which is a product of the government's unstable educational policies. As a result, parents are faced with two choices: to stay and spend a great amount of money on private education, or to go abroad. Sohn (2005) has found that parents are more likely to choose the latter if they are (1) more highly educated, (2) place greater value on education, (3) have higher incomes, and (4) work in the service sector.

Second, many extensive qualitative studies have been conducted on *kirogi* fathers, possibly owing to the fact that South Korean scholars have easier access to these fathers, who are in the same country. This string of research has mainly investigated the problems and challenges experienced by *kirogi* fathers while living alone in South Korea, and the strategies they use to cope with stress and difficulties they encounter (e.g., Kim, 2005; Kim, 2006; Lee & Koo, 2006). Kim (2006), for example, has argued that there are three main types of problems that *kirogi* fathers are likely to confront: (1) family relationship problems coming from isolation; (2) psychological problems resulting from loneliness; and (3) economic problems related to financial pressure and a drop in economic status. While such findings tend to support the popular belief that fathers are the real sufferers in the *kirogi* families, there are also studies that discuss the positive effects of separation: for instance, *kirogi* fathers can focus more on their work and may develop a stronger emotional attachment to their families (see Lee & Koo, 2006).

Third, past literature has focused on *kirogi* children, mainly the effect on them of studying abroad at an early age (e.g., Cho, 2000; Lee, 2010; Yeom, 2008). The central question has been whether the benefits of going overseas for an English education offset the risks involved, such as the father's absence in the early socialization process. There has also been interest in children's re-integration after they return to Korea; however, the findings in this area of research have been mixed. For example, in her qualitative study with two *kirogi* children, Yeom (2008) argues that there is as much negative as positive impact on children from *kirogi* families. Such a finding is not surprising, given that the *kirogi* family is a recent phenomenon, and authors agree that more time is needed for the findings in this area to mature (Lee, 2010; Yeom, 2008).

Despite this growing interest in *kirogi* families in academia, few studies have discussed *kirogi* mothers. Existing studies on *kirogi* mothers are generally one-dimensional: they are simply described as sacrificing their lives for the sake of their children (see Chew, 2009; Cho, 2004; Choi, 2006). These narrow descriptions and the prevailing negative stereotypes about *kirogi* mothers motivated our study. In South Korea and among Korean ethnic communities abroad, *kirogi* mothers are often seen as women who have abandoned their husbands and parents-in-law, and are interested only in the well-being of their children (Kim, 2005). Moreover, the South Korean media occasionally portray *kirogi* migration as a strategy that wives can use to flee and avoid burdensome duties in their homeland (Park, 2004). In addition, *kirogi* mothers are subject to anything-could-have-happened-there suspicions once they return to South Korea.

The second motivation underlying our investigation into mothers' perspectives is to offer an alternative narrative to the existing literature, particularly research produced by South Korean scholars published in both Korean and English. Many authors have argued that this unique familial arrangement is likely to lead to the deterioration of relationships between family members (Chew, 2009; Choi, 2006; Kim, 2006). For example, Cho (2004) has argued that during the *kirogi* arrangement, a father tends to become nothing more than a money supplier to his family, ignored and excluded from most family affairs. Eventually, men will lose their paternal status in the family (Kim, 2006). Despite these findings and the contributions of previous authors, we believe a full assessment of the *kirogi* family process cannot be complete without considering the voice of *kirogi* mothers. This chapter aims to address the issue by providing women's perspectives on their experiences as *kirogi* mothers and women.

Methodology

In-depth interviews were conducted with thirty *kirogi* mothers in a mid-size Canadian city. Interviews lasted for sixty to ninety minutes, and each interview was audio-recorded and transcribed. All interviews were conducted in Korean by the first author of this study, who is Korean Canadian. Interviews took place at either the interviewee's home or local coffee shops. The thirty *kirogi* mothers were recruited by snowball-sampling procedures, which proved to be highly effective. Snowball sampling is a referral-sampling method, which uses a process of chain referrals (Singleton & Straits, 2005). The researcher was first introduced to two *kirogi* mothers through an acquaintance of his at the local Korean church. These first study participants introduced other *kirogi* mothers to the interviewer. The women ranged in age from thirty-four to fifty-two years at the time of the interview, with an average of 43.1 years. The average period of separation was two years and eight months, with a range from six months to seven years and ten months of separation. The women had, on average, 2.1 children, and all mothers had university degrees. A brief profile of the thirty *kirogi* mothers who took part in this study is provided in table 14.1.

The data collection for this study was carried out from August 2009 to April 2010. The interview guidelines asked study participants mainly about their pre-migration background, decision to migrate, family relationships before and after the migration, daily activities, social networking in the host country, and the difficulties and challenges they faced. Although many questions related to intimacy and private family matters, most participants answered them in great detail. For many, talking out their problems during the interview helped to relieve their stress. Also, some mothers were hoping that the negative image of *kirogi* mothers perpetuated by the South Korean media could be changed through the publication of this research. Interview transcripts were analysed thematically with the assistance of the N-Vivo software. The study was approved by the Research Ethics Board of the home institution of the authors.

Findings

We structure our analysis by examining three sets of relationships: wife-husband, mother-children, and father-children. In discussing their family relations, study participants referred to how these relationships evolved over the migration process. In fact, when situating the decision to migrate in their lives and in assessing the current status of their relationships, interviewees spontaneously discussed their family circumstances and relationships prior to migration. When assessing their lives in Canada, they frequently compared "now" and "before" to emphasize the direction of change or stability in their relationships. In her study of astronaut mothers living in Vancouver, Waters (2002) discusses the need to approach gender power relations among transnational families as evolving over time. She documents how, in the early settlement process, astronaut migration may disempower women and deepen their financial dependency on their husbands. When analysing women's lives after a number of years in Canada as astronaut mothers, she documents how women became empowered and gained a sense of independence and freedom, despite being financially dependent on their husbands (Waters, 2002). In the analysis below, we focus on the relationships following migration. In the discussion that follows, we link the present with the past in an attempt to propose a typology of families. While our findings seem to be coherent with what many others find, we propose a framework for understanding the interplay between international migration and family relationships among transnational nuclear families at the micro level.

Table 14.1. Profile of the *Kirogi* Mothers Study Participants

Case Name	Age	Length of Separation	Education	Previous Occupation	Current Occupation	Husband's Occupation	Number of Children	Total Household Income (CAD)	Status in Canada
Alexis	41	1 year 6 months	MA	Cellist	–	Researcher	2	$75,000	I–L
Allison	46	6 years 9 months	BA	Florist	–	Professor	2	$100,000	I–L
Cecilia	44	3 years 2 months	BA	–	Cashier	Business	2	$50,000	I–L
Claudia	52	6 months	BA	–	–	Business	3	(N/A)	I–L
Crystal	34	1 year 3 months	BA	–	–	Business	3	(N/A)	I–F
Cynthia	43	1 year 6 months	PhD	Professor	–	Engineer	2	$75,000	I–F
Daniele	45	2 years	BA	–	–	Banker	1	$120,000	I–F
Ellen	44	1 year 3 months	MA	Piano Tutor	Student	Professor	2	$120,000	I–F
Eva	45	5 years	BA	–	–	Journalist	2	$85,000	I–F
Helen	35	1 year 2 months	BA	Private Tutor	Cafeteria	Investor	2	$120,000	I–L
Janette	51	7 year 10 months	BA	Banker	–	Business	2	$100,000	I–F
Jessica	39	1 year	BA	–	–	Consultant	2	$90,000	I–L
Juliana	49	2 years	MA	Nutritionist	–	Researcher	2	$70,000	I–L
Laura	48	2 years 7 months	BA	HS Teacher	–	Professor	1	$90,000	(N/A)
Lily	40	5 years	BA	–	–	Business	2	$90,000	I–L
Maggie	49	6 years 6 months	BA	–	–	Consultant	2	(N/A)	Study
Margaret	42	2 years 3 months	BA	–	–	Architect	3	$100,000	I–L
May	42	2 years 9 months	BA	–	Cashier	Business	2	$100,000	I–L
Melinda	42	4 years	BA	–	Student	Foreign Trade	2	(N/A)	Study
Melissa	43	1 year 3 months	BA	–	–	Business	2	$95,000	I–F
Melonie	38	1 year	BA	Business	–	Business	2	$125,000	I–F
Mindy	43	2 years 3 months	MA	Programmer	–	Executive	2	$80,000	I–F
Nicole	40	1 year	MA	Instructor	Student	Instructor	2	$80,000	I–F
Sammy	48	3 years 4 months	BA	–	–	Professor	2	$100,000	I–L
Sandy	41	1 year 1 month	BA	Sales	Cashier	Business	2	(N/A)	Study

Table 14.1. Profile of the *Kirogi* Mothers Study Participants (*concluded*)

Case Name	Age	Length of Separation	Education	Previous Occupation	Current Occupation	Husband's Occupation	Number of Children	Total Household Income (CAD)	Status in Canada
Shannon	43	1 year 8 months	BA	Pharmacist	–	Pharmacist	2	(N/A)	I–L
Stephanie	45	5 years	BA	Illustrator	–	Journalist	2	$80,000	I–L
Susan	42	1 year	BA	–	–	Business	2	$90,000	I–F
Terra	38	3 years 2 months	BA	–	–	Consultant	3	$50,000	I–L
Terresa	41	1 year 10 months	Ph.D.	Professor	–	Banker	2	$130,000	I–L

*Note: Age at the time of interview

I–L: Landed Immigrant, I–F, Immigration applicant with application file number only, Study: on study visa.

Spousal Relationships

The literature on transnational Asian families that resemble *kirogi* families (e.g., for astronaut mothers in Canada, see Waters, 2002; for Taiwanese "study" mothers in the United States, see Chee, 2003) underscores the diversity of experiences reported by women who took part in these studies with respect to their marital relationships after migration. We find that most women reported that their relationships either improved or deteriorated after migration, but some reported no change. These results are similar to Chee's (2003) findings in her study of a group of Taiwanese women who migrated with their children to the United States for educational purposes. We noted that among our interviewees, women who experienced greater emotional distance and more frequent conflicts after migration also talked about their pre-migration relationship as being troubled and unstable.

One recurrent theme in the narratives was that husbands felt like strangers during reunions. For women in these relationships, the feeling of strangeness and the realization that they had become very accustomed to living without their husbands stood as the most negative aspect of the physical distance. Mindy provides an example: "But it was after my husband's first visit here ... like, after he left ... that's when I really ... like, really missed him for the first time. I mean, it felt so hard to be here by yourself, do everything on your own. That realization was hard to take, but the thing is, after his second and then third visit, things became much easier for me to handle. I mean, ... you get to ... like, you don't miss him that much, and you start thinking, or I did ... life without a husband is not that bad after all. And you get used to this kind of thinking" (forty-three-year-old mother).

For others, however, the physical distance proved to be beneficial. This group of women experienced greater emotional intimacy and enhanced sharing with their husbands after migration. For them, the separation provided spouses with an opportunity to appreciate each other more. Women said that their husbands became much more understanding and generous and showed greater care after migration. Living alone in Korea, some men realized how important their wives were. In addition, as breadwinners, the husbands experienced a sense of pride and felt very responsible, a situation that women viewed as being beneficial for their relationship. According to Jessica, "Our relationship has gotten so much better since I moved here with my children. I mean, I never would have imagined how much I was going to miss him. The separation has been a good time for me to reflect upon our marriage, and now I realize how bad a wife I was. And I think my husband also realized how important I was in his life. So this past summer, when we visited Korea, everything was so nice that we couldn't be nicer to each other ... it was almost like a new marriage" (thirty-nine-year-old mother).

Improvements in the spousal relationship after migration need to be contextualized in family life before migration. For many of these women, living together in South Korea did not mean that they saw their husbands often or spent time with them; the prolonged absence of their husbands was not something new. The work culture of the middle and upper classes in South Korea requires that men work and socialize with other male colleagues, usually while consuming alcohol, every day until late evening. Married men go home when everyone is sleeping, and they are often the first ones to leave in the early morning. Frequently their obligations spill over into the weekends with work-related activities, like golfing or other events; not surprisingly, family members rarely spend time together, and children may see their fathers once a week, typically on Sundays. Some men did not engage in daily family affairs (see discussion, below, for further developments on different patterns of pre-migration gender relationships). In this sense, some *kirogi* mothers experienced the transnational family arrangement positively because the real absence of the husbands meant no expectations, which were usually a source of struggle before the separation. As Alexis said,

> In Korea, I spent too much time simply waiting for my husband. He would normally come home after midnight because he was so busy with his work. And I would have to just wait for him ... like, doing nothing ... so in a way, it's just a waste of time. And on the weekends he would usually go "business golfing," so again, we don't get to spend much time together. Every weekend, there will be this false hope of maybe we can do this or that together, but that rarely happened. And this made me so mad all the time. But here in Canada, you don't have to worry about all that. I don't need to waste my time waiting for my husband, because here you just do everything on your own. You can schedule your life around you. You can spend your free time doing what you like to do. There's no more waiting for your husband until late at night ... there's no husband here. (forty-one-year-old mother)

Women elaborated on how they maintained or improved their relationships through frequent communication with their husbands. Daily Internet conversations, generally with webcams, often resulted in more frequent and better perceived quality time spent together *after* rather than *before* migration. In nearly all cases, spouses were engaging in ritualistic communication, calling each other at least twice a day. Some men were described as being very keen to know about everything that happened to the family. Many mothers said that this renewed interest on the part of their husbands resulted in daily in-depth conversations between spouses, which rarely happened in South Korea. Ellen had such an experience: "Because he's not here with us, he wants to know about everything that happens in a day. When I was in Korea, he never bothered asking me, and really, what's the fun of telling him anyway, right? Most of the things are just usual businesses; they're boring to listen to. But I guess now, even the boring stories are fun stories. We would tell each other about everything. So I think we both know much more about each other, like, after all these years there was still some part of me he didn't know about" (forty-four-year-old mother).

Overall, our findings on the spousal relationship paint a rather positive picture. Women migrants and their husbands in South Korea acted resourcefully in creating a sense of closeness through the use of communication technology. From the women's perspective, the physical separation was a source of loneliness and suffering, but it also resulted in a better emotional bond, mutual appreciation, and understanding. The overall assessment, at the time, was positive rather than negative. Interestingly, physical distance provided a space where gender relations could be redefined. This process is further illustrated by changes in father-children relations.

Father-Children Relationships

Despite the physical separation between the fathers and children, most mothers believed that the relationships improved. Similar to the way they described their spousal relationships, most of these mothers pointed out that their husbands had spent very limited time with their children in South Korea. Stephanie's husband was typical; as a photojournalist, he was so busy "even on the weekends" that he had failed to develop any kind of bond with his children:

And while my children were growing up ... at one point, I just thought, you know what? We're just going to live our own lives. I mean, not like having a divorce or anything, but we're not going to just wait for him to come to go somewhere … you know what I mean? Like, if we want to go on a trip, we will just go by ourselves. And that's what we really did. Like, most of the trips we made, it was just me and my children. If my husband could join us, great, but if he can't, so be it, we'll still go, you know. But the thing is, maybe this wasn't such a great idea. Because, I mean, at some point, I think my children had forgotten who their father was. It was just like to them, father was just someone they would see sometimes at home … not like a real father, you know. (forty-five-year-old mother)

However, many mothers said the separation has brought a change in their husbands; they became much more accessible. Fathers called their children regularly, and they engaged in many more discussions than they did when living together in South Korea. Fathers also became more interested in their children's education. In fact, some mothers said their husbands spent more time physically with their children after the separation than before. Maggie, living apart from her husband for more than six years, said, "He visits us about three times a year. The funny thing is, though, you know, when he's here he spends time with us … like, twenty-four hours a day, right? We're always together, and he wasn't like that when we were in Korea. So I think, in a way, the children spend much more time with their father than the time we lived in Korea. They talk more and stuff, you know. I mean, in Korea … you know, how the lives are so busy, right? Like, there are so many 'weekend' families … the kids never get to see their dads. We were lucky to eat out together once a week, but when he's here, he has really nothing else to do but spend time with us … with the children" (forty-nine-year-old mother).

In addition, many mothers said their husbands had become friendlier and more generous with their children. Several mothers, including Sammy, explained that her husband "doesn't get to see the little mistakes" of his children; as a result, he is more affectionate and understanding toward them (forty-eight-year-old mother). Children, in turn, liked their "new dad" and missed him even more. The close involvement of *kirogi* fathers in their children's lives after migration reported in our study echoes the results of Lee and Koo (2006) in their study of *kirogi* fathers. Many participants in this earlier research were continuing to be active members of their families, often guiding their children's education, despite the physical separation; an emotional attachment between fathers and children could be nurtured (Lee and Koo, 2006).

On the other hand, a few mothers said the relationship between their husbands and children worsened after migration. These mothers, in general, expressed concerns over how the children became accustomed to their father's absence. Melonie, thirty-eight, for example, was worried about her children, who started to avoid their father's phone calls. Nonetheless, as a whole, interviewees from our sample reported enhanced relationships between children and their fathers following migration. Fathers abandoned their rigid role of authority figure. Instead, they entered their children's lives with daily time spent communicating and exchanging information. The transnational family space provided them with a place to become more emotional, involved, and present – a contrast to the way the family was together in Korea. This finding powerfully speaks to the fact that international migration can reconfigure family relations in a positive way.

Mother-Children Relationships

As was the case with the father-children and husband-wife relationships, most interviewees felt that their relationship with their children improved following migration. Here, three major themes could be identified from the mothers' narratives.

First, the relationship changed because both mothers and children felt less pressure for the children to excel academically in Canada. Many mothers said their lives are "easier" here because there is no intense competition between students in school, which was often the source of struggle between mothers and children in South Korea. There, it is mothers' responsibility to produce highly achieving offspring (see Kim & Yoon, 2005; Sohn, 2005; also, for general discussion on the education system in South Korea, see Lee & Larson, 2000). For example, in South Korea the ideal was that children study at private institutions until late at night, but after migrating to Canada, most mothers could dispense with the need to push their children to the limit. Students enjoy themselves more in schools here and, most important, they are free from the pressure of academic performance. As a result, mothers and children are able to spend much more time together, which has led to a creation, or in some cases a re-creation, of tighter bonds between mothers and their children. Margaret related her experience:

> In Korea, I could never relax, 'cause I was always nervous over my children … like when you see them watching television or hanging out with

their friends, you think, are they really supposed to be doing that? I mean, their peers could be studying right now … and, yeah, we used to have troubles because of that. Since coming to Canada, I don't feel that anxious anymore. I mean, I don't really care anymore. You see these Canadian kids … they enjoy their lives, you know … so I am also, like, so be it … let's enjoy, too. So here I have been actually trying to create fun memories with them – like going on a trip – and they like that. And the funny thing is, they're still pretty good in school. So, yeah, I am much more relaxed now … like, I am relaxed enough to actually hear their stories out and understand them more. (forty-two-year-old mother)

On the other hand, mothers who continued to push their children academically in Canada reported their relationships to be distant. This was especially true for mothers who came to Canada for only a short-term stay. Jessica, for example, was very worried about her children "falling behind" their peers in South Korea, and expressed the need to continue to be a very demanding and a "mean mother" to her children.

Second, the relationship between mothers and their children flourished because the children matured after the separation, perhaps much more than their peers in South Korea. Many mothers said their children had "grown up" and had come to understand their parents who were making great sacrifices for the sake of their children's future. Also, the difficulties arising from the father's absence made them realize the importance of family. In turn, these "matured" children were accommodating their mothers to the best of their ability. This change was especially true for May, forty-two, who was an employee at the local convenience store at the time of the interview. She said her children were actually arranging their timetables around her work schedule, and they even prepared a meal for her from time to time.

Third, some mothers discussed how close they felt to their children since migration because they had rediscovered motherhood after coming to Canada. Most of these mothers had careers before leaving South Korea and had limited time with their children. After their migration to Canada, they became stay-at-home mothers, and the relationship with their children improved. This was particularly true for Laura, a former high school teacher, who had worked very long days helping other children yet felt she was neglecting her own. "You know how Korean education is crazy these days, right? Like, it is super hardcore, which means that as a high school teacher you really don't have a life. I was so busy all the time and was never able to give my only son enough attention, and I really feel bad about it now because eventually it led us here. I mean, my son was so struggling in school, and while I was helping other students to get better, I could never offer that kind of help to my own kid. How bad is that? So he hated it when he knew it was going to be just us in Canada. He likes his dad a lot more, you know. But I am happy that I was finally able to become a real mother, and I guess that helped me a lot to bridge our gap" (forty-year-old mother).

Although most mothers felt they had become closer to their children after the separation, another recurring theme was that rearing sons in the absence of their fathers was difficult. Many mothers said their sons had become harder to control, especially when they reached puberty. They are "grown up in head" and "act like husbands." Some mothers expressed particular difficulties in engaging their sons in conversation, especially when the subject of sexuality came up. In contrast, few mothers expressed discord with their daughters during puberty. Eva had been apart from her husband for five years. "[Have you had any conflicts or troubles with your children since coming to Canada?] With my son – he's always the trouble. [Why?] Because he's in puberty now, right? And we have many arguments, especially about his girlfriend. It just drives me crazy sometimes. I mean, I could never imagine him to be this disobedient – he used to be this very good kid, you know, but since some time ago, he now stands up to me every single time. I mean, I really understand why father is so important for boys, because he would never be like that in front of him. He's very scary, you know" (forty-five-year-old mother).

Overall, mother-children relationships were related to the sense of empowerment and freedom that mothers experienced in Canada. Because women who worked outside the home in South Korea prior to migration had such demanding schedules, they felt that combining work and family life was impossible. After migration, however, this tension no longer existed, and they experienced a significant reduction in their level of stress and valued their new, more balanced lives. At the same time, they devoted more time to social networking and leisure. Some pursued paid work to complement the family income or as a way to socialize and build their networks.

Making Sense of Evolving Family Relationships after Migration

To identify changes or level of stability in relationships before and after the *kirogi* migration that emerge from interviews, we created a typology of three family types. These types refer to the situations of the families prior to the migration. As with any schematic typology, these three types of families should be seen more as a continuum than as discrete and mutually exclusive categories. Despite its shortcomings, this approach allows us to identify patterns of experiences among study participants.

Using the participants' level of dependence on their husbands prior to the migration as a measure, we can distinguish three family types. By *dependence*, we refer to both financial and emotional dependence. All families were patriarchal in the sense that the fathers were primarily breadwinners and had limited involvement in domestic work or their children's education. We define the three categories of husband-wife relationships and families as follows. The analysis is summarized in table 14.2.

Traditional Patriarchal Families

In these families, wives were *highly dependent* on their husbands prior to migration. Husbands often treated their spouses like "babies" or "kids" (these labels are taken from the interviews) and were the sole decision makers for their families. The roles and responsibilities of women in these families were limited to so-called women's work: child rearing and domestic chores. They rarely stepped out of their very circumscribed private spheres and did not work outside the home. Fathers were most likely to be present in these families. From the women's accounts, we see that the fathers/husbands tried to be around their families as much as possible (or perhaps had a job that gave them more flexibility). They performed many tasks in the household, from changing light bulbs to managing and controlling all family finances (i.e., recording daily expenditures). Often, they were involved in their children's education. In fact, many husbands in this group were actively engaged in their children's lives, performing tasks such as searching for better private educational institutions or summer camps. They were also generally the initiators of the *kirogi* migration for their families. For these reasons, the pre-migration relationships in these families were, in general, very stable. Marriage partners experienced positive relationships, and women talked about how they appreciated their partners' care and affection.

However, study participants in this group revealed that following migration, they had to become much more independent of their

Table 14.2. Comparisons of Changes in Family Relations across Three Types of Pre-Migration Korean Families

	Pre-Migration Relationship	Key Adaptive Changes	Post-Migration Relationship	
			Positive Change	Negative Change
I. Traditional Patriarchal Families				
A. Overall family relationship	Highly stable	Wife gains more autonomy	Overall: Relationships remain unaffected	
B. Spousal relationship	Good and stable relationship between spouses	- Wife in charge – doing "everything" herself - Wife discovers identity through new roles - education, voluntary work	Both husband and wife appreciate the role changes gained autonomy for wife	- Husband refuse to accept changes in wife - Wife not acculturated - Wife burnout
C. Parent-child relations	Good and sable relations with children		Children accept and accommodate changes in mother	Children dislike and reject "busy" mother
II. Modern patriarchal families				
A. Overall family relationship	Highly stable	Wife gains more freedom	Overall: Mixed results	
B. Spousal relationship	Husband-wife: stable	- Wife is free of familial duties, filial piety - Wife's increased investments in self-education, leisure - Reduced stress from school competition	- Newly discovered affection - Space to avoid conflict - Wife's improved quality of life – more time for leisure (e.g., golf)	- Husband becomes a "stranger" - Wife refuses to return to Korea
C. Parent-child relations	- Father-children: distant - Mother-children: tense	- Decreased presence of father - Reduced pressure from mother for academic excellence		- Diminished role and authority of father - Conflict between mother and children

Table 14.2. Comparisons of Changes in Family Relations across Three Types of Pre-Migration Korean Families (concluded)

	Pre-Migration Relationship	Key Adaptive Changes	Post-Migration Relationship	
			Positive Change	Negative Change
III. Progressive Patriarchal Families				
A. Overall family relationship	Unstable		Overall: Improved relationships	
B. Spousal relationship	Husband-wife: tense	Rediscovered fatherhood and motherhood - Significantly increased communication between spouses and between parents and children - Wife's role change from working mom to stay-at-home mom - Wife becomes more dependent financially	- Newly discovered affection - Greater appreciation of husband as earner - Wife find new identity as mother	- Husband becomes nuisance and forgotten - Wife feels loss of self-identity - Wife is depressed - Unstable pre-migration relationship continues or gets worse
C. Parent-child relations	- Father-children: very distant - Mother-children: very good	- Father is more aware of the interests of other members of the family - Mother has more time for children	- Father becomes more generous and caring - Children like "new dad" - Mother-children relationships remain good and stable	- Children loose respect for father - Father becomes a "stranger"

spouses. In a foreign country without their husbands, these *kirogi* mothers had to do everything by themselves, and they suddenly became responsible for activities they had never managed before, such as driving, shovelling snow, and putting gas in their cars. The somewhat forced and sudden need to be independent resulted in many a participant (re)discovering her own "self" and taking charge of her life apart from her husband. For some mothers, the *kirogi* migration opened up new opportunities – some enrolled in colleges or worked for the first time since getting married.

Overall, this group's family relationships remained stable after migration. Among families that experienced an improvement, the husbands appreciated and respected their stronger, more independent partners. Women were proud of themselves for having undergone such a rapid change. The women's new sense of self was also reported to have a positive influence on the relationship with their children. In some cases, however, study participants experienced a deterioration of family relations because the husbands did not accept the level of independence gained by their wives, a situation that created conflict and a lack of mutual trust. Finally, some mothers did not become independent; they continued to be highly dependent on their husbands even while abroad. For instance, some could not fill out forms and had to fax everything to their husbands. Others relied heavily on their eldest child for English-language interactions, and even after a number of years, did not attain the level of autonomy that other women acquired. These mothers expressed strong feelings of loneliness and resentment toward their Canadian lives.

Modern Patriarchal Families

In these families, wives were *dependent, but active* beyond the family sphere. Husbands were breadwinners, while wives were in charge of everything that happened in the family, including the affairs of extended family and kin. They were financially dependent but relatively independent socially and emotionally. While the big decisions were usually made by their husbands, other smaller decisions were theirs to make. Most of the participants belonging to these families spoke of their extremely busy daily lives in South Korea prior to migration. They had "many businesses to take care of," both inside and outside their homes. Women not only were responsible for their own family matters, including their important duties as daughters-in-law, but they were also actively involved in finding any "edge" for their families, particularly regarding their children's education. They ensured that their children would get the best possible education, obtain the highest possible results, and eventually get into the very best schools. Such extreme pressure put on children and enforced by mothers often led to very difficult mother-children relationships. With such heavy social expectations looming large, mothers and children struggled to create healthy relationships. On the other hand, husbands were, in general, "never interested in the school things" of their children. Such imbalance sometimes caused conflicts and tensions between spouses.

Following migration, many participants felt a tremendous relief. First, they did not have to handle their in-laws and all the responsibilities of good daughters-in-law. Second, they did not have to deal with the South Korean education system and the corresponding social expectations. Overall, they were freer and finally had time to enjoy their lives. Since they no longer felt obligated to enforce long study hours on their children, participants felt they had become good mothers.

Overall, participants in this group experienced mixed results with respect to their family relationships after migration. In families with improved relationships, spouses felt that they had rediscovered each other, and that affection, empathy, and love had been revived. In other cases, however, mothers and children realized that they had become very accustomed to the absence of their husbands/fathers, and thought that this level of independence was harmful to the overall family cohesion and unity. Husbands and wives became strangers to each other, and some mothers reported that they were "too comfortable" without their husbands.

Progressive Patriarchal Families

In these families, wives were *very independent*, both financially and emotionally. Most participants in this group were income earners and had demanding careers. However, despite being in the workforce while raising children, these women had husbands who were not involved in family affairs. Therefore, in addition to their traditional responsibilities, women had to perform many "manly" tasks, such as maintaining the vehicles or taking the children on weekend trips. Such new responsibilities led to very high stress levels and mixed feelings toward their roles as mothers and workers. They often felt that they failed to be good mothers because of the multiple demands put on them.

Most of the participants coming from these families reported tense family relationships prior to migration. In many cases, the main reason was the father's complete absence from family affairs. However, mothers and children in this family type differed from the other study participants in that they were already used to living their own lives without their husbands/fathers prior to migration. As Stephanie's earlier narrative indicates, these mothers in general believed that "if there's no expectation, there's no pain." A mother's independent life naturally resulted in a difficult spousal relationship, but often the father-children relationship was the more troubling; fathers became "not a person, but a title" to their children. Because the husbands were so absent, the mothers grew very close to their children, despite being working mothers.

As was the case with modern patriarchal families, most mothers in this group said that their husbands had changed since the migration. Fathers were much more interested in the daily lives of their family members and were usually the ones making frequent phone calls. Overall, the change in the behaviour and attitudes of the husbands/fathers brought much improvement to family relationships in this group. In fact, we observed the most striking changes in these families. As in the modern patriarchal families, progressive fathers became more generous and caring, and they were able to be emotionally expressive with their children. In addition, wives became completely financially dependent on their husbands after migration, a situation most had not experienced before. This type of dependency bothered some women who had worked prior to migration, but, overall, it fostered a new sense of appreciation for their husbands (see Chang & Darlington, 2008, for similar patterns in astronaut wives). Finally, women who no longer worked outside the home and became stay-at-home mothers after migration talked about rediscovering motherhood and viewed themselves as being better mothers in Canada than they had been in South Korea.

Conclusions

This study was triggered, in part, by past literature on *kirogi* families, which generally emphasizes the negative consequences of this transnational familial arrangement (e.g., Chang & Darlington, 2008; Chew, 2009; Falicov, 2007). Despite the efforts of transnational family members to keep the family intact, the emotional costs of separation have been suggested to often outweigh the benefits (Waters, 2002). In addition, as family members become accustomed to the absence of their parents, children, spouses, and so on, the reunion of once-separated family members has been described as the "meeting of strangers" (Falicov, 2007). *Kirogi* families have been viewed negatively, especially in South Korea; many authors have argued that this unique familial arrangement likely leads to the deterioration of relationships among family members (Chew, 2009; Choi, 2006; Kim, 2006). Our results provide an alternative narrative emerging from the perspectives of a group of *kirogi* mothers.

One contribution of our analysis is to situate family relationships after migration in continuity with relationships prevailing prior to migration. Our analysis thus shows that to understand how transnational spaces created by international migration may offer an opportunity for gender and power relations to be transformed, closer attention must be paid to family gender and power relations in the pre-migration period. Our chapter puts forward a typology of families according to the study participants' level of dependence on their husbands and reveals a complex set of relationships among *kirogi* family members. We see that any change in their relationships was affected by the family process *both* before *and* after the migration. Overall, this particular type of transnational familial arrangement was presented in a positive light by study participants, with the majority of participants reporting continued stability or even improvement in their family relationships. Such consequences were especially apparent for progressive patriarchal families in our study, where we saw the most positive changes.

Based on the narratives of *kirogi* mothers in our research, our results suggest that there are three main factors seemingly essential in maintaining or improving *kirogi* family relationships after migration. First, we find that the emotional well-being of the *kirogi* mothers plays a key role in influencing the overall relationship among *kirogi* family members, and this was most visible among traditional patriarchal and modern patriarchal families. Since coming to Canada, most of our study participants felt relieved of the constant pressure and stress of familial duties and from the competitive nature of the education system in South Korea. Because Korean mothers generally play the mediator role between family members, these freer mothers were now positively affecting their family relationships.

Second, the change in the fathers' behaviours and attitudes toward their families after migration stands as particularly significant. As discussed previously, most study participants spoke of their husbands' not being around their families in South Korea. Since migration, how-ever, fathers who were previously absent rediscovered fatherhood by becoming much more caring and interested in family affairs overseas. Both mothers and children appreciated the change, and the spousal and father-children relationships were restored for many families. Improved relationships were most visible among progressive patriar-chal families.

Finally, the extensive use of ICT seems to have successfully created virtual intimacy for *kirogi* families (Wilding, 2006). Wilding (2006, p. 132) has argued that the use of ICT can construct "connected relation-ships" between transnational family members and "enable them to overlook their physical separation by time and space." Such an argu-ment certainly seems applicable to the *kirogi* families in our research. Participants' narratives suggest that sustained and quality time spent through Internet phone and webcam communications have become habitual in these families' lives, what Falicov (2003) calls "rituals of con-nections." Despite the twelve-hour time difference, fathers, mothers, and children make daily time to be together. As Licoppe and Smoreda (2005) argue, it is not necessarily the content of the communication but simply the fact that they are communicating that maintains the fam-ily unit. While some authors emphasize the idealization of others that often accompany virtual intimacies (Yeoh et al., 2005), many women in our study articulated that they had experienced improvements in their family relations.

In conclusion, *kirogi* families are claiming legitimacy as a family type in South Korea and within Korean ethnic communities abroad. Despite the distance that separates family members, *kirogi* families defy criti-cisms and pessimistic predictions very prevalent in previous research. In our study, we find that many *kirogi* families are stable and enjoy improved relationships; however, we do not know the impact that being part of a *kirogi* family has on the subsequent permanent reunion. Whether greater father involvement in child rearing and a greater sense of empowerment for mothers will continue in the post-*kirogi* period remains to be studied.

REFERENCES

Chang, M., and Darlington, Y. (2008). "Astronaut" wives: Perceptions of changes in family roles. *Asian and Pacific Migration Journal, 17*(1), 61–77.

Chee, M. (2003). Migrating for the children: Taiwanese American women in transnational families. In N. Piper and M. Roces (Eds.), *Wife or worker? Asian women and migration* (pp. 137–56). Lanham, MD: Rowman & Littlefield.

Chew, P. (2009). In pursuit of linguistic gold: Mothering in a globalised world. *English Today, 98, 25*(2), 33–9.

Cho, M. (2000). The migration of Korean students to English speaking countries and its influence on Korean families (in Korean). *Kyungwon College Journal, 22,* 173–98.

Cho, U. (2004). Korean families on the forefront of globalization (in Korean). *Economy and Society, 64,* 148–71.

Cho, Y. (2007). *The diaspora of Korean children: A cross-cultural study of the educational crisis in contemporary South Korea.* (Doctoral dissertation, University of Montana.) Available from ProQuest Digital Dissertations. (AAT 3278274).

Choi, Y. (2006). The phenomenon of "geese-families": Marital separation between geese-fathers and geese-mothers (in Korean). *Journal of Family and Culture, 18*(2), 37–65.

Falicov, C. (2003). Immigrant family processes. In F. Walsh (Ed.), *Normal family processes: Growing diversity and complexity* (pp. 280–300). New York/London: Guilford Press.

Falicov, C. (2007). Working with transnational immigrants: Expanding meanings of family, community, and culture. *Family Process, 46*(2), 157–71.

Kim, H. (2005, 8 April). Foreign country and the lonely Kirogis' deviance (in Korean). *Weekly Kyunghyang.* Retrieved from http://weekly.khan.co.kr/.

Kim, K., & Yoon, H. (2005). Traits of the families having the likelihood of migration for children's education (in Korean). *Korean Journal of Sociology of Education, 15*(3), 29–50.

Kim, S. (2006). The "Kirogi" fathers' changes of lives and adaptation problems (in Korean). *Journal of Korean Home Management Association, 24*(1), 141–58.

Korean Educational Development Institute (2009). *Number of Korean students studying abroad (2001–2008), Destinations of Korean students studying abroad (2008)* (in Korean). Retrieved from https://www.kedi.re.kr/.

Lee, D. (2010). A study of the life and culture of young Korean students studying in the United States. *Educational Research and Reviews, 5*(2), 78–85.

Lee, Y., & Koo, H. (2006). Wild geese fathers and a globalised family strategy for education in Korea. *International Development Planning Review, 28*(4), 533–53.

Lee, M., & Larson, R. (2000). The Korean "examination hell": Long hours of studying, distress, and depression. *Journal of Youth and Adolescence, 29*(2), 249–71.

Licoppe, C., & Smoreda, Z. (2005). Are social networks technologically embedded? How networks are changing today with changes in communication technology. *Social Networks, 27*, 317–35.

Park, S. (2004, 17 October). Kirogi families at the risk of dissolution. *Sisa Magazine 2580*. Seoul: Munhwa Broadcasting Corporation.

Parrenas, R. (2005). *Children of global migration: Transnational families and gendered woes*. Stanford, CA: Stanford University Press.

Pe-Pua, R., Mitchell, C., Iredale, R., & Castles, S. (1996). *Astronaut families and parachute children: The cycle of migration between Hong Kong and Australia*. Canberra: Australian Government Publishing Services.

Portal, J. (2000). *Korea: Art and archaeology*. London: British Museum Publications.

Pratt, G., & Yeoh, B. (2003). Transnational (counter) topographies. *Gender, Place and Culture, 10*, 156–66.

Sheppard, M. (1998). *The "astronaut" family and the schools* (Doctoral Dissertation, University of Toronto, Department of Adult Education, Community Development and Counselling Psychology). Available from ProQuest Digital Dissertations. (AAT NQ33927).Singleton, R., & Straits, B. (2005). *Approaches to social research* (4th ed.). New York: Oxford University Press.

Sohn, J. (2005). Sociological analysis on the phenomenon of Korean students studying abroad (in Korean). *Korean Journal of Sociology of Education, 15*(2), 95–120.

Vertovec, S. (2009). *Transnationalism*. London: Routledge.

Waters, J. (2002). Flexible families?: "Astronaut" households and the experiences of lone mothers in Vancouver, British Columbia. *Social & Cultural Geography, 3*(2), 117–34.

Wilding, R. (2006). Virtual intimacies? Families communicating across transnational contexts. *Global Networks, 6*(2), 125–42.

Yeoh, B., Huang, S., & Lam, T. (2005). Transnationalizing the "Asian" family: Imaginaries, intimacies and strategic intents. *Global Networks, 5*(4), 307–15.

Yeom, J. (2008). The light and shade of early studying abroad from children's experiences (in Korean). *Open Children Education Research, 13*(6), 241–59.

Contributors

Danièle Bélanger, PhD, is a sociologist and demographer with a special interest in Asia. She is currently the director at the Graduate Collaborative Program in Migration and Ethnic Relations at the University of Western Ontario. As the holder of the Canada Research Chair in Population, Gender, and Development, she studies the links between demographic and social change in the Asian context. In her research, funded by the Social Sciences and Humanities Research Council (SSHRC) and the International Development Research Centre (IDRC), Dr. Bélanger investigates how new migration opportunities within Asia affect women and their families. She speaks four languages fluently and has lived and worked in several countries of the developing world. This experience makes it easier for her to conduct much of her research through first-hand fieldwork.

Chedly Belkhodja, PhD, is a professor in the Department of Political Science at the Université de Moncton. His research focuses on the questions of managing immigration in smaller cities and in areas with low immigration, and the discourse and representations of cultural, religious and ethnic diversity. He has published articles in *Canadian Ethnic Studies*, *Canadian Journal of Political Science*, *Politique et Sociétés*, *Argument*, *Francophonie d'Amérique*, and *Lexicometrica*. He has also contributed many chapters to collective works. From 2003 to 2006, he served as Director of Research at the Atlantic Metropolis Centre, and he has been one of the Centre's directors since 2006. He also directed two films produced by the National Film Board of Canada: *Tableaux d'un voyage imaginaire* (Imaginary Journeys) in 2001 with the filmmaker Jean Chabot, and *Au bout du fil* (Hanging On) in 2006.

Elic Chan is a PhD candidate in the Department of Sociology at the University of Toronto. His dissertation examines the implications of ecological and group characteristics on the development of Asian charitable organizations in Canada. His major areas of interest include immigration, ethnic communities, and labour market participation. Chan's research has been published in *International Migration Review*, *Sociological Forum*, and *Sociological Quarterly*.

Susan S. Chuang, PhD, is an associate professor in the Department of Family Relations and Applied Nutrition at the University of Guelph. She received her BA in criminology and sociology at the University of Toronto. At the University of Rochester, she received an MSc in elementary education, and an MSc and a PhD in human development. She was a postdoctoral fellow at the National Institutes of Health, Maryland. Her lines of research encompass parenting, fathering, parent-child relationships, child and adolescent development, school readiness, and immigration in various socio-cultural contexts. Recently, her publications include co-edited books, *On New Shores: Understanding Immigrant Fathers in North America* (2008), *Immigrant Children: Change, Adaptation, and Cultural Transformation* (2011), *Gender Roles in Immigrant Families* (in press), and two special issues of *Sex Roles* (2009) and the *Journal of Family Psychology* (2009). She is currently writing a book, *Tigers or Dragons: Asian Parenting in America Today,* and organizing her fifth international conference on immigrant families. She is currently the series editor for Springer Science+Business Media Publishers' *Advances in Immigrant Family Research*.

R. Frank Falk, PhD, is the Director of Research at the Institute for the Study of Advanced Development in Denver, Colorado, and Professor Emeritus of Sociology at the University of Akron. He has chaired the Departments of Sociology at two major universities, the University of Denver and the University of Akron. He also served as Chair of the Classical Studies, Anthropology, and Archaeology Departments while at Akron and was University Vice-President of Research in 1993. He specializes in research methodology with an interest in social psychology and adult emotional development. He has authored or co-authored nine books and monographs, twelve chapters in books, twenty-six peer-reviewed journal articles, and delivered more than seventy-five presentations at professional meetings, including the National Association for Gifted Children, Social and Emotional Needs of the Gifted, and the

World Conference on Gifted. Since 1980, he has conducted research on the personality traits of gifted and talented students and adults, using both qualitative and quantitative approaches. His most recent publications involve the measurement of overexcitabilities in Dabrowski's theory. His chapter on cross-cultural studies appears in S. Mendaglio (ed.), *Dabrowski's Theory of Positive Disintegration.*

Eric Fong, PhD, is a professor of sociology at the University of Toronto. He has published widely in the area of race and ethnic residential patterns and ethnic businesses.

J.D. Han, PhD, is an associate professor of economics and finance at King's University College, University of Western Ontario. He has been studying East Asian economies, including Korea and China, and has recently been collaborating with Dr Peter Ibbott on the international migration of Koreans, with an emphasis on students. He is the representative in Canada for the Korean Association for Canadian Studies (KACS) and serves as an editorial member of its journal. He is also a research associate for the Centre for the Study of Korea at the University of Toronto.

Peter Ibbott, PhD, is associate professor of economics at King's University College, University of Western Ontario. His research is in the areas of demography, migration, living standards, intellectual property, and public economics. His recent papers have appeared in the *Journal of American-Canadian Studies, Canadian Studies in Population, American Journal of Law and Medicine,* and *Canadian Journal on Aging.*

Aya Kimura Ida, PhD, is an assistant professor in the Department of Sociology at California State University–Sacramento. Using social psychology frameworks, her research investigates how group identity impacts the mental and physical health of racial and ethnic minorities. In a current project, she analyses data collected among Japanese immigrants and sojourners to assess how psychosocial resources (e.g., social support) affect their psychological well-being as they make the transition to life in the United States. Her recent work has been published in *Sex Roles, Journal of Black Studies,* and *Sociological Focus.*

Mihyon Jeon, PhD, is an assistant professor in the Department of Languages, Literatures and Linguistics at York University. Her research is directed toward understanding the process of the development of a second or a foreign language, focusing on sociolinguistic applications to language education in the areas of heritage-language maintenance in North America and English-language education in Asia. Her recent papers have appeared in *Modern Language Journal, Language, Culture and Curriculum, Language Awareness,* and *Heritage Language Journal.*

Junmin Jeong is currently pursuing his PhD in sociology at the University of Toronto. Before beginning his graduate studies in Canada, he worked as a journalist in Korea. His main research interests are the integration of immigrants and their children, transnational migrant networks, and immigration and crime. His papers have been presented at scholarly conferences such as the Canadian Sociological Association, Academy of Criminal Justice Sciences, and the Canadian Asian Studies Association.

Ann H. Kim, PhD, is an assistant professor in the Department of Sociology at York University. Her research is largely motivated by questions related to the immigrant and ethnic integration process, and the factors that contribute to differing paths of integration. Her research interests include Korean migrants and transnational families in Canada, Asian panethnicity, immigrant seniors, and urban inequality. Her recent papers have appeared in the *American Journal of Sociology, Canadian Journal of Urban Research,* and *Canadian Studies in Population.*

Guilsung Kwak, PhD, is currently working as an international migrant community organizer after receiving his PhD in social work at the University of Calgary. His work is based on identifying issues and barriers that inhibit the adjustment and integration of newly settled migrants in Korea. His primary interest is in how Korean social work practice and immigration policy play constructive roles in building supportive networks and services for immigrants and their families.

Min-Jung Kwak, PhD, is a human geographer who is currently teaching in the Urban Studies Program at the University of Toronto. Her research interests broadly cover the areas of globalization, transnational migration, immigrant entrepreneurship, urban housing and labour market issues, and family and gender relations. She has been particularly interested in Korean-Canadian communities in major Canadian cities, and her research findings have been published as policy reports, book chapters, and journal articles. Her most recent publication was in the *Journal of International Migration and Integration*.

Young In Kwon, PhD, is a research professor at Yonsei University, Seoul. Rooted in family sociology, and in the lifecourse framework, her research interests focus on culturally diverse family relationships and on men's life-long role and identity development within multi-layered socio-cultural contexts. Her current scholarship examines the role, identity, and relationship development of paternity in Korean and Korean immigrant contexts. She recently worked at the University of Guelph as a postdoctoral fellow to investigate the construction of fatherhood among Korean immigrant men in Canada.

Daniel Lai, PhD, RSW, is a professor and Associate Dean (Research and Partnerships) of the Faculty of Social Work at the University of Calgary. For years his teaching and research have focused on relationships between culture, health, and the well-being of aging immigrants and culturally diverse populations, family caregiving issues, and social policy issues related to population aging. Dr Lai is a prolific researcher who held the Alberta Heritage Health Scholar Award between July 2003 and 2009. He has received research funding from the SSHRC, the Alberta Heritage Foundation for Medical Research, and the Canadian Institutes of Health Research (CIHR). Dr Lai's publications include more than eighty peer-reviewed journal papers and book chapters, and over three hundred conference papers and invited presentations. He was the Social Policy and Practice Section Editor for the *Canadian Journal on Aging* between August 2003 and July 2007. Between 2004 and 2008, he served on the Advisory Board of the CIHR Institute of Aging.

Nancy B. Miller, PhD, brings a sociological perspective to the assessment of children at the Gifted Development Center in Denver, Colorado. In her work at the Center, she is committed to fostering children's social and emotional development at home and at school. She also serves as editor for *Advanced Development*, a journal on adult giftedness. She was Executive Officer for Sociologists for Women in Society from 2002 to 2006 at the University of Akron. Her research focuses primarily on emotional development, gender and giftedness, and women's social support and adjustment.

Pyong Gap Min, PhD, is Distinguished Professor of Sociology at Queens College and the Graduate Center of the City University of New York. He also serves as Director of the Research Center for the Korean Community at Queens College. His areas of specialization are immigration, ethnicity, immigrant businesses, immigrants' religious practices, and family and gender, with a focus on Korean and Asian Americans. He is the author of five books, including *Caught in the Middle: Korean Communities in New York and Los Angeles* (1996) and *Preserving Ethnicity through Religion in America: Korean Protestants and Indian Hindus across Generations* (2010). Both books won two separate book awards. He is the editor or co-editor of seven books, including *Asian Americans: Contemporary Trends and Issues*, Second Edition (2006).

Miea Moon is a PhD student in clinical psychology at the University of Windsor and a research analyst at the Centre for Addiction and Mental Health (CAMH) in Toronto. Her research focuses on mental health among culturally diverse populations.

Marianne S. Noh, PhD, is a postdoctoral scholar at the University of Western Ontario in the Arthur Labatt Family School of Nursing. She completed her graduate studies in sociology at the University of Akron. Her research focuses on the health consequences of intimate partner violence. Currently, she is examining complex interactions among social statuses and social contexts such as ethno-racial status, immigrant status, and rurality to predict outcomes in help seeking and physical and mental health among abused women. Her previous research has included a content analysis of print media to investigate social constructions of abused women and the battered-woman syndrome, multivariate analyses of depressive symptoms among immigrants living with the chronic health condition HIV/AIDS, and a comparative analysis of ethnic and gender identity formations among second-generation immigrant youth in the United States and Canada.

Samuel Noh, PhD, currently holds the David Crombie Professor of Cultural Pluralism and Health in the Department of Psychiatry at the University of Toronto. Within the department, Dr Noh serves as the Head of the Culture, Community and Health Studies (CCHS) Program. He is also a Senior Research Scientist and the founder and Head of the Social Equity and Health Research Section at CAMH. Educated in medical sociology and social epidemiology, he focuses his research on social and cultural determinants of immigrant and minority health. His research interests include cultural sensitivities in assessing social stress and mental health, social disparities and health equity, psychosocial processes of racial and ethnic discrimination and mental health, stigma and service utilization among Asian Canadians, cross-cultural investigations of depression and addiction problems, micro-businesses and immigrant health, and HIV prevention in immigrant communities. He was the principal investigator of more than twenty research and training grants, including a postdoctoral research fellowship program in the social determinants of mental health. His research-based publications appear in leading book series and peer-reviewed journals, including the *Journal of Health and Social Behavior, Social Science and Medicine, American Journal of Public Health, Journal of Nervous and Mental Disease, Youth and Adolescence, Journal of Community Psychology,* and *Journal of Addiction Research and Theory.* He has made over 120 presentations at international and national conferences, and delivered more than eighty invited special lectures, seminars, and workshops around the world.

Jungwee Park, PhD, is a senior analyst at Statistics Canada. Trained as an applied sociologist, he has studied various issues related to social policy. His recent projects focus on workers' health, training, and retirement. As well, Dr Park, as an outside faculty member, teaches at the University of Ottawa and Lakehead University.

In-Jin Yoon, PhD, is a professor in the Department of Sociology at Korea University in Seoul. His research interests are social psychology, minorities, international migration, and multiculturalism. His major publications include *On My Own: Korean Businesses and Race Relations in America; Korean Diaspora: Migration, Adaptation, and Identity of Overseas Koreans;* and *North Korean Migrants: Lives, Consciousness, and Support Policy for Resettlement.* His recent papers have appeared or are forthcoming in the *Journal of Ethnic and Migration Studies, Korea Observer, Korean Journal of Sociology,* and *International Journal of Public Health.*

Index